New Islamic Urbanism

New Islamic Urbanism

The Architecture of Public and Private Space in Jeddah, Saudi Arabia

Stefan Maneval

UCLPRESS

First published in 2019 by
UCL Press
University College London
Gower Street
London WC1E 6BT

Available to download free: www.uclpress.co.uk

A CIP catalogue record for this book is available from The British Library.

ISBN: 978-1-78735-644-3 (Hbk.)
ISBN: 978-1-78735-643-6 (Pbk.)
ISBN: 978-1-78735-642-9 (PDF)
ISBN: 978-1-78735-645-0 (epub)
ISBN: 978-1-78735-646-7 (mobi)
DOI: https://doi.org/10.14324/111.9781787356429

For Jakob

Contents

List of figures ix
Preface xii
Acknowledgements xvii

Introduction 1

1. **A brief history of Jeddah in the nineteenth and twentieth centuries** 22
   City of merchants and pilgrims 22
   Architecture and urban development from the pre-oil era until today 28

2. **Public and private spaces in Jeddah in the first half of the twentieth century** 40
   From the harbour to the bazaar: Topography of a trading town 42
   Places of encounter: Mosques, open spaces and coffeehouses 45
   Visible, but unseen: Women and public space 49
   Residential architecture: One building, multiple functions 54
   Theoretical reflections (1): The problem of translation 61
   Theoretical reflections (2): Approaches to public and private space in Arab-Muslim societies 66
   Privacy in an open house 71
   Strong publics, weak publics and public space 77
   Conclusion 81

3. **The transformation of urban space in the early oil era, 1950s and 1960s** 86
   Malcolm X in Jeddah 88
   Spatial differentiation 91
   New residential architecture 97
   Conclusion 106

4. **Architecture and religious reform: Architectural discourse from the 1970s to the 1990s** 108
Islamic architectural criticism: A case study 110
Social connectedness 114
Privacy 117
Westernisation versus Islam 121
Islamic Revival 122
Frames of reference: New Urbanism and the Islamic City paradigm 130
Conclusion 134

5. **Residential architecture, from the 1970s to the early twenty-first century** 139
New Islamic Urbanism in practice 141
Facets of enclosure (1): Fear and safety 153
The changing architecture of social life 155
Facets of enclosure (2): Don't trust the concrete 160
Conclusion 167

6. **Navigating urban space: Jeddah, early twenty-first century** 170
Routine human encasement in Jeddah 171
Urban design and state control 174
Cars 180
Encounters on the stairs: Strategies of avoiding *khalwa* 182
Debate on *ikhtilāṭ* 185
Masculine, feminine: The duplication of spaces 187
Negotiating gender segregation (1): A man's world 191
Negotiating gender segregation (2): Encounters in cyberspace and the city 195
'Street Pulse': A public sphere utopia? 198
Claiming public spaces: Protest and resistance 201
Gated publics, counterpublics 205
Conclusion 212

7. **Conclusion** 217

References 227

Index 239

List of figures

Figure 1.1	Map of Jeddah in 1762, from C. Niebuhr's *Reisebeschreibung nach Arabien und andern umliegenden Ländern* (vol. 1).	24
Figure 1.2	Arrival of pilgrims in the port of Jeddah. Postcard, around 1900.	25
Figure 1.3	Al-Shām quarter in the northwest of Jeddah, 1917. Photo: Raphaël Savignac.	29
Figure 1.4	Village of huts outside the walled city, east of the Mecca Gate, 1917. Photo: Raphaël Savignac.	30
Figure 1.5	Building with open balconies in al-Shām quarter, 1917. Photo: Raphaël Savignac.	30
Figure 1.6	Map of Jeddah, *c.* 2009, indicating unplanned settlements and vacant land.	34
Figure 1.7	Map of the old town of Jeddah in the early twenty-first century.	37
Figure 1.8	Ruin of an old residential building in al-Balad, 2012.	38
Figure 2.1	Market street in Jeddah, 1918. Photo: Charles Winckelsen.	41
Figure 2.2	The customs house, photographed from an arriving boat, 1926. Photo: van Voorthuysen.	43
Figure 2.3	View of the town and an open space behind the customs house, around 1900.	44
Figure 2.4	Al-Qābil Street, with al-ʿUkāsh Mosque to the left and al-Miʿmār Mosque in the background (centre). View from the terrace of the post office, 1918. Photo: Charles Winckelsen.	44
Figure 2.5	Open space with a sitting area next to al-Bāshā Mosque in Ḥārat al-Shām, 1918. Photo: Charles Winckelsen.	46

Figure 2.6	A boy dancing in front of a group of children dressed up for the ʿīd al-fiṭr at the end of the fast of Ramadan, around 1900.	47
Figure 2.7	Coffee house next to the Dutch consulate. Photo: van Voorthuysen 1926.	48
Figure 2.8	Prison inmates, 1917. Photo: Raphaël Savignac.	49
Figure 2.9	Women in the street, 1917. Photo: Raphaël Savignac.	50
Figure 2.10	Poor woman of African origin with a baby in the harbour, 1918. Photo: Charles Winckelsen.	51
Figure 2.11	Ground floor office in the Dutch consulate in a typical old building, around 1900.	55
Figure 2.12	A *mirkāz* next to an entrance and another one in an open space in front of a row of houses, around 1900.	56
Figure 3.1	Mass accommodation for pilgrims at the old airport.	87
Figure 3.2	Concrete building, constructed around 1960, in al-Hindāwiyya.	92
Figure 3.3	A lane in al-Kandara district.	95
Figure 3.4	Small residential units constructed on an ad hoc basis in al-Thaghr district.	97
Figure 3.5	Apartment building, constructed around 1960, to the northeast of the old town: Yasemin's home when she grew up.	98
Figure 4.1	Maha Malluh's art installation 'Food for Thought' at the 2012 Edge of Arabia exhibition in Jeddah.	129
Figure 5.1	Living room/reception hall with windows covered by several layers of opaque materials, during the daytime.	140
Figure 5.2	Villa in al-Sulaymāniyya district, combining neo-classical columns and a rustic crenellated tower.	143
Figure 5.3	Wall surrounding a villa in al-Sulaymāniyya district.	143
Figure 5.4	Blends of iron sheet between single-family houses.	144
Figure 5.5	An upper middle-class family's reception hall.	145
Figure 5.6	An apartment building in al-Ḥamrāʾ district.	146
Figure 5.7	Apartment building, built around the 1960s, in al-Kandara district.	146

Figure 5.8	Screen in front of the entrance to a small residential building in al-Hindāwiyya district. Men sitting in a *mirkāz* by the entrance.	148
Figure 5.9	Men sitting in a *mirkāz* in front of their clubhouse in al-Hindāwiyya district.	149
Figure 5.10	Wood panels, window panes and air conditioner: a *majlis* turned office in the old Nūr Walī building.	150
Figure 5.11	Entrance to a gated community in northern Jeddah.	152
Figure 5.12	Abdulnasser Gharem's 'Concrete Block', at the 2012 Edge of Arabia exhibition in Jeddah.	161
Figure 5.13	Discussion in a *majlis* held in the reception hall of a residential building.	166
Figure 6.1	King Fahd Street, also known as Sittīn Street.	172
Figure 6.2	A woman jogging on the roadside.	177
Figure 6.3	Youths playing table football along the roadside.	178
Figure 6.4	The Jeddah Rush Housing Project. In the foreground: facilities of the pilgrims' city at the old airport.	183
Figure 6.5	Amusement park in northern Jeddah.	192
Figure 6.6	Families picnicking at the Corniche.	193
Figure 6.7	Telephone number written on the rear window of a car.	195
Figure 6.8	Ahmad Angawi's 'Street Pulse' installation at the 2012 Edge of Arabia exhibition in Jeddah.	200
Figure 6.9	A beach resort in Obhur.	206
Figure 6.10	Girls riding bicycles in the Durrat al-ʿArūs holiday resort. Photograph from Olivia Arthur's *Jeddah Diary* (2012)	208
Figure 6.11	A group of veiled women posing for Olivia Arthur's camera. Photograph from Arthur's *Jeddah Diary* (2012)	209

Preface

In the conservative cultural climate in Saudi Arabia of the 1980s and 1990s, a specific architectural style emerged: New Islamic Urbanism. The emphasis on privacy protection and the blocking of views characteristic of this architecture, although originally derived from a conservative Islamic imagination of social coexistence, enables, as I argue throughout this book, a broad variety of alternative social practices. Some of these may even be in conflict with the prevailing attitudes to gender relations, piety and moral conduct. New Islamic Urbanism thus facilitates both a conservative and a liberal way of life. Moreover, it allows for the constitution of counterpublics that challenge and renegotiate the boundaries between the public and the private.

Although the notion of societal change is essential to the research presented in this book, returning to Jeddah seven years after finishing my fieldwork I was surprised at how different life in this city had become. The present described in the last chapters of this book had become history, and it struck me that some of the forces of change described there must in fact have been more powerful than I had unconsciously assumed. Since the demise of King ʿAbdullāh in 2015 and the rise to power of crown prince Muḥammad bin Salmān, gender segregation had been abolished in many places, such as cafes and shopping malls. As an unaccompanied man, I was no longer denied access to the food courts and upper floors of shopping centres. At the Medd Cafe and Roastery, Jeddah's first 'third wave' coffee shop which opened at the northern edge of the corniche in 2015, where half a pound of coffee beans cost 77 Saudi riyal (approximately 18 euros), a mixed crowd of students, artists and hipsters gathered every night. They enjoyed a lifestyle and an atmosphere of freedom previously known only from trips abroad. On the occasion of Medd Cafe's third anniversary, a programme of events had been set up in March 2019, including public talks on topics such as 'healthy living', a stand-up comedy show and a speed networking event, in which 10 men and four women spontaneously participated while others were watching.

All events, attended by mostly young men and women, took place on the upper floor of the cafe, which normally served as the women's or family section, in contrast to a largely, but not exclusively, male downstairs section. The concept of gender segregation still survived here and elsewhere in Jeddah, but it had become more of a choice, resulting in blurred boundaries between what were formerly two strictly divided spheres. Women had officially been granted the right to drive cars and work in a large variety of jobs, from saleswomen and waitresses to customs officers. In spring 2019, driving schools were booked out half a year in advance, and the first women could already be seen driving. At the recently finished expansion of the corniche walkway – a new recreational area of a size and quality unprecedented in Jeddah – women riding bicycles had become a common sight, and so had mixed groups of young men and women, chatting, going for a walk, spending time together. Several art exhibitions, galleries and an annual art festival, called '21,39', had been established, providing forums of exchange and inspiration for a thriving art scene. In January 2019, the first cinema in town was inaugurated, following one on the campus of the King Abdullah University of Science and Technology (KAUST) and three in Riyadh, after a 35-year ban on cinemas. Two months later, the movie *Roll'em*, set and shot in Jeddah, was the talk of the town, or rather of the educated elite. It tells the story of a young filmmaker struggling to make a film about Jeddah, and his encounter with an old cinematographer whose filmmaking career ended in the 1970s in a country without cinemas.

It may appear tempting to correlate the recent opening of the country with the country's new unofficial ruler, crown prince Muḥammad bin Salmān (whose father, King Salmān, is in his mid-eighties and purportedly suffering from 'mild' dementia). Only 31 years old when appointed crown prince in June 2017, Muḥammad bin Salmān soon made it into the global news by arresting some 200 princes, ministers and wealthy businessmen for corruption charges, confining some of them in the Ritz-Carlton in Riyadh and not treating them gently for several weeks. Corruption is an odd accusation in a country where the king rules by decree and appoints all ministers and other key offices in the state, traditionally favouring members of his own family. The ruling family has amassed tremendous wealth over the past decades, neglecting and exploiting significant parts of the population while sedating others with well-paid public sector jobs in a blown-up state apparatus. Although the real driving force behind the 2017 purge seems to have been a demonstration of power and the seizure of control over a political system based on nepotism, the buying of loyalty and unhindered personal enrichment, rather than the fight against corruption, the crown prince managed to portray himself as a reformer destined to propel his country into a direction often described as 'forwards' – as if any possible other position was either wrong or 'behind'. He was celebrated as such not only in the self-censored local news, but also by US president Donald Trump,[1] the *New York Times* (e.g. Friedman 2017) and the *Independent* (e.g. McKernan 2018), to name only a few influential voices of our time.

Muḥammad bin Salmān has indeed reduced the power of the religious police, established an Entertainment Authority and promoted reforms that paved the way for the changes described above. Among his major projects is the 'Vision 2030' plan, which is based on a McKinsey report. Seeking to diversify the Saudi economy, its main goal is to end the country's dependency on oil (Khashan 2017). While the crown prince might well have a 'vision', this arguably entails first and foremost a strategy for securing the Āl Saʿūd's, i.e. the ruling clan's, hold on power by appeasing the Saudi populace. Rather than actually granting civil liberties, such as freedom of expression or political participation, the crown prince's reforms allow certain parts of the population to breathe the air of a liberal lifestyle. In fact, many political activists, among them several women's rights activists, have been detained during Muḥammad bin Salmān's reign. The significant number of such cases, the ill-treatment of political prisoners and their families, and especially the brutal murder of the journalist Jamal Khashoggi on the premises of the Saudi consulate general in Istanbul spread fear among Saudis of being spied upon, persecuted or arrested on unpredictable allegations. It may seem contradictory that the crown prince persecutes activists who advocate the kind of reforms he himself is pushing forward with. Yet it is not the first time in history that the Saudi regime has applied a twofold strategy of silencing dissenters while meeting some of their demands, thus trimming its sails to the wind. In the early 1990s, for example, this policy led to a number of conservative reforms serving to demonstrate the Saudi government's concern for the public implementation of Islamic law and the religious principle of Commanding Right and Forbidding Wrong (see chapter 4). So far, this strategy has proved successful for the Saudi rulers, and it is hence unsurprising that it is once more vigorously deployed.

The recent reforms address primarily a generation of the under thirties, who constitute more than 50 per cent of the population, according to a 2016 survey of the Saudi General Authority for Statistics. They have affected, in the first place, a relatively small group of middle- and upper-class Saudis – those who can afford a hand-brewed drip coffee at prices comparable to those in Paris or London, who have often studied abroad, are fluent in English and do not share any of the anti-Western sentiments that nurtured the Islamic Revival movement one generation ago. It is the same milieu that I describe in more detail in chapter 6 as proponents of a lifestyle which, until recently, was in conflict with the official gender policy and, until today, challenges prevailing moral standards.

The fact that the Saudi regime, under the leadership of Muḥammad bin Salmān, adapted its gender policy to the desires of the cultural elite of the younger generation does not make the crown prince a pioneer of liberalisation. In contrast, it shows how powerful the counterpublics described in this book are. They have been enacting, often in the shelter of the architecture of New Islamic Urbanism, alternative gender roles and concepts of publicness and privacy for years. By ceaselessly promoting, through particular bodily practices and public displays, their own visions of social order, appropriate behaviour and male–female relationships, they have caused the Saudi state to respond. Rather than being at the forefront of social renewal and liberalisation, as the crown prince likes to see himself, Muḥammad bin Salmān should be regarded as the first powerful member of the royal family who understood that the demands of the younger generation should no longer be ignored.

The reforms that took place in recent years are relevant in the first place, as mentioned above, to a relatively small group of liberal-minded Saudis and expats of the middle and upper classes. They have by no means altered the entire picture as I describe it in this book. This is due to the fact that gender segregation in Saudi Arabia is not simply imposed on the Saudi people by the government or religious leaders, but supported by large parts of the society, by conservatively minded men and women alike. Even if gender segregation is now abolished in certain places, many unwritten rules regulating men's and women's interactions and movements are still valid. I experienced this in spring 2019, when I visited one of the most popular shopping malls in Jeddah, the Mall of Arabia. No longer was I, as a single man, prevented from entering the central food court, which previously used to be demarcated as a 'families only' space, i.e. accessible only to women, or men accompanying female relatives. Yet, while looking for a vacant table in one of the self-service restaurants there, carrying my meal and a cup of tea on a tray, I noticed that navigating gendered spaces had not become much easier. When I placed my tray on the first vacant table, a woman sitting at the next table wearing an *ʿabāya* and a *niqāb* lifted her head, as if troubled by the prospect of me facing her. Her husband, sitting opposite to her, noticed this and turned around to see who was attempting to sit down behind him. In anticipated respect of their feelings, I lifted my tray again to look for a better place.

Unable to find a place where I would not have faced a woman at a neighbouring table, I opted for a table next to three unaccompanied women, not entirely sure whether they accepted me sitting there because they did not mind, or only tolerated my presence because they barely had another choice. In other instances, I observed one man asking another not to look at his wife or daughter or to sit down elsewhere. The mutual caution required of men and women to avoid visual contact described in what follows has thus not become obsolete, but rather spread to formerly gender-segregated places where the principle of *ikhtilāṭ* (mixing of men and women) has recently been introduced.

Whereas the case study provided in this book ends approximately with the demise of King ʿAbdullāh, its purpose is not only to document the societal changes that took place until then, but also to challenge widespread assumptions about public and private spaces in Saudi Arabia and other Muslim contexts where gender segregation is an important principle of social order, as well as to contribute, by presenting an analytical framework and a case study, to academic debate on public and private spaces in non-Western societies (cf. Qian 2014).

Note

1. Donald J. Trump on Twitter: 'I have great confidence in King Salman and the Crown Prince of Saudi Arabia, they know exactly what they are doing ... Some of those they are harshly treating have been "milking" their country for years!' 6 November 2017.

Acknowledgements

I feel a profound sense of gratitude toward Professor Ulrike Freitag, for inspiring me and awakening my interest in the city of Jeddah and also supporting me in finding a research topic that has fascinated me for several years. Her confidence and interest in my work was an invaluable source of encouragement. I am greatly indebted to the Berlin Graduate School of Muslim Culture and Societies, Freie Universität Berlin for a four-year scholarship that allowed me to research and write the dissertation on which this book is based. I would like to thank Professor Gudrun Krämer, Bettina Gräf, Gabriele Freitag and all members of the BGSMCS for providing an inspiring environment to conduct my research.

This book is the outcome of a journey of 10 years, during which this project has evolved a great deal. Particularly helpful in this process were the advice and comments I received from my advisors and mentors Heike Delitz and Schirin Amir-Moazami. Heike's sociological work changed my way of looking at architecture, and Schirin's questions and critical remarks were essential in narrowing down the focus of my research and sharpening my arguments. I am likewise grateful to Birgit Krawietz for her support, critical comments and encouragement, particularly in the phase of turning the dissertation into a book. In this respect, I am also appreciative of the remarks and suggestions on a previous version of the manuscript that I received from two anonymous reviewers.

Many thanks go to King Abdulaziz University, in particular Professor Hisham Mortada. Without his tremendous effort and support, my fieldwork in Jeddah in 2011 and 2012 would not have been possible. Thanks go also to the Effat University in Jeddah, especially Lisa Zuppé, and the King Abdullah University of Science and Technology, particularly Dominik Michels, for inviting me as a research fellow in April 2012 and March 2019 respectively. Thanks to the remarkable support of Lisa Zuppé and Gerald Naughton at the Effat University, I was able to conduct interviews with a group of young women and to visit, and travel within,

Saudi Arabia with my family, which allowed me to gain new insights into gender-segregated public and private spaces.

In Jeddah, where I conducted fieldwork, I have a debt that I can never repay. I am grateful to all the Jiddawis, permanent or temporary inhabitants of the city, who agreed to talk with me. Because of the sensitive issues some of them touched upon and the persecution of what the Saudi authorities perceive to be dissidents, I must not mention their names here, which I sincerely regret. Their generosity, hospitality, trust and interest in my work will never be forgotten.

Special thanks are due to Benedikt Pontzen and Omar Kasmani, who commented on some chapters of the manuscript at various stages, and to the participants of Ulrike Freitag's research colloquium, particularly Julia Clauß, Leyla von Mende, Katharina Mühlbeyer and Antonia Bosanquet, who did likewise. My colleagues at BGSMCS have contributed to this project in various ways, discussing and suggesting analytical comments. I presented earlier versions of several chapters of this book at conferences and workshops, and I would like to express my gratitude especially to Nora Lafi, Steffen Wippel, Christian Steiner and Philippe Pétriat for offering opportunities to do so. The feedback I received on these occasions improved the manuscript. I would also like to say a big thanks to Fatin Abbas for her attentive proofreading and thoughtful comments. Her support and patience were an enormous help in a very stressful period of my life.

This book would not be the same without the photographs from the Christiaan Snouck Hurgronje collection in Leiden and the Raphaël Savignac collection in Jerusalem. I am thankful to Arnoud Vrolijk from the Leiden University Libraries and Jean-Michel de Tarragon from the École biblique et archéologique française de Jérusalem for giving me permission to reproduce these images. I am particularly thankful to Olivia Arthur for allowing me to use some of her magnificent pictures from Jeddah that inspired me to write an important section of chapter 6. Thanks go also to Tariq Alireza, who shared digital copies of his collection of historical postcards from Jeddah with me. The argument presented in chapter 2 is informed by a close reading of these and other visual sources. I also thank Adnan Abbas Adas for the permission to reproduce a map of the Old City of Jeddah that is both detailed and well designed.

At UCL Press, I am grateful to Chris Penfold for his professional support. Accompanying the publication of this book, his confidence in my work was extremely encouraging. Warm thanks to Robert Davies for his copyediting and thoughtful comments.

Special thanks go to Luca Bertoldi for offering me a residency at Wunderkammer Trento in the final phase of writing the first draft of this book. His hospitality was as overwhelming as the heat of the summer in Trento. The moments we shared and the inspiring conversations we had while I was going through a hectic phase of obsessive writing are unforgettable.

Last but not least a very big thank you to my parents for fostering, while raising me, the curiosity that constitutes the driving force behind my research, and to Sarah Quappen, Matthias Nebel, Gregory Carlock, Johannes Greger, Hassan Haddad, Martin Gronemeyer, Ying Huang, Konstantin Klein, Eva Dingel, Frans Willems, Vasco Kretschmann, Stephan Frielinghaus, Brian P. Long, Dennis Halft, Lars Ostermeier, Yunus Yaldiz, Sven Karge, Sakina Abushi, Janet K. Miller and Yu Yamamoto for their friendship and support.

Finally, I dedicate this book to my son Jakob. Thank you for being a source of joy, thank you for being the way you are.

Introduction

The only sign indicating an entrance to the Effat University in Jeddah said 'Ladies' Entrance'. I had come, in February 2012, in order to conduct interviews with a group of students, and I knew that it was a private university for women. I was also aware that, being in Saudi Arabia, I could not just walk into a women's campus, so I had contacted university authorities prior to my visit, which was then minutely planned by one of the university's assistant professors. But as I could not see any other entrance, I went to the one for women. Before I reached it, a security guard yelled at me, telling me not to enter. I called Gerald, the assistant professor, on the phone and asked him what to do.

'Try once more to get in there', he said, which I did. The security guard asked about the purpose of my visit, inspected my passport, had me write down my name and passport number in a list, and finally showed me to the men's entrance, which was not indicated as such. In the room behind the gate a woman in uniform told me to take a seat and wait. A few minutes later, a veiled woman came to pick me up and led me through the campus to Gerald's office.

While we were walking across the courtyard, passing several buildings on our way, the veiled woman repeatedly shouted '*rijāl!*', Arabic for 'men', to warn students and female staff of my presence. She did so whenever we came to the corner of, or entrance to, a building and when women were in sight. The students did not seem to be very bothered by this. Some did not react at all, others indifferently put on their headscarves, too slow and negligent to hide their hair properly before I passed by. Occasionally, this prompted the woman accompanying me to shout in a more insistent voice: '*rijāl, yā banāt!* [hey girls, men are here]!' When we arrived at the corner of another building, she asked me to wait until she had cleared the way.

Prior to my visit to Effat University, I had become aware that I, as a man, was denied access to certain buildings and places in Saudi Arabia – in contrast to the widespread assumption that gender segregation in

Saudi Arabia solely limits the mobility of women and leads to their exclusion from a masculine public sphere. Yet, unlike Gerald, who received me a couple of minutes later in his windowless office, I was still not accustomed to the precautions taken to guide a man through a women-only space. Gerald told me that, on the way to his office and out again, he went through the same procedure every day. I realised that Effat University's architecture – the high walls that surrounded it, the gate, the guard's room serving as a control point, the lack of windows in Gerald's office – had many things in common with residential buildings I had passed on my way to the university. The concealment of women – or their hair, or certain forms of display of their bodies – behind the veil, or behind walls and corners of buildings, was also familiar to me from Saudi homes I had previously visited. I had often been entertained in a particular reception room which female family members did not enter as long as I was present. Furthermore, the vigilante's shout, *'rijāl, yā banāt!'*, reminded me of what I had learned about life in the old buildings in Jeddah in the past: that men climbing stairs had to utter words to warn unrelated female household members to stay away. It struck me that, in terms of architecture and social practice, the university bore a striking resemblance to private space.

On the other hand, the chance encounters in the university courtyard, as well as what students told me later in interviews, seemed to prove that a Saudi university can be considered as much a public space as any other university in the world. These women in their early twenties did not only come to Effat University to study. They got to know other people and made friends there, socialised, showed off fashionable clothes, engaged in various leisure activities and discussions, and were introduced, through their studies, to academic discourse on a variety of subjects. They communicated with students, faculty members and visiting lecturers from all over the world, thus gaining exposure to opinions and ways of thinking different from their own. Far from their families, who would not know if they did not don the veil when a man passed by, these students enjoyed some degree of independence and a public life at the university.

Complexities such as these caused me to rethink my own presumptions about the distinction between the public and private. I gradually understood that these categories do not necessarily denote two distinct spheres, which are spatially divided. As I argue throughout this book, these spheres should be regarded as intertwined, because our notions of privacy determine the way we construct public spaces, and our perception of the public realm shapes the architecture of private space.

Moreover, what appear to be a means to protect the private sphere can at the same time enable the constitution of publics.

Disentangling the changing relationship between public and private space in Jeddah over the course of the twentieth century is the aim of this book. The episode at the Effat University campus does not only provide an example of how notions of private and public are simultaneously enacted within the same space. It also reflects my own position as a researcher. I will discuss this point in the next section, before I elaborate on how I aim to contribute to academic and wider public debate on Muslim forms and conceptions of publicness and privacy. As my focus is on the architecture of public and private space, the third and last section of this introduction deals with my approach towards a sociology of architecture.

Reflections on research in a gender-segregated context

At the time of my visit to the Effat University I had spent a total of approximately three months in Jeddah. I had developed my own routines and rituals of fieldwork, become a regular at some restaurants and coffee shops, discovered the city by car and on foot, taken thousands of pictures with my camera, talked to various people about how they experienced the city, but situations such as the one at Effat University were still new to me. The way I spent my time in Jeddah differs critically from my way of life in Berlin, where I normally live. In many regards I adapted to my new surroundings: to mobility dominated by individual motor vehicles, to gender segregation, regular prayer times, the heat, and the local architecture which separates and connects people and activities in a specific way. All these factors, along with many others, affect the lives of all people staying in Jeddah. They are part of what the sociologists Helmuth Berking and Martina Löw (2008) have dubbed the inner logic (*Eigenlogik*) of the city. Perceived as normality or, rather, as undeniable reality, this inner logic is constantly being reproduced by residents of the city, whether temporary or permanent. I consider my research also as an attempt to understand some aspects of the local specificity and inner logic of Jeddah or, rather, of the social production and negotiation of public and private space there.

Although I regularly partook in certain activities with permanent residents of Jeddah and visited many places together with them, our everyday lives in the city did not have much in common beyond some shared moments. I lodged at a university-owned gated housing development for students, but I did not attend classes, have lunch or pray with those living in the same building. I accompanied several men, aged between 25 and 50, on a variety of leisure or professional activities to get an impression of where their lives take place, whom they meet, and how, in their conversations and social practices, they construct the city. I observed from a close distance and I listened to their stories. Even if I became something like a friend to some of them, my role always remained that of an outsider. However, in a societal context where a large percentage of the population consists of foreigners, the insider/outsider question is difficult to answer and, I assume, less important than the researcher's awareness of his or her own bias. My perspective is that of a male, non-Muslim Westerner, and as such it is certainly biased, but no more so than that of, say, a Muslim woman.

The scope of my study is certainly limited by the fact that I only had access to male and a few mixed spaces, not to exclusively female ones, the only exception being my visit to Effat University. The account of that visit given above illustrates that the constitution of public and private space is gendered, especially in a country like Saudi Arabia, where the politics of gender plays a crucial role in the formation of subjectivities and the constitution of space. I was denied access at the gate of the university because I am male, and my presence caused the female students to change their behaviour, or at least it was expected that it would. This implies that my material is gendered too, particularly with respect to data collected by means of anthropological methods. Furthermore, the majority of my primary sources – autobiographies, travel accounts, studies in architecture and urban development – were produced by men.

I used a variety of strategies to handle the gender bias in my archive. First, in my reading of sources I have paid special attention to the role of women in order to avoid reproducing the inherent gender bias of these texts. This also implied being attentive to the absence of women from some accounts and images.[1] Second, I arranged interviews with women to counterbalance to a small degree at least the prevalence of data obtained from personal conversations with men. Third, I indicate in my writing as much as possible whom I speak about and who produced the information I draw on, especially with regard to gendered spaces.

After all, so much excellent research on women in Saudi Arabia has been produced already that I felt I did not have to rehash well-trodden ground but could in many instances rely on the findings of other scholars: anthropologists Soraya Altorki (1986) and Mai Yamani (1996; 2000; 2004) have written about the changing social life of three generations of women in Jeddah with a focus on the elite. Both scholars observe that the nuclear family and the conjugal couple gained importance and autonomy vis-à-vis the extended family in the course of the twentieth century. Whereas Altorki argues that, as a consequence of this trend, women began to enjoy more social freedoms, Yamani is critical of the fact that women of the younger generation are tied to the domestic sphere much more than before. Eleanor Doumato (1992; 1999; 2000), who conducted fieldwork in Riyadh in the conservative cultural climate of the 1990s, is even more sceptical with regard to women's changing role in society. Women's opportunities, she contends, have been significantly reduced since the Saudi–Wahhabi conquest, not least because the Saudi state makes use of a restrictive gender policy to lend religious legitimacy to its claim to power. In the twenty-first century, Amélie Le Renard (2008; 2011; 2014; 2015), Madawi al-Rasheed (2013; 2015) and Annemarie van Geel (2016; 2018) have examined how new media, new urban spaces and changes in the government's agenda in relation to gender and women's issues have allowed for the emergence of new forms of public expression for women. While Le Renard and van Geel study gender segregation and women's public sociability from an anthropological point of view, al-Rasheed traces the position of women in the Saudi nation state.

Considering that Saudi society in general is still fairly unexplored by Western scholars compared to other Middle Eastern countries, such as Egypt or Lebanon, the topic of women in Saudi Arabia has been relatively well researched. Academic literature on Saudi Arabia also covers certain types of men, mostly those belonging to the royal family,[2] and radical Islamists.[3] Ordinary men, those who neither govern nor challenge the Saudi state in one way or another, seldom feature in most accounts of the history and society of Saudi Arabia. Anthropological studies dealing with Saudi men are particularly scarce (with the notable exception of Menoret 2014). Even though I chronicle major differences in the constitution of public and private spaces of men and women, my contribution to the production of knowledge on Saudi Arabia is stronger with regard to men.

It seems to be a widely accepted truth that men in Saudi Arabia are the ones who benefit from the rigid segregation regime the country is known for. My argument, as developed in this book, is that this assumption is a gross simplification that overlooks the fact that gender segregation serves to constrain the movements not only of women but also of men. At the same time, gender segregation provides opportunities for some men and some women: on the one hand many jobs, from taxi driver to judge, are reserved for men. On the other hand, present-day 'women-only' workspaces, universities, leisure spaces and so on enable a significant proportion of women to engage in activities which, in Saudi

Arabia, would be considered unsuitable for them in a mixed environment, and which were in fact inaccessible to them in the past, when an exclusively female infrastructure had not yet been created.

Public and private space

The topic of public and private space in a predominantly Muslim urban setting such as Jeddah deserves, I believe, more attention. A discourse on what, in Muslim societies, is hidden and what is visible as well as on who has and who does not have access to the public sphere already exists (see e.g. Göle 1997; Göle and Ammann 2004; Salvatore and Eickelman 2004). This discourse, which occurs in the Western mass media, academia, public discussions and private dinner conversations, tends to have a normative overtone. According to a widespread assumption, women in Muslim societies are excluded from the public sphere, especially in places where their physical visibility is limited by the veil and rules of gender segregation. As a means to render women invisible, the veil is often interpreted as a symbol of gender inequality or even of the subjugation of women, and gender segregation is interpreted as a manifestation of a patriarchal, misogynist social order.[4] There is hardly anywhere where women are less visible than in Saudi Arabia; and one thing almost everyone seems to know about that country is that women's lives there are miserable, not least because they are married to and ruled by conservative Muslim men.

Many women in Saudi Arabia indeed perceive their exclusion from certain public spaces as unjust. For several decades, for example, some women activists protested against the ban on driving because it limited their mobility. Yet the fact that these women found – and still find – opportunities to publicly express their opinion on these and other issues (see Schmid 2010; al-Rasheed 2013: chapters 4, 5) and, furthermore, that a large number of women do not want to do away with gender segregation at all (see Le Renard 2014: 138; al-Rasheed 2013: 159–63), indicates that things are more complex than is commonly held. I assume that, by reducing this complexity to a one-sided account of the subjugation of Muslim women, the normative discourse on women's rights or, generally speaking, on public and private spaces in Saudi Arabia and other Muslim contexts serves to confirm the superiority of Western values (see Abu-Lughod 2002; Ahmed 1992; Mahmood 2005). By stating this, I do not mean to deny or justify gender inequality in Saudi Arabia. Rather, the aim of this book is to provide a more nuanced account of the negotiation of public and private spaces there, an account that does not focus solely on women, but also on men. In doing so, I want to speak back to Western normative discourse on publicness and privacy in Muslim contexts and challenge the assumption that gender segregation and veiling necessarily lead to the exclusion of women from the public sphere.

Reservations about the use of the terms 'public' and 'private' as analytical categories in Muslim contexts have repeatedly been voiced by scholars of the Middle East with a feminist background (e.g. Joseph 1997; vom Bruck 1997). Their sceptical attitude often derives from a critical reassessment of an orientalist tradition that viewed Muslim societies as divided into a male public and a female private sphere (see Joseph 2000: 25–7; Nelson 1974; Stolleis 2004: 14–16). A discussion of this tradition is provided in chapter 4 in a section on the paradigm of the so-called Islamic city. From the 1980s on, a growing number of researchers began to investigate female forms of public life, resistance to male dominance and the influence of women on the political sphere in the Middle East (e.g. Abu-Lughod 1986; 1990; Altorki 1986; Chatty and Rabo 1997; Hale 1986; Hegland 1986; Joseph 1983; Peteet 1986). Their findings have called schemes of binary oppositions between house and market or female and male, as well as private and public, instituted by generations of researchers of both urban and rural Muslim communities into question.

In light of the observation that much of women's public activity takes place within the domestic sphere, some feminist scholars have suggested that the categories of public and private are inappropriate within a Middle Eastern context. Such a conclusion, however, is informed by the presumption that the home is equivalent to private space whereas public spaces are generally to be found outside the home. As Friederike Stolleis (2004: 18–19) has argued with regard to Damascus, we should rather consider meetings of women inside homes, which can frequently be observed in many Muslim urban communities, as genuine publics. Their activities turn the rooms where they convene into public spaces. Such an interpretation requires a dynamic, relational conception of space formulated, among others, by Martina Löw (2001) or Doreen Massey (2005). Both authors argue that space should not be regarded as a fixed physical entity but as the changing relationship between material objects and human beings. A home, or a part of it, can temporarily lose its character of a private space if it is used to house a public.

The phenomenon that public assemblies can be held in residential buildings was observed by Jürgen Habermas in *The Structural Transformation of the Public Sphere*, originally published in 1962. In the era of the Enlightenment, private persons convened in reception halls of bourgeois homes to engage in rational-critical debate on the common weal, thus constituting what Habermas labelled the bourgeois public sphere. When the book was translated into English, as late as 1989, feminist scholars such as Seyla Benhabib (1992a), Nancy Fraser (1992) and Mary P. Ryan (1992) criticised it for idealising a historical variety of the public sphere while failing to notice how far it was characterised by exclusion based on gender, class, race or religion. They also highlighted the importance of taking other, less official publics into consideration, that is to say formal or informal networks and discursive circles which differed from the authoritative publics of men of high social status only in their limited power of decision making. Scholars of the Middle East, on the other hand, to whom Habermas's model of the bourgeois public sphere appeared Eurocentric, set off to expand it to include various historical and geographical Muslim contexts. Miriam Hoexter, Nehemia Levtzion and Shmuel N. Eisenstadt (2002) analysed civic institutions concerned with the tasks of deliberating on issues of general public interest, providing advice, determining what is right and wrong in cases of dispute, and administering public funds in the so-called classical period of Islam, roughly speaking until the thirteenth century. Emphasising that the public sphere can have a religious dimension, they identified the *ʿulamāʾ*, or religious scholars, as main actors of the public sphere in the Muslim societies under scrutiny. A similar approach from a comparative perspective which, besides Islam, includes Catholicism and liberal modernity has been followed by Armando Salvatore (2007). Dale Eickelman and Jon W. Anderson (2003) explored how new mediums of communication led to the emergence of new publics in the Muslim world. Also dealing with contemporary society are the books edited by Nilüfer Göle and Ludwig Ammann (2004), as well as Armando Salvatore and Dale Eickelman (2004). They examine the relationship between religion, the public sphere and public space, as well as different forms of public expressions of Muslim identity.

Hardly any of these authors is concerned with physical aspects of public space, or the material framework of the publics under scrutiny. Hans Christian Korsholm Nielsen and Jakob Skovgaard-Petersen's (2001) edited book, *Middle Eastern Cities 1900–1950: Public Places and Public Spheres in Transformation*, while focusing on architecture and urban development, does not provide a theoretical reflection on the meaning of publicness, public space and the public sphere in the context of the Middle East. It seems to take a universal, yet unspecified definition of these concepts for granted. Nor do most of the above-mentioned authors appear to have taken notice of the feminist criticism of Habermas's model of the bourgeois public sphere or of feminist scholarship on women's publics in Muslim contexts (an exception being Göle 1997). Only a few of them take into consideration the many social groups who are or were excluded from the publics they define and analyse, groups which often constitute their own publics and counterpublics. Exclusion from authoritative publics based on social status and gender as well as the constitution of alternative publics have to be considered in order to gain a more comprehensive picture of the conception of public space in Jeddah, past and present. As critical studies of masculinity have shown, this argument is valid not only for women but also for various groups of subordinated masculinities and subcultural movements (see Carrigan, Connell and Lee 1985; Connell and Messerschmidt 2005; Ghoussoub and Sinclair-Webb 2000; Hirschkind 2006; Lagrange 2000; Menoret 2014): for slaves and poor African immigrants in Jeddah in the first half of the twentieth century, for example, and for migrant workers, religious minorities, political dissidents and gay people in Saudi Arabia today. In fact, the Saudi state hinders the creation of many publics. It does not grant citizens civil liberties, such as freedom of assembly, freedom of association, freedom of opinion and freedom of expression, and it is known for its harsh treatment of dissidents and critics. It is on these grounds that I consider Saudi Arabia to be an authoritarian state. Exploring how, in the political context of Saudi Arabia, publics can be formed, is another objective of my book. I discuss this question in chapters 5 and 6, which deal with contemporary Saudi society.

An attempt to derive from Habermas's model of the bourgeois public sphere general principles of the notion of a public in order to elaborate it and apply it to other cultural contexts as well as to groups of people who, due to their sexual orientation, gender, class or ethnic identity constitute a minority, has been made by Michael Warner (2002). '[T]he notion of a public enables a reflexivity in the circulation of texts among *strangers who become, by virtue of their reflexively circulating discourse, a social entity*', Warner observes (2002: 11–12, emphasis added). Independent of social categories such as gender and class, Warner's definition allows one indeed to speak about publics in a broad variety of cases that are not included in most studies of Muslim institutions equivalent to Habermas's model of the bourgeois public sphere. I found Warner's *Publics and Counterpublics* particularly insightful with regard to spaces where the private and the public overlap. In Saudi Arabia, but not only in that country, people often gather at home or in other privately owned and visually protected spaces. Sometimes they make public – by means of photographs, videos and the internet – activities accepted only within the private domestic realm. Warner's concept of counterpublics provides the theoretical framework for my analysis of these activities. I argue in chapter 6 that they aim at renegotiating the border between public and private in the society of Saudi Arabia.

It is important to note that, by 'circulation of texts', Warner does not mean written texts alone. Making use of semiotic terminology, he refers rather to all forms of communication – written and oral texts, visual media, clothes, body language and so on. This makes his concept fruitful for a study not just of the discursive formation of publics but also of public space as an 'assemblage' (Deleuze and Guattari 1987) of material objects and human beings which allows for or encourages communication between strangers. The topic of public space in Middle Eastern societies with an emphasis on urban places of encounter has been investigated by a number of scholars, of whom I summarise here only those who were particularly inspiring for my own work. Nilüfer Göle (2000) has shown how a growing popular desire to follow an explicitly Islamic way of life changed the constitution of public urban spaces and caused the emergence of an entirely new architecture of public space. The example she gives to illustrate this point is a hotel in western Turkey which caters especially to the needs of pious Muslims. In her studies on changing consumer culture in Egypt, Mona Abaza (2001; 2006) argues that shopping malls, which, in recent decades, have proliferated in Cairo as well as in other Middle Eastern cities and also in Jeddah, brought about new forms of public sociability. Particularly important for my inquiry into public spaces within a Saudi context are the anthropological studies conducted by Amélie Le Renard (2008; 2011; 2014) and Pascal Menoret (2014) on the capital of Saudi Arabia. Conceiving of public space as a sphere of encounter and person-to-person communication between strangers rather than, in the sense of Habermas, as a sphere of rational-critical debate, Le Renard provides valuable insights into young women's sociability in places such as universities, shopping malls and restaurants. Menoret, in his exceptional book *Joyriding in Riyadh*, treats the connection between urban development in the oil era and male youth subculture. He interprets the phenomenon of car drifting – that is, performing dangerous manoeuvres with usually rented or stolen cars in the streets of Saudi cities – as a political act aiming to destroy the official image of Saudi Arabia as a safe and orderly country.

In contrast to the vast array of literature on publics and public space in Muslim societies in various historical and geographical contexts, the topic of privacy is strikingly under-researched. The authors discussed thus far, indeed, hardly touch upon this issue. As if cautious not to intrude into the private sphere of their subjects, scholars of the Middle East largely eschew inquiring into conceptions of privacy among Muslims. Are they worried that they might find evidence for the outdated assumption that the private sphere in Muslim cultures is the women's realm? A similar observation has been made by Deniz Kandiyoti (1996) with regard to the relatively unexplored topic of sexuality in Middle Eastern societies. As Kandiyoti suggests, this can be explained by 'resistance against delving into culturally taboo areas and a reaction against the gender essentialism implicit in some radical feminist theorizing which bears some resemblance (albeit with different implications) to the categories deployed by Islamic fundamentalism' (1996: 14).

A handful of publications on notions of privacy in Islam or in Muslim societies indicate that gender essentialism can be avoided. Michael Cook (2000), Eli Alshech (2004) Mohammad Hashim Kamali (2008) and Christian Lange (2012; 2013) have written on the topic from the perspective of Islamic law. They offer valuable insights into the textual sources informing Muslim conceptions of privacy and, in the case of Alshech, the variety of interpretations of these texts. Abraham Marcus (1986) has used legal documents to explore how private space was conceived and socially produced in eighteenth-century Aleppo. I provide a discussion of these approaches and their respective merits in chapter 2. Suffice it to say at this point that an adequate debate on private space in Muslim societies has so far not taken place, and that the few authors who have addressed this topic are mostly concerned with the legal dimension of privacy. In order to gain an understanding of how private space is constructed and experienced in daily life, we must take social practice and material culture into consideration, especially architecture, as it has the capacity to separate and enclose people, screen them from view and hide their bodies, personal belongings and secrets.

It is taken for granted that studying publics, especially Muslim or feminist publics, is a legitimate project. As the literature on these subjects suggests, this is due to the agency involved in activities associated with the public sphere: discussion, the expression of one's opinion, deliberation on the common good, the forging of alliances, the fight for one's rights. Why should it be useful to study private space? Privacy obviously involves a great deal of concealment and locking away; it comprises that which is withdrawn from all a public has to offer. Private life is, by definition, the opposite of being in public and, as such, not thought of in connection with agency. The writings of several Saudi architects and urban planners, however, suggest a different perspective on privacy (e.g. Abu-Gazzeh 1996; Jomah 1992; al-Mutawea 1987; al-Nafea' 2005;

al-Shahrani 1992). Drawing by and large on the same textual evidence as Alshech (2004), Cook (2000) and Kamali (2008), they argue that privacy in Islam is a religious value. For them, maintaining one's own and respecting other people's privacy according to the rules of Islamic law is a pious virtue and a way to please God. Living up to this ideal of privacy requires the conscious efforts of attentive believers, especially when the social environment is perceived to be threatening it. Privacy has to be protected, defended and striven for. Understood in this way, it is not just a mere negative of publicness, but a quality achieved through personal endeavour which involves a great deal of agency.[5]

Transferring concepts which have a definite origin and tradition in Western thinking, such as public and private, to another cultural context presupposes a process of translation. I deal with this problem in more detail in chapter 2. At this point I want to define what actually is to be translated, that is to say what I mean when I write about public and private spaces in Jeddah. With regards to publics, I follow Michael Warner's definition of an imaginary social entity that comes into being through communication, or 'reflexively circulating discourse' (2002: 11–12). Public space, then, is the place and material framework that enable the constitution of this social entity. In the past, communication between strangers in Jeddah happened for the most part on the level of person-to-person interaction. My starting point in chapter 2 is therefore not a particular discourse, but the places of sociability themselves. In recent decades, new media of communication have given rise to new publics. In my inquiry into contemporary public spaces in chapter 6, which is far from a comprehensive analysis of these new media, I deal with Facebook, YouTube, TV and the press in order to explore how diverse categories of people seek publicity through different channels.

With regard to the notion of privacy, I am concerned with culturally dependent conceptions of an individual's personal sphere of non-interference with strangers. Private space, then, is a dynamic assemblage of human bodies, material objects and pieces of information which, in a particular cultural context, is concealed from outsiders. Concealment and protection is provided by human beings; artefacts such as walls, curtains or clothes; social practice; and texts of all kinds, from verbal communication to body language and the law. The question of whether a material object, such as a house or a letter, is protected from intrusion because of its content – occupants in one case, information in the other – or because the object itself is considered to be part of someone's private sphere is often difficult to answer and primarily of juridical concern. Rather than giving a precise list of who and what is regarded as private,

I am interested in understanding how, in an interplay of architecture, human bodies, social practice and discourse, private space is constituted in Jeddah by different groups of people at different times.

Investigating private spaces in a social context where great value is attached to a particular concept of privacy offers the opportunity to better understand the spatial arrangements of coexistence in that society. Assuming that the spheres of the public and the private are interwoven, I suggest that we can develop a better understanding of each of these concepts if we examine them simultaneously. Such an investigation allows us to comprehend why certain categories of people are excluded from particular publics, for example, or why certain publics convene in specific places and in particular architectural settings. This is particularly useful if we wish to challenge popular discourse on what is concealed and what is visible in Muslim communities and cultures. I choose to investigate a long trajectory in a relatively large and heterogeneous field, an entire city in the course of approximately one century. This approach offers the opportunity to survey the transformation of society on a larger scale, albeit at the expense of some detail. The focus on the architecture of public and private space is nevertheless based on a selection of cases and sources. I leave other forms of privacy, such as privacy of correspondence or information, mostly aside.

My inquiry into the transformation of the city of Jeddah in the course of the twentieth century, I suggest, can be helpful for the rethinking of common notions of publicness and privacy in Muslim contexts in general. My intention is not to say that my observations from Jeddah apply to the entire Middle East, nor that places as diverse as Riyadh, Doha and Cairo all followed the same path. My point is rather that the case presented here is capable of improving our analytical framework for the interpretation of public and private spaces in Muslim societies, especially in gender-segregated contexts. The reason is not only that Saudi Arabia is known for its strict segregation regime, enforcement of public morals and anti-liberal politics, and for exporting all of this to Muslim communities all over the world, from Indonesia and Pakistan to Nigeria, Morocco and Denmark. Viewed as an extreme, yet characteristic example of Islamic patriarchy, the case of Saudi Arabia also challenges both Western understandings of gender equality and liberal-secular assumptions concerning the freedom of the individual, which are key within both public sphere theory and Euro-American critique of Islam. As a consequence, the inquiry into public and private spaces in Jeddah presented in this book offers insights into radically different ways of defining the boundary between the public and the private realms, as well as into the interconnections between the religious, the public and the private. By highlighting disputes between conflicting notions of the public and the private, and by tracing changes in the conception of these categories, I aim to avoid an essentialist view of cultural differences. It is in this sense that I believe the material presented here, and my interpretation of it, may offer alternative perspectives on public space and privacy in gender-segregated Muslim contexts and in societies where political participation is severely restricted by the state.

Architectural sociology

I have explained above why studying conceptions of public and private in Jeddah can be of great value. In what follows I will elucidate why I chose to explore the architecture of public and private space – and not other forms of publicness and privacy – and which methods I used to do so.

Architecture surrounds us more or less all day long and profoundly affects our connection with the environment. As Maurice Halbwachs observed in his seminal work, *The Collective Memory*, originally published in 1939: 'The group not only transforms the space into which it has been inserted, but also yields and adapts to its physical surroundings. It becomes enclosed within the framework it has built' (Halbwachs 1980: 130).[6] Besides providing shelter from the forces of nature, buildings influence the flow of air as well as visual and acoustic signals, and they regulate the movement of people and goods.

This point is illustrated in Michel Foucault's analysis of prison architecture in *Discipline and Punish* (1977). The watchtower in the middle of the circular building as well as cells arranged along radial corridors in Jeremy Bentham's panopticon enabled anonymous, invisible prison guards to exercise physical control over inmates. The panopticon thus not only reflects changing notions of punishment and surveillance, crime and control in the Enlightenment era; this new type of building also helped to establish new relations of power – specifically because of the way in which it regulated views and framed bodies. Since a large variety of institutions – schools, the army, hospitals – were restructured in a similar mode, the particular interplay between architecture and human bodies in the panopticon is, according to Foucault, a distinctive feature of the emerging disciplinary society. Foucault's exemplary analysis, while not originally conceived as a study in architectural sociology, reveals the central role that architecture plays in defining society.

For many decades, sociologists were reluctant to address architecture and other artefacts. Those sociologists who have dealt with the built environment, for example Norbert Elias (1983) or those associated with the Chicago School (e.g. Park 1915; Park, Burgess and McKenzie 1967 [1925]), tended to see it as a reflection or an expression of social differences (cf. Delitz 2010: 39–61). Architecture can in fact be read and studied this way. In recent years, however, some scholars have begun to broaden this perspective, claiming that architecture not only passively reflects the structure of a society but also provides a framework for social practices (e.g. Delitz 2010; Fischer 2004; Fischer and Delitz 2009; Gieryn 2002). Furthermore, as these authors emphasise, architecture renders hierarchies and social differences visible and tangible, thus enabling or enforcing them rather than merely mirroring them.

If notions of public and private enable different degrees of access to people, spaces, material objects and information, architecture represents an important means of regulating relations between people and access to spaces categorised as public and private. This does not mean that a particular type of architecture determines the use of a building for public or private purposes. On the contrary, architecture is flexible in terms of use, and notions of public and private are contextual. That is to say, the same building and the same room can be a private family space and house a meeting where matters of public concern are discussed at different times. Architecture is involved in producing private space in much the same way as clothing, for example, allows us to maintain privacy while in public: we would not attend a public gathering unclothed. Just as the maintenance of our privacy with the help of clothes is, in most instances, a precondition for joining a public, architecture in Jeddah can, for example, fulfil the function of protecting the privacy of a group of women by screening them from view while they are, at that very moment, constituting a public.

While a building can be used for different purposes at different times, the architecture itself channels flows and movements more or less constantly in the same way. Whereas institutions are subject to fluctuation and change because individuals move, grow older, change their minds, lose their jobs, are replaced and eventually die, their physical framework of materials such as stone, brick, steel, glass, concrete or even wood and other organic materials remains relatively stable (Gieryn 2002: 35–41). The permanence of buildings provides the social institutions of public and private life with a tangible, visually recognisable and durable structure (Delitz 2010: 91–123, 130–2, 178–84; Eco 1986; Löw 2001: 166–98, 226). Owing to its omnipresence, endurance and ability to connect and segregate people, architecture plays a vital role in reproducing the local specificity of public and private space.

The ability of architecture to resist nature's forces of change is, of course, only relative. Ancient monuments deteriorate. We can tear down a house and build a new one, or we can alter an existing building to suit our needs. The written and unwritten laws of 'how things are supposed to be done' (Berking 2008: 27; my translation) in a particular city can be rejected and changed. As much as buildings reproduce existing behaviour patterns and power relations, new architecture has the ability to induce new social practices and transform the social fabric (Delitz 2010: 174–90; Löw 2008; 2009: 345–46). If we recognise that architecture, alongside human beings, is an integral part of society, we must consider that significant modifications in the built environment are accompanied by societal change (Delitz 2010: 140, 150–2).[7] In line with these considerations, I suggest that a sociologically informed study of architecture can contribute to a better understanding of social transformation.

Some of the changes that have occurred in Saudi Arabia since the beginning of the oil era are plainly visible to anyone roaming the streets of Jeddah. While exploring the city, I perceived the contrast between the building tradition that was maintained until the wealth of the oil economy swept the country and the residential architecture of today as striking. Tower houses constructed out of coral, limestone and wood have been replaced by apartment blocks, detached single-family houses and gated communities made of concrete, steel and glass. While the facades of old buildings contained large openings covered by wooden gratings that allowed air and light to enter while preventing people in the streets from seeing those inside, windows in contemporary homes are small and often covered by impermeable materials. And whereas photographs of Jeddah from the early twentieth century show a vibrant street life, new neighbourhoods seem to be devoid of human beings. Judging from the appearance of the architecture, the streets and open spaces, I understood that the notion of home, the perception of the urban environment and, moreover, conceptions of public and private space must have changed considerably during the last 60 years or, roughly speaking, within two generations. As none of these changes are well documented and researched, studying them became the aim of my research on which this book is based.

While architecture has in recent years become the subject of an increasing number of sociological and socio-historical studies (e.g. Fischer and Makropoulos 2004; Glover 2008; Grubbauer 2011; Jones 2011), to my knowledge the most profound and comprehensive theoretical reflection on architectural sociology has been presented by Heike Delitz (2009; 2010; 2017; Fischer and Delitz 2009). My empirical approach to the study of the architecture of public and private space in Jeddah is to a large extent informed by her work. Delitz draws on the Bergsonian tradition of sociological thinking, primarily the work of Gilles Deleuze and Félix Guattari (1987). She borrows the idea of the assemblage (in French, *agencement*) from Deleuze and Guattari – a concept they use to describe a material system of animate bodies and inanimate objects that interact, selecting and directing forces in the process just as Bentham's panopticon does.

Elaborating upon the specificity of an architectural assemblage, Heike Delitz (2010: 126–35) combines the Deleuzian notion of the assemblage with the theory of architecture presented by Deleuze's student Bernard Cache (1995), an architect and philosopher. According to Delitz, an architectural assemblage consists firstly of walls that frame and separate spaces and activities. The walls and roof of a building establish a physical barrier between a group of people and a mass of others. They define the visible, tangible and durable border of a social entity, thus making a particular mode of inclusion and exclusion part of people's lived reality. Secondly, windows, doors and other openings in walls have to be considered. They connect interior space with its surroundings. The perforation of walls and the permeability of openings determines the degree to which the occupants of a building can communicate with, or are isolated from, the outside world. Surprisingly, telephone and internet are not mentioned by Delitz in this context. Enabling communication with the outside world independently of openings in the walls, or through holes no wider than an electric cable, they are capable of bringing about significant changes in architectural assemblage. In my opinion, these means of communication should therefore be taken into consideration as well. A third aspect of the architectural assemblage are the floors and surfaces as well as furniture inside a building, a category which includes stairs, heating or cooling systems and other technical equipment. Surfaces and furniture affect visual and acoustic signals as well as thermal flows within a building. They guide people's movements through direct physical contact with the human body, thus making certain activities possible while hindering others (see Cache 1995: 22–30). In sum, architecture can be considered as the material framework of social practices.

The material aspects of built space have an affective quality. In other words, the way that walls and windows, floors and furniture made of specific materials are arranged has an impact on the human body (Delitz 2010: 144–9; cf. Ballantyne 2007: 41–2; Bille and Sørensen 2007;

Böhme 2006; Sennett 1994).[8] For Delitz, who follows Deleuze's use of the term, affects are the movements and forces resulting from the interaction between bodies and artefacts, or the effects produced by an architectural assemblage. This concept of affect is not to be confused with the assumption of 'an inbuilt behavioral-physiological response' to physical objects, a response that is sometimes constructed as universal, unconscious, involuntary and noncognitive, as Ruth Leys (2011: 437–8) sums up another strand of affect theory advocated by S.S. Tomkins, B. Massumi and N. Thrift, among others. The affect produced by a window grating can be the intentional blocking of views of neighbours while allowing a fresh breeze to enter the house. The affects produced by architecture can also be on the emotional level. As Georges Bataille pointed out with respect to palaces, churches and prisons, some architecture evokes fear and imposes silence (see Hollier 1992: 46–7). Other types of architecture provide people with a feeling of safety, even if this safety is only an illusion, as Setha Low (2003) and Wendy Brown (2010) have shown in their respective studies of gated communities in the United States and new nation-state walls, such as on the US border with Mexico or in Israel. As these examples illustrate, these emotions and bodily responses are neither universal nor necessarily unconscious, but contextual and subject to dispute: one and the same wall can evoke feelings of safety among some people and anxiety and despair among others. These contrasting emotional responses can both be considered as affects.

Architectural assemblage is, like any other type of material or 'machinic assemblage', connected to the discourse or 'collective enunciations' of the institutions themselves (Deleuze and Guattari 1987: 504). In the case of Bentham's panopticon, Foucault identifies a related discourse in public debate on criminal law. He draws a parallel between the new prison architecture and eighteenth-century military reform as well as the establishment of the human sciences. These collective enunciations, which contributed to the development of new bodies of knowledge, illuminate the purpose of the panopticon and the meaning attached to this particular type of architecture in the society which produced it. Discourse not only on the architecture itself but also on social practice and moral standards linked to it has to be taken into consideration in order to understand how changes in architecture correspond to overall societal change or, in my case, varying conceptions of public and private space.

These theoretical reflections have implications with regard to my methods. Investigating how architecture in a society, city or milieu frames, separates and shapes public and private social activity requires recognising who occupies the buildings under scrutiny and how access to them is regulated. Furthermore, we need to know how the materials and technical elements of this particular architecture block and permit views and the flow of air, light and sounds. Quantitative data providing information about the movement and flows of various elements, both animate and inanimate, which either enter or are prevented from entering a building are useful for gaining insights into the relationship between the design and materiality of buildings and their occupants. I found valuable data of this kind in studies conducted by architects from Jeddah. Abdulla Bokhari (1978) and Hisham Jomah (1992), for example, provide detailed descriptions of the residential architecture of Jeddah in the past. Ahmet Eyuce (n.d.) calculated the proportion of windows in the facades of old buildings and compared it with the proportions in contemporary architecture. Apart from these sources I studied travel accounts, autobiographies, floor plans, sections and building schemes, as well as historical photographs. Another important way I attained knowledge at this stage of my research was through architectural surveys of different districts of the city, which I documented in photographs, sketches and journals. Such information contributes to what may be defined as the phenomenology of architectural assemblage (cf. Delitz 2010: 211–13).[9]

Architectural assemblage cannot be understood in isolation from social practice. My phenomenological description of architecture of different periods in Jeddah is therefore interlinked with observations of what people do in a particular architectural framework, whether residential architecture, cafes and shopping malls or streets. In this respect, my work is also inspired by Michel de Certeau (1984), who emphasises the social and political significance of everyday practices, even of minute, often unconscious and seemingly irrelevant movements and activities. I used anthropological methods of data collection, such as qualitative interviews or informal conversations and non-participant observation, to collect information about the present and recent past. A few interviews were recorded and later transcribed, but much informal conversation was not, because I soon found out that my voice recorder created a formal interview situation that irritated many of my interlocutors. After a few failed interviews with otherwise talkative and open-minded informants, I decided to refrain from using a voice recorder, with only two exceptions. Instead, I kept written records from memory immediately after the conversation. In the case of more distant historical periods, I have turned to written sources, especially travelogues and memoirs. I also analysed photographic archives, particularly those of Christiaan Snouck Hurgronje, Charles Winckelsen and Raphaël Savignac, to learn what people in the past did in certain architectural settings.

In order to explore how the architectural assemblage – including its construction, style and material, and social practice connected to it – relates to relevant discourse, I turned to unpublished theses, working papers and journal articles produced by architects and urban planners from Saudi Arabia. In my discussion of how their narratives of Jeddah's transformation during the oil era relate to other public debates, I draw on a wide range of studies dealing with the political climate of the 1980s and 1990s. Public debate on gender segregation and mixing in the twenty-first century is also relatively well researched, and I relate my own anthropological data to this discourse as documented by other scholars.

Finally, I consider the question of affects evoked by architecture. I found anthropological observation most useful for studying how people react to architectural settings. I also refer to findings from a human science perspective concerning the implications of certain physical conditions on human bodies. Language-based sources, oral inquiry and written text were the only options available for gaining insight into the perception of architecture and environments of the past. Capturing affectivity is certainly the most difficult task in a study in architectural sociology. My aim is not to cover affects produced by every building or building type under scrutiny. Rather, I focus on examples of how new architecture, as 'a new fold in the social fabric' (Deleuze 1995: 158), introduces a difference in society, requiring social practices to adapt to new material frameworks and conceptions of public and private space to be revised (cf. Delitz 2010: 150–2).

The first chapter of this book presents an outline of the general history of Jeddah with a focus on urban development. It provides background information especially for readers unfamiliar with the history of Jeddah. Chapters 2 to 6 follow, roughly speaking, a chronological order. Chapter 2 begins with Jeddah in the first half of the twentieth century. In this chapter, I also discuss in greater detail the problem of translating the concepts of public and private. The massive growth and transformation which the city experienced in the first two and a half decades after the Second World War is explored in chapter 3. From the mid-1970s on, an increasing number of Saudi architects and urban planners criticised the architecture and urban development of Jeddah in the oil era. Their discourse as well as the cultural climate from which it emerged is the topic of chapter 4. Since the spheres of the home and the outside world became increasingly divided during the second half of the twentieth century, I discuss changes in residential architecture and urban space separately in chapters 5 and 6. While chapter 5 deals with architectural and societal change from the 1970s to the present, chapter 6 focuses primarily on the twenty-first century.

From 2009 to 2012, I spent a total of four months of fieldwork in Jeddah, with each visit lasting between 10 days and four weeks. I travelled mostly alone, but on my last trip in April–May 2012 my then wife Sarah and my son Jakob, at that time three years old, accompanied me. This gave me the opportunity to gain insights into 'families-only' spaces otherwise inaccessible to me. Visas for Saudi Arabia are difficult to obtain. I received them through the German consulate general, King Abdulaziz University and Effat University Jeddah. King Abdulaziz University also provided me with free accommodation in the student housing compound in spring 2011 and winter 2012. Whereas the Saudi authorities are generally highly suspicious of researchers writing on Saudi Arabia, and can censor unwanted opinions (Maneval 2014), none of the institutions which enabled my fieldwork in Jeddah controlled or limited my research or influenced the content of my book in a restrictive way.

Notes

1. There are certain parallels between this strategy and methods employed by the Subaltern Studies Project, which produces accounts on the history of subjects who did not write their history themselves, above all the peasantry in colonial India (e.g. Guha 1996, 1999).
2. e.g. Fürtig (2007), Glosemeyer (2002), Hertog (2011), Kechichian (2001), al-Rasheed (1996).
3. e.g. Commins (2006), Dekmejian (1980, 1994), DeLong-Bas (2004), Fandy (1999a), Lacroix (2011), Teitelbaum (2000).
4. For a critique of this discourse, see Amar 2011; Amir-Moazami 2007; Dornhof 2011; Fernando 2009; Mahmood 2001.
5. This perspective on my sources and findings was inspired by Saba Mahmood's *Politics of Piety* (2005).
6. For a discussion of the fruitfulness of Halbwachs's work for a sociological study in architecture, see Markus Schroer (2009).
7. A noticeable study in architectural history emphasising this point was presented by Erwin Panofsky as early as 1957. Equally pioneering is Pierre Bourdieu's (1967) preface to the French translation of Panofsky's *Gothic Architecture and Scholasticism*. Indeed, Bourdieu borrowed the concept of habitus from Panofsky in order to develop it further.
8. Due to the ability of architecture and other artefacts to affect people's emotions and to guide bodily movements, some theorists ascribe agency to buildings (e.g. Gieryn 2002; concerning the agency of inanimate objects in general see e.g. Gell 1998). The term agency, however, is disputed with regards to the question of intentional action: should we speak about the agency of inanimate objects in spite of their obvious lack of intentionality (see Morphy 2009: 6)? I prefer to speak about the affectivity of architecture instead, which is less ambiguous.
9. For a study in architectural sociology from a phenomenological point of view, see Frers (2007).

1
A brief history of Jeddah in the nineteenth and twentieth centuries

According to popular legend, in the year 26 AH/647 CE caliph ʿUthmān decided that Jeddah was to be the port of Mecca (Pesce 1976: 61; Ṭarābulsī 2008: 147). The origins of this legend can be traced back to the third/ninth century (Hawting 1984). What appears to be true is that, since the rise of Islam, the city of Jeddah has served as a transshipping location for merchants and as a transit point for pilgrims on their way to Mecca, around 70 km away.[1] By the late nineteenth century, the city of Jeddah was organised in a way that facilitated the passage from the port to Mecca and Medina, two cities that are holy for Muslims. The inhabitants of Jeddah seem to have been well aware of this function of their city. In his autobiography, ʿAbdullāh Manāʿ writes: 'We knew since our childhood that [our city] was the entrance hall (*dihlīz*) or the gateway to the two Holy Cities' (2008: 69).

Providing a historical overview of the nineteenth and twentieth centuries, this chapter shows how trade and the pilgrimage (*ḥajj*) constituted the main pillars of Jeddah's economy, secured the city's survival in spite of unfavourable climatic conditions, and shaped its demography and physical layout.

City of merchants and pilgrims

Jeddah gained particular importance as a trade city as early as 1425, when the Mamluks decided to use the harbour of Jeddah as the main port of entry to their realm, forcing merchants to call at Jeddah and pay a duty on their imports, especially spices and coffee. The city kept its function as a port of entry under the Ottoman Empire (1517–1918), especially in the early nineteenth century (Freitag 2007: 66). The entire city was oriented towards the sea, while appearing relatively secluded on the three sides facing the land, where a wall protected it against Bedouin invaders. A map produced by Carsten Niebuhr in 1762, which can be considered to be the first map of Jeddah that was based on scientific measurements, indicates two rows of houses parallel to the shoreline (Figure 1.1).[2] Among them were the customs house and later, in the second half of the nineteenth and early twentieth century, other administrative buildings. Merchants from other cities, from the Eastern Mediterranean to the Indian Ocean, had their trading posts in Jeddah, and some of them resided there.[3]

Although the opening of the Suez Canal in 1869 led to a general increase in shipping traffic in the Red Sea region, the harbour of Jeddah became less important as a port of call in the last quarter of the nineteenth century. This was a result of the shipping industry's transition from sailing boats to steam-powered boats. Steamships soon became capable of travelling longer distances, making an intermediate stop for merchant ships travelling between Suez and the Indian Ocean unnecessary. Jeddah remained the most important port in the Ḥijāz region, which encompasses the cities of Mecca, Medina, Jeddah and Taif, but commerce, especially exports of traded goods, declined significantly. Imports started to grow again towards the turn of the twentieth century, as the number of pilgrims and the amount of money they brought with them to cover their expenses increased. Since agriculture is hardly possible in the desert of the Tihama, as the strip of land between the Red Sea and the mountains of the Ḥijāz is called, Jeddah depended heavily on the import of goods of various kinds. Hence, imports outnumbered the city's exports by far and, over the course of the second half of the nineteenth and the early twentieth centuries, to an increasing degree (Ochsenwald 1984: 63–5; Freitag 2007: 68–9). The economy of Jeddah in this period thus rested increasingly on the pilgrimage (Figure 1.2).

Whereas Jeddah itself has no ritual significance in the *ḥajj*, the proximity to Mecca shaped the city's layout: one of the most important market roads in the old town, the Sūq al-ʿAlawī, led straight from the harbour in the west to the Mecca Gate in the east. At the Mecca Gate (Bāb Makka), pilgrims would find caravans – of camels and donkeys, in the past, and later of buses and trucks – to Mecca. As an extension of the Sūq, a few huts on either side of the road in front of the gate were set up by camel drivers and vendors of agricultural produce and cattle (Burckhardt 1829: 13; Tamisier 1840: 131). In the early nineteenth century, according to a travel report by Johann Ludwig Burckhardt (1829: 24), who stayed in

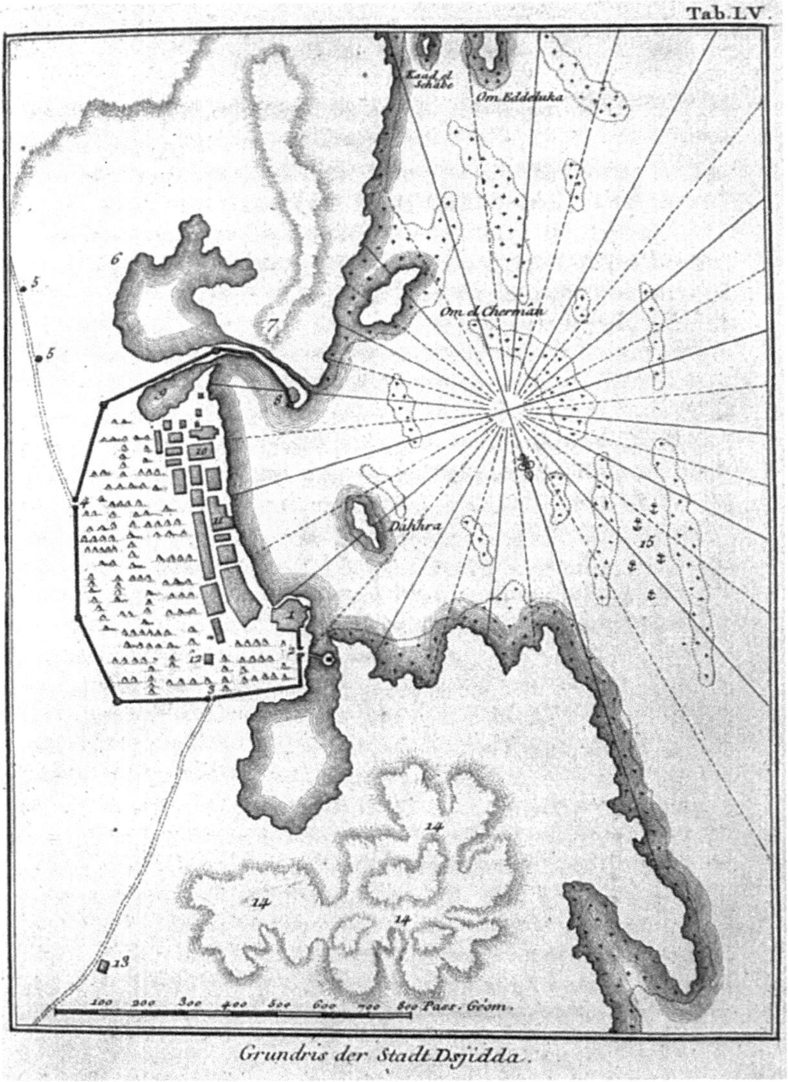

Figure 1.1 Map of Jeddah in 1762, from C. Niebuhr's *Reisebeschreibung nach Arabien und andern umliegenden Ländern* (vol. 1). Note that south is at the top, and that Niebuhr did not see the western parts of the walled city area. The numbers in the map refer to: 1) the house of the Pasha, 2) Bāb Sharīf, 3) Bāb Jadīd, 4) Bāb Makka, 5) watchtowers on the road to Mecca, 6) a plain where salt is collected when the seawater evaporates, 7) Christian cemetery, 8) ruins of a tower with battery, 9) the so-called Port of the Galleys, 10) Niebuhr's and his companions' house, 11) the customs house, 12) the house of the *kiḫya* (the Pasha's lieutenant), 13) Eve's tomb, 14) large hills of coral limestone and shells, 15) anchorage of ships from India and Suez. © Universitätsbibliothek Kiel (Q 527-1).

Figure 1.2 Arrival of pilgrims in the port of Jeddah. Postcard, around 1900. © Leiden University Libraries, C.S. Hurgronje collection (Or. 12.288 K: 2).

Jeddah in 1814, caravans to Mecca left Jeddah between twice a week and every night, depending on the season. The route to Medina, in comparison, was far less frequented.

Social life was also influenced by the thousands of pilgrims passing through annually, many of whom ended up settling in the town permanently. The highly regarded pilgrimage guides (*muṭawwif*, pl. *mutawwifūn*), house owners who were able to rent out accommodation, dock workers and peripatetic water sellers all profited from pilgrims (Manāʿ 2008: 74). Even today, more than 90 per cent of pilgrimage traffic passes through the airport of Jeddah. In order to allow for millions of pilgrims to travel in and out within a short period of a few weeks each year, one of the biggest airport terminals in the world was opened to the north of the city in 1981. While in the past many pilgrims were unable to return home to their own countries for lack of money and so stayed in Jeddah until the end of their lives, today many Muslims from poor countries make use of the pilgrimage to obtain a visa to enter Saudi Arabia, where they stay to earn money.

At the beginning of the twentieth century, Jeddah experienced three different ruling dynasties in quick succession. Until the First World War the town was part of the Ottoman Empire and was ruled by an Ottoman governor. A barracks set up around 1830 to the north of the town housed

Ottoman troops (Didier 1857: 130; Ṭarābulsī 2008: 56). In parallel with the Ottoman administration, there were regional institutions of social order, at the head of which was the Hashemite sharif and his representative (*wakīl*) in Jeddah (Ochsenwald 1984: 5–9; Freitag 2015b: 113–14). When the Ottoman Empire collapsed after the First World War, the Sharif of Mecca declared independence. However, the Hashemite ruling family was able to hold onto power for barely a decade because in 1924–5 the Ḥijāz was conquered by the troops of ʿAbd al-ʿAzīz bin Saʿūd. After a siege, the city of Jeddah surrendered to the founder of what is today the Kingdom of Saudi Arabia on 23 December 1925.

A significant factor that led to Jeddah's fall to the invaders was the shortage of water in the city. The groundwater is of poor quality, and some years there is no rain at all. Water from rare but sometimes massive downpours was formerly collected in cisterns outside the gates of the town and underneath some of the houses (Bokhari 1978: 182–3; Manāʿ 2011: 112–13; Rathjens and von Wissmann 1947: 84–9). Water sellers charged residents, pilgrims and other travellers high prices for the commodity (al-Faḍlī 2010: 40–3; Ṭarābulsī 2008: 140–2). The first seawater desalination plant was set up in 1907, still within the period of Ottoman hegemony, and it was rebuilt and expanded several times in subsequent years (Ṭarābulsī 2008: 138–40). Even today the supply of water represents a major challenge for the municipal administration of Jeddah. More than 97 per cent of the requirement for potable water is met by the output from desalination plants. The daily production of these plants was around 1 million cubic metres per day in 2010.[4]

Despite the lack of water, trade and pilgrimages ensured that travellers from the entire Muslim world and beyond settled in Jeddah. As reported by the traveller Johann Ludwig Burckhardt, 'The inhabitants of Djidda, like those of Mekka and Medina, are almost exclusively foreigners' (Burckhardt 1829: 14). The names of many of the families that have lived in Jeddah for generations indicate, even today, an origin in other parts of the world: the Bā ʿIshn, Bā Junayd and Bā Qādir families, to name but a few, from Hadhramout in present-day Yemen; the famous ʿAlī Riḍā (Alireza) family from Iran; as well as numerous families who adopted names that refer to the place of origin of their ancestors, such as al-Ifrīqī ('the one from Africa'), al-Banjābī ('the one from Punjab') or al-Asmarrī ('the one from Asmarra').

Red Sea traders and pilgrimage guides (*mutawwifūn*) enjoyed wealth and status in Jeddah (Ṭarābulsī 2008: 173–5). Other, less lucrative professions represented in Jeddah in the past included retail trade, fishing, boatbuilding, oil pressing, textiles, gastronomy, housebuilding and building-related labour, metalwork, construction of donkey-drawn carts, shipping, carrying of goods, the extraction of building material in limestone quarries and prostitution (Anṣārī 1982: 226–7; al-Faḍlī 2010: 36–54; Jomah 1992: 113–15; Ṭarābulsī 2008: 152–68). The income and living conditions of representatives of these professions varied considerably (Manāʿ 2008: 21–6).

Not even every labourer in Jeddah had an income. Although the slave trade was officially prohibited in the entire Ottoman Empire in 1890, slavery in the Arabian Peninsula continued to exist for several decades thereafter (Ochsenwald 1984: 117–21; Toledano 1982: 224–48; Toledano 1998: 10–11; Pétriat 2016: 134–40). In her memoirs of the late 1940s and early 1950s, Marianne Alireza (2002: 139–41) mentions several slaves working in the household of the Alireza family in Jeddah at the time.[5] Enslaved men and women usually lived in the houses of their owners. They could be bought in the market in Jeddah until slavery was finally abolished as late as 1962, when Prince Fayṣal ordered the release of all remaining slaves and compensated their owners (Ṭarābulsī 2008: 261–2). Male slaves in Jeddah were exploited for hard physical work, such as pearl diving or carrying limestone, water or flour. Others were employed in bakeries and coffeehouses, or as servants assisting in the family business. The majority of slaves in Jeddah, just as in the Ottoman Empire in general, were female domestic servants (Altorki 1986: 31; Ochsenwald 1984: 117; Toledano 1998: 6–7; Toledano 2007: 79).

The inhabitants of Jeddah distinguished between four residential quarters (*ḥāra*, pl. *ḥārāt*) that the city comprises: Ḥārat al-Baḥr facing the sea in the west, Ḥārat al-Shām in the northwest, Ḥārat al-Maẓlūm in the northeast and the centre of the city, and Ḥārat al-Yaman in the southeast. In the past, every quarter was officially represented by its own shaykh, also known as *ʿumda* in Jeddah, who was elected by a council of elders (Ṭarābulsī 2008, 180–90). Community ties within a *ḥāra* were imagined rather than manifested in gates or other physical barriers as is common in other cities in the Middle East and North Africa. The border between neighbouring quarters was invisible, and marriage between families residing in different quarters was not uncommon (Thābit 1998/9: 86; Jomah 1992: 175; Manāʿ 2011: 130–1). Consequently, kin were sometimes living in different quarters (see Manāʿ 2008: 26–7). Yet people identified strongly with their respective quarter, to the extent that there were sometimes rivalries between groups of men from different quarters and, on occasion, even fights (Freitag 2016a; Jomah 1992: 200–1; Manāʿ 2011: 201; Ṭarābulsī 2008: 182, 290).

Architecture and urban development from the pre-oil era until today

In the first half of the nineteenth century, the poorer population within the walled city of Jeddah lived in simple huts (Burckhardt 1829: 9; Tamisier 1840: 89), more affluent families in stone buildings. The latter were built of coral limestone, locally called *ḥajar manqabī*, and imported timber (Figure 1.3. See Pesce 1976: 105–30; King 1998: 32–51). The facades of these multi-storey buildings were whitewashed and many of the large window openings had wooden oriel windows called *rūshān* (pl. *rawāshīn*) in Jeddah. By the 1940s, a few rich merchants had already commissioned foreign engineers to build them new mansions out of concrete (Anṣārī 1982: 34).

According to a travel report by Heinrich von Maltzan, who claims to have stayed in Jeddah twice (in 1860 and 1870), the settlements of huts within the walled city were torn down after an epidemic of cholera in 1864–5.[6] Their inhabitants were driven out of the town and settled down in villages of huts a few kilometres from Jeddah (Figure 1.4. See von Maltzan 1873: 47). Information on life within these settlements is scarce, as most chroniclers and European travellers did not find them worthy of detailed description. It is only reported that a large part of the populace of at least some of the villages was of African origin (Didier 1857: 130; Savignac 1917: May 8 and 9; Tamisier 1840: 131–2). As the population of Jeddah grew towards the middle of the twentieth century, more and more people, mostly from other parts of the Arabian Peninsula and foreign countries, settled in these neighbourhoods *extra muros* (Ṭarābulsī 2008: 117). In the 1940s, mud brick was used there as a cheap alternative to the costly limestone preferred as building material by more affluent homeowners (al-Faḍlī 2010: 33–4; Jomah 1992: 57–8; Sijeeni 1995: 141). One decade later, concrete replaced mud brick as the primary building material for low-cost dwellings (al-Anṣārī 1982: 35–6; Bokhari 1978: 279–80, 338–40; Ṭarābulsī 2008: 117).

According to travelogues by Burckhardt (1829: 9), Tamisier (1840: 89–90) and von Maltzan (1873: 47), the settlements of huts inside the town area that were destroyed in 1864–5 had been situated on the fringes of the walled city, mainly in the north. The demolition of these quarters cleared the ground for new stone buildings. Some of them were constructed in a new style, with open balconies replacing the gratings of the *rawāshīn*, as historical photographs indicate (Figure 1.5). Some housed offices previously unknown in Jeddah, for example consulates and an expanding Ottoman administration. Foreign diplomatic entities – initially

Figure 1.3 Al-Shām quarter in the northwest of Jeddah, 1917. Photo: Raphaël Savignac. © École biblique et archéologique française de Jérusalem.

the consulates of the United Kingdom and France, and somewhat later those of Italy, the Netherlands and other European countries – were set up in Jeddah from the 1840s onwards (Didier 1857: 144; Freitag 2015b: 114; Ṣabbān n.d.: 29–34). Simultaneously, in a period of administrative reform known as Tanzimat, the Ottoman Empire strengthened its

Figure 1.4 Village of huts outside the walled city, east of the Mecca Gate, 1917. Photo: Raphaël Savignac. © École biblique et archéologique française de Jérusalem.

Figure 1.5 Building with open balconies in al-Shām quarter, 1917. Photo: Raphaël Savignac. © École biblique et archéologique française de Jérusalem.

presence in Jeddah, albeit not to the same degree as in other provincial capitals.[7] Almost all consulates and administrative buildings constructed in the late Ottoman period were concentrated in al-Shām quarter in the north.

By the middle of the twentieth century, the number of residents had grown to an estimated 50,000 (Duncan 1987: 84; Anṣārī 1982: 115). In anticipation of further growth, the wall encircling a town area of approximately 1 km² was torn down in 1947. One of the reasons for the demolition was an increasing number of cars in the city: only one out of a total of five city gates was wide enough to allow for the passage of cars (Krause 1991: 22; Sanger 1954: 3–4).[8] After the demolition of the wall, cars were able to move in and out of town easily. This can be seen as a harbinger of a much larger transformation of the city which was still to come.

After the Second World War the social structure and the appearance of the city changed radically with the onset of commercial exploitation of oil in Saudi Arabia, initially with American help. The wealth that was brought into the country by the oil economy attracted migrant labourers from all over the world. Since then, the ceaseless influx of large numbers of migrant workers has caused a high demand for housing. Foreign architects, engineers and construction workers helped to alleviate the lack of housing, by introducing new building materials and techniques. From the 1950s on, new settlements built of concrete came into being, ranging from exclusive villa quarters to densely populated neighbourhoods with low-cost dwellings for the poor. Today, around 4 million people live in Jeddah, making it the second-largest city in Saudi Arabia, after the capital Riyadh. As a result of several extensions of the harbour, Jeddah is the most important port in Saudi Arabia today. Within six decades the area of the city grew from 1 km² to 1,765 km². In comparison, the city of Berlin, where approximately 3.5 million people live, occupies an area only half as large; and London's 8.5 million inhabitants live in an area smaller than that of Jeddah, of approximately 1,570 km². Still there is no end in sight to the rapid expansion of the city.

The first new neighbourhoods that emerged in the oil era were characterised by irregular street patterns, relatively small attached houses and high population density. Al-Ruways, al-Hindāwiyya, al-Kandara, al-Sabīl and al-Nuzla al-Yamāniyya districts, for example, replaced former villages of huts when unskilled workers in need of inexpensive dwellings constructed their houses on squatted land in a belt around the city centre. In 1959 the Saudi government, lacking native expertise in city planning, asked the United Nations for help in solving urgent problems pertaining to the infrastructure of the city, such as shortages of housing and public facilities, urban sprawl and traffic congestion. The United Nations appointed ʿAbd al-Raḥmān Makhlūf, a town planner from Cairo who had earned his Ph.D. two years earlier in Munich, to produce the first development plan for Jeddah (Mandeli 2008: 520–1; Hassan 2001). The impact of Makhlūf's master plan is difficult to assess, as hardly any information about it is available. It seems to have focused on select problems of urban planning, such as the street network and the integration of the suburbs, rather than providing a comprehensive vision for the future of the city in terms of either architectural style or socio-economic dynamics. Abdulla Bokhari, an urban planner from Jeddah, comments on the building activity up to the early 1970s as follows: 'one can safely state that the period was characterized by a hysterical architectural frenzy in which anybody was allowed to build anything anywhere' (1978: 292).

In 1969, 10 years after Makhlūf's first master plan, the Department of Municipal Affairs of the Ministry of Interior commissioned the British consultancy company Robert Matthew, Johnson-Marshall & Partners (RMJMP) to produce a 'Regional Physical Plan and Master Plans and Detailed Plans of the Major Cities – Mecca, Medina, Jeddah, Taif and Yanbu – in the Western Region of the Kingdom of Saudi Arabia' (Duncan 1987: 52). After a preparatory phase of one year, the master plan for Jeddah was officially approved in 1971 and subsequently put into practice. It covered a vast array of topics, from housing needs, industry, business and employment, to civic, cultural and religious life, education, tourism, the conservation of the historic city centre, the connection of Jeddah to other cities via roads and the harbour, transport within the city, public health, power supply and utilities, as well as land use (Duncan 1987: 57–64, 130–2).

From 1948 to 1962, the city had grown from an estimated 50–60,000 inhabitants to 114,000 (al-Anṣārī 1982: 115–17). RMJMP conducted a socio-economic survey based on a 5 per cent random sample which established that the number of inhabitants was 381,000 in 1971 (Duncan 1987: 82). Unexpected events led to a population boom that exceeded even the highest estimates. In the course of the Arab-Israeli war in October 1973, Saudi Arabia, then under the rule of King Fayṣal, tried to exert pressure on the pro-Israeli US government by initiating in the OAPEC (Organization of Arab Petroleum Exporting Countries) a drastic increase in the price of oil. Since the US did not change its position in the Arab-Israeli conflict, the prices remained at the same high level, and Saudi Arabia's oil revenues grew (Champion 2003: 79–80; al-Rasheed 2002: 136–41; Vassiliev 2000: 393–4, 401). Economic growth and abundance of employment opportunities attracted migrant workers on an unprecedented scale. As a consequence, the population of Jeddah doubled every five years from 1973 on (al-Turkī and Bāqādir 2006: 75; Duncan 1987: 185–6). In 1974, an official census counted 495,900 inhabitants (Abdulgani 1993: 52). According to a second socio-economic survey conducted in 1978, the population had reached 916,000 – a figure approximately twice as high as the authors of the RMJMP master plan had anticipated (Duncan 1987: 151–2, 185).

The rapid development of the country, in particular its major cities, generated high labour demands, and the increasing number of immigrants who constituted the majority of the workforce led to even higher pressures on infrastructure. The shortage of housing prompted the Saudi government in 1974 to establish the Real Estate Development Fund (REDF). Providing interest-free loans to Saudi citizens, it enabled them to invest in the construction of private homes and buildings of a commercial nature, such as apartment buildings, hotels and offices. The loan, up to 300,000 riyals, would be reduced by 20 per cent for repayment within 20 years and by another 10 per cent for early repayment. But not everyone profited from the REDF. Many people were not able to meet the requirements for acquiring a loan: Saudi citizenship, landownership and a down payment of 30 per cent (Duncan 1987: 407; Mandeli 2008: 524–5; Tuncalp and al-Ibrahim 1990: 113–15). The fund not only caused a boom in construction activity and the creation of thousands of new residential units, but it also fuelled speculation in real estate and brought about skyrocketing land prices (Bokhari 1978: 334–8; Fadan 1983: 210–19, 246–54). As landowners speculated on higher future values, many central areas already enclosed by the network of roads remained undeveloped for years – a trend that continues today, albeit to a lesser degree. In fact, in the mid-1970s the construction of roads prior to the actual development of an area became an important strategy deployed by the Jeddah Municipality in order to expand the road network while avoiding the destruction of buildings and compensation of their owners (Bokhari 1978: 324–7, Duncan 1987: 376; Krause 1991: 29).

Due to the unforeseen population increase, only some parts of the city were developed according to the RMJMP master plan, while uncontrolled urban sprawl prevailed in other areas of the city (Figure 1.6. See Abdulaal 2011; Duncan 1987: 174–7; al-Hathloul and Mughal 2004). The outcome of this dual process can be seen in the urban fabric and on the map. In an attempt to make the city easily accessible by car – thus following the ideal of the automotive city – RMJMP introduced a network of streets in a grid pattern (Bokhari 1978: 296; Mandeli 2008: 521; Sijeeni 1995: 89). RMJMP also recommended the establishment

Figure 1.6 Map of Jeddah, *c*. 2009, indicating unplanned settlements and vacant land. The red hexagon indicates the location of the Old City and approximate area of Jeddah in the first half of the twentieth century. Based on data from the Jeddah Strategic Plan 2009. © Stefan Maneval.

of a public transportation system (Duncan 1987: 311–20) but, with the exception of a few bus lines, nothing like it has been established as yet. Soon districts with straight lines of streets and rectangular plots of land alternated with so-called irregular or informal settlements of the lower social classes, where houses were constructed on an ad hoc basis. The latter, so-called *ʿashwāʾiyyāt* (sing. *ʿashwāʾiyya*), can be found on the eastern fringes and in the vicinity of major industrial complexes, such as an oil refinery, and near the harbour to the south of Jeddah. At the time of their establishment, these neighbourhoods were located outside the boundaries of city administration. Their inhabitants chose to settle there in order to avoid the regulations of the municipality (Duncan 1987: 45, 96, 174–5, 187; al-Faḍlī 2010: 10–13; al-Hathloul and Mughal 1991: 271–2; Sijeeni 1995: 81–2, 141–3).

Although the first two Saudi kings, ʿAbd al-ʿAzīz and Saʿūd, had built a palace known as Qaṣr al-Khuzām (Khozam Palace) to the south of the city in al-Nuzla al-Yamāniyya (Bokhari 1978: 281–2; Mashāṭ 1998/9), the southern districts were soon not very attractive to the well-off. Anyone who could afford to settled in the north of the city (Duncan 1987: 90; Mortada 1992: 168–72; Sanger 1954: 12). In the past, real estate facing north within the walled town was more expensive than real estate and land oriented southwards, because of the prevailing direction of the wind (Manāʿ 2011: 77). In the hot climate of Jeddah, the cool northern wind is regarded as pleasant. The area north of the historic city centre was further developed when Prince Fayṣal, later the king (1964–75), chose to build his palace on Medina Road in the 1940s (Bokhari 1978: 281; al-Shahrani 1992: 73). Other members of the royal family followed suit and invested private money in the development of the area (Zaʿzūʿ 2004: 90–1). Embassies were set up in the vicinity of the Amīr Fayṣal residential compound and upper-class families settled there (Duncan 1987: 90, 100; Bokhari 1978: 283; Sijeeni 1995: 82). Addresses in the northern districts are associated with prestige even today. Since the growth of the city is limited by the mountains of the Ḥijāz to the west, Jeddah has expanded primarily parallel to the coastline, reaching a length of approximately 80 km on the north–south axis.

The Saudi Ministry of Municipal and Rural Affairs did not allow the consultants of RMJMP to revise their plan. Instead, in 1977 the consultants Sert Jackson International/Saudconsult were appointed to produce a follow-up study and new development plan (Duncan 1987: 334–75). In 1980, after a preparation period of three years, the 'Jeddah Master Directive Plan' was completed. Adapted to the actual growth of the city and addressing some of the shortcomings of the previous plan, it largely followed the paradigms set by RMJMP. The same can be said of the subsequent development plans, prepared by Al-Soumat Engineering Service and Al-Beeah Consultancy Offices in 1987 and 1995 respectively (Mandeli 2008: 525–9; Sijeeni 1995: 95–100). In the 1980s, limiting urban sprawl and increasing population density in developed areas became a major aim of city planning in Jeddah and other Saudi cities. The Saudi government implemented urban growth boundaries (UGB) in 100 Saudi cities to achieve this aim. The strategy of UGBs involved providing facilities only in designated areas of cities in order to discourage building activities outside the developed areas. While the overall success of this policy is disputed (al-Hathloul and Mughal 2004; Mandeli 2008: 526–7), one of its outcomes is an increase in land value within the UGBs and a decrease in real estate prices outside their confines. Due to the relatively low land prices at the northern fringes of Jeddah, for example, building activity can still be observed in these areas today, although houses will remain disconnected from the water and wastewater system as well as other public services for years.

In sum, the history of urban planning in Jeddah reads like an endeavour to gain control over the urbanisation process, an endeavour constantly challenged by rapid population growth. The authorities attempted to control urban development because they wanted to reduce the cost of facilities and services (al-Hathloul and Mughal 2004: 612). Low-income groups, on the other hand, tried to reduce their costs of housing by circumventing building regulations and squatting on undeveloped land on the outskirts of the city. From a different perspective – offered, for example, by James Scott (1998: 55–7) – the Saudi government's attempts to produce a regular urban landscape, with straight, wide streets and rectangular plots of land of equal size, are also aimed at controlling the populace. The negligible number of public squares and open spaces in Jeddah – the walkway along the corniche constituting the only noteworthy example – must be considered in this context too. The Saudi state does not grant its citizens the right of assemblage. It is not surprising that it does not provide the inhabitants of major Saudi cities with any public space that would allow larger gatherings of people (see chapter 6).

Throughout the 1970s, the old core of the city, specifically the western part, remained the main commercial centre of Jeddah (Figure 1.7). Office buildings, shops, warehouses, hotels and banks had been erected in the area known as the Central Business District, and the most valuable land in the entire city was located there (Bokhari 1978: 300, 310–11; Duncan 1987: 176–7). This trend changed beginning in the 1980s. Emphasising mixed land use, the 1980 master plan promoted the

Figure 1.7 Map of the old town of Jeddah in the early twenty-first century. The map indicates where the city wall once stood before being demolished in 1947, the main market streets and some landmark buildings: 1) the Shurbatlī house, 2) the Bā Junayd house, 3) the Jār house, 4) the Dhākir house, 5) the Bā ʻIshn house, 6) al-Shāfiʿī mosque, 7) al-Shāfiʿī *waqf* building, 8) the Nūr Walī house, 9) the Naṣīf house, 10) al-Balad house. Originally published in Telmesani, Sarouji and Adas (2009). © Adnan Adas, reproduced with the permission of the author.

Figure 1.8 Ruin of an old residential building in al-Balad, 2012. Photo: © Stefan Maneval.

proliferation of business and commercial centres as well as community services within new neighbourhoods or along main streets (Sijeeni 1995: 92–5). As a result of this policy, it is perfectly possible to live in Jeddah today without ever visiting the historic city centre, and although the densely populated mixed-use area is still highly frequented by consumers, members of the middle- and upper-income groups seem to avoid it.

Known as al-Balad today the old town is inhabited almost exclusively by migrants from Sudan, Somalia, Pakistan, Bangladesh, Yemen and other relatively poor countries. The former population deserted the old structures between the mid-1950s and the 1980s in favour of a more comfortable lifestyle in the modern city areas (Bokhari 1978: 278–80; Sijeeni 1995: 81). Yet the houses and land in the historic city centre are still in the possession of these families. Demolishing the old buildings is not permitted, but the land on which they stand is more valuable than the decrepit structures themselves. For that reason, most of the once-magnificent houses are on the brink of collapse, and more profitable modern apartment blocks, hotels or offices will eventually be built in their place (Figure 1.8). While RMJMP counted a total of around 1,300 old buildings that were still standing in 1970, there are only around 300 remaining today, on the basis of current estimates. In June 2014, the historic city centre of Jeddah was given UNESCO world cultural heritage status.

But fires and occasional heavy downpours continue to take an annual toll on even more houses, so the preservation of the old town is still a race against time (Maneval 2012a; Figure 1.8).

Notes

1. In terms of its dual function for the Red Sea trade route and the connection between the land and the sea, Jeddah resembled other port cities in the region, such as Mocha in what is today Yemen (see Um 2009) and Massawa in today's Eritrea (see Miran 2009).
2. The emphasis given to these structures in Niebuhr's map may be misleading, because Niebuhr and his companions were not allowed to come near to the Mecca Gate and explore the eastern part of the city (see Pesce 1976: 105).
3. For a history of Jeddah from 1850 to 1950 focusing on merchant families, see Pétriat 2016.
4. In Berlin a similar number of inhabitants require on average around 560,000 cubic metres of water per day. The demand in Jeddah is substantially higher because, among other things, 20 per cent of the water is lost due to leaks in the supply network.
5. For another account of a purportedly enslaved man in Saudi Arabia in the 1950s, see Lecocq (2015).
6. The veracity of von Maltzan's purported journey to Mecca and stay in Jeddah in 1860, of which he gives an account in his book *Meine Wallfahrt nach Mekka: Reise in der Küstengegend und im Inneren von Hedschas*, published in 1865, is questioned by Ulrike Freitag (2017) based upon a comparison of von Maltzan's published travelogue and his unpublished diaries. The journey in 1870, however, is not in doubt.
7. On the Tanzimat reforms and their impact on Ottoman provincial capitals, see e.g. Hanssen et al. 2002; Weber 2009: 29–46, 114–59; Ochsenwald 1984: 7–8, 167–9.
8. The city gateways were Bāb al-Madīna and Bāb Jadīd in the north, Bāb Makka in the east, Bāb Sharīf in the south and Bāb al-Bunṭ in the west.

2

Public and private spaces in Jeddah in the first half of the twentieth century

In the first half of the twentieth century, the most important market road in Jeddah, known today as Sūq al-ʿAlawī, led pilgrims from the harbour in the west to the Mecca Gate in the east. The regular stream of pilgrims made this street the most lucrative location for shop owners, especially where it intersected the city's north–south axis, Sūq al-Nadā (Krause 1991). Historical photographs of the market area in Jeddah show shopkeepers sitting or standing next to the entrance of their shops, displaying some of their stock on the street in front of them, and ambulant merchants selling their goods on wagons, trays or mats on the ground. One can see a steady stream of people passing by the shops in the early twentieth century: customers looking at goods on display and negotiating prices with salesmen, porters carrying large baskets or sacks on their heads, donkey drivers, camel riders and heavily loaded water sellers, as well as residents and workers trying to find their way through the crowd (Figure 2.1). Women, however, are almost completely absent in photographs of the streets and markets in late nineteenth- and early twentieth-century Jeddah.

In the past, observations such as these led Western scholars of the Middle East to the conclusion that cities in Muslim contexts were characterised by a clear physical separation of the private domestic sphere from the public realm, and that women in these cities were excluded from the public sphere (recently, e.g. Ammann 2004; Wirth 2000). This argument has been challenged by a generation of feminist scholars since the 1980s, yet the impression that women in gender-segregated Muslim contexts do not participate in public life and are confined, more or less, to the private, domestic realm lingers in public discourse. It is based upon two Eurocentric assumptions: first, that publics convene only in public spaces, while residential buildings are essentially private; and second,

Figure 2.1 Market street in Jeddah, 1918. Photo: Charles Winckelsen. © bpk / Ministère de la Culture – Médiathèque du Patrimoine, Dist. RMN-Grand Palais.

that gender segregation restricts the movements and freedoms only of women. This chapter looks into the relationship between public and private spaces in the city of Jeddah in the first half of the twentieth century. It argues that the architecture in Jeddah did not provide fixed boundaries between public outdoor and private interior spaces, but helped in the constitution of gendered publics both inside and outside the home. The division between the public and private realms was immensely important, demanding that men and women alike strictly observed gender-specific rules of conduct.

The chapter begins with a stroll through the city, moving eastward from the harbour to the bazaar area, the mosques and the open spaces in the city centre. The fictional walk through the old city then continues inside the typical tower houses, starting on the ground floor and moving up the stairs all the way to the roof terraces. Looking deeper into questions of gender, such as the one touched upon above concerning the visibility or invisibility of women in certain places, this survey of the city is divided into four sections. Investigating public and private spaces in a particular city, especially a city in the Middle East, requires a critical reflection on the concepts of public and private, which is provided in the next two sections: the first deals with the problem of translating the terms 'public' and 'private' into Arabic, and the second discusses the meaning of these concepts in the local context under scrutiny. Applying the analytical categories of 'public' and 'private' to the observations from the survey of the city, the last two sections in this chapter offer a synthesis of the preceding parts, with the first being dedicated to private spaces and the second to different forms of public space in Jeddah in the past.

From the harbour to the bazaar: Topography of a trading town

Until the middle of the twentieth century, most merchants, pilgrims and other travellers arrived in Jeddah by boat (Sanger 1954: 11). Their first view of the city was a cluster of white houses of different sizes, enclosed by a wall.[1] On land, travellers first had to pass through the customs house and a health check in the maritime health office (Figure 2.2). These facilities were situated on the shore among a row of other official buildings: the quarantine station, the post office and, further north in a building known as Bait al-Baghdādī, the Foreign Office (al-Ḥārithī 2003/4: 233–5; Manāʿ 2011: 30, 97; Ṭarābulsī 2008: 159–60). Behind these buildings was an open space where petty traders and Bedouin sold their goods (Figure 2.3). Traversing the square along a dirt road, travellers came to the western city gate, known as Bāb al-Baḥr (Gate of the Sea) or Bāb al-Bunṭ (Harbour Gate). The gate opened onto Qābil Street, the widest street in town and, since its modernisation in the Hashemite era (1916–25), one of the city's major market streets (Figure 2.4; Ṭarābulsī 2008: 235).[2] Qābil Street was bordered by a large mosque, named Masjid al-ʿUkāsh, in the north. South of Qābil Street was a lively bazaar area known as al-Sūq al-Kabīr, the 'Large Market' (Manāʿ 2011: 211–50; Ṭarābulsī 2008: 236–7). At its eastern end, Qābil Street was intersected by Sūq al-Nadā, the city's main north–south axis.

Instead of diving into the bustle of the bazaar, most visitors would first look for a place to stay in a quieter area. Having crossed Sūq al-Nadā, they would continue eastward along the extension of Qābil Street, called Sūq al-ʿAlawī,[3] and probably ask for lodging in a caravanserai.[4] Offering ample space for commodities, caravanserais were used particularly by merchants. They were often strategically located close to city gates or along the main street of Jeddah (Burckhardt 1829: 44; Ṭarābulsī 2008: 241–4). An increasing number of modern hotels have replaced them since the 1940s.[5] Before mass accommodation for pilgrims was

Figure 2.2 The customs house, photographed from an arriving boat, 1926. Photo: van Voorthuysen. © Leiden University Libraries, C.S. Hurgronje collection (Or. 12.288 B: 10).

constructed beginning in 1950, pilgrims and other travellers often found lodging in private homes. The city's economy depended heavily on the pilgrimage, and the accommodation of pilgrims was one way for the inhabitants of Jeddah to profit from the annual flow of people through the city. Pilgrimage guides (*mutawwifūn*, sing. *muṭawwif*, also referred to as *wukalā*, sing. *wakīl* = agent) rented additional rooms, sometimes entire buildings, if their own houses did not offer enough space to accommodate customers (Manāʿ 2008: 72–6; Ṭarābulsī 2008: 173, 620). Some

Figure 2.3 View of the town and an open space behind the customs house, around 1900. Unknown photographer. © Leiden University Libraries, C.S. Hurgronje collection (Or. 26.365: 12).

Figure 2.4 Al-Qābil Street, with al-ʿUkāsh Mosque to the left and al-Miʿmār Mosque in the background (centre). View from the terrace of the post office, 1918. Photo: Charles Winckelsen. © bpk / Ministère de la Culture – Médiathèque du Patrimoine, Dist. RMN-Grand Palais.

pilgrims, Africans for the most part, slept on the streets (Manāʿ 2008: 75; Sanger 1954: 11).

Sūq al-ʿAlawī was the east–west artery of Jeddah (Manāʿ 2011: 143).[6] Sloping uphill towards the east, it led pilgrims and travellers through the city to Bāb Makka, the Mecca Gate. The street divided Jeddah into two northern and two southern quarters. The former were Ḥārat al-Shām in the northwest and Ḥārat al-Maẓlūm in the northeast, the latter Ḥārat al-Baḥr facing the sea and Ḥārat al-Yaman to the southeast. Rathjens and von Wissmann (1947: 77) indicate Sūq al-ʿAlawī and some adjacent streets as the city's main market area.

Places of encounter: mosques, open spaces and coffeehouses

In the first half of the twentieth century, seven major mosques and an undefined number of small prayer houses existed in Jeddah. All available sources indicate that Masjid al-Shāfiʿī in al-Maẓlūm quarter is the oldest of the existing mosques. Built around the middle of the thirteenth century, Masjid al-Shāfiʿī seems to have ceased to be the city's only central Friday mosque in the course of the centuries, as foreign and domestic merchants as well as different Ottoman governors often funded the construction or extension of other mosques (Krause 1991: 52–3; cf. Pesce 1976: 120; Sijeeni 1995: 74–5; Ṭarābulsī 2008: 287–97). In principle, a mosque is open to every Muslim, and believers often simply choose the nearest mosque to pray in. Before the Saudi–Wahhabi conquest, however, adherents of the various Muslim schools and sects used different mosques and spaces to conduct their respective rituals. Maurice Tamisier (1840: 78–9), for example, reports that Sufi dervishes used to gather and sing for three to four hours in the Sulṭān Ḥasan Mosque (also known as *Masjid al-Bāshā*, or Pasha Mosque)[7] during pilgrimage season. Charles Didier (1857: 136) mentions Sufi gatherings with music and singing in the house next to the one in which he resided in al-Shām quarter. It may have been one of the many Sufi *zāwiyas*, places where Sufis conducted their collective rituals (Ṭarābulsī 2008: 298–9), or a gathering of Sufis at home. Sufism was – and still is – a widespread phenomenon in the Ḥijāz, and many *ʿulamāʾ* (Muslim scholars) and other notables adhered to a Sufi convent (*ṭariqa*). Under the rule of King ʿAbd al-ʿAzīz (1926–53), many *zāwiyas* were destroyed and numerous Sufi shaykhs left the Kingdom or moved to areas where Wahhabi influence was weaker. Others,

Figure 2.5 Open space with a sitting area next to al-Bāshā Mosque in Ḥārat al-Shām, 1918. Photo: Charles Winckelsen. © bpk / Ministère de la Culture – Médiathèque du Patrimoine, Dist. RMN-Grand Palais.

however, stayed in the Ḥijāz, adopting less visible ways to perform their rituals (Sedgwick 1997: 360–1).

Apart from serving religious purposes – daily prayer, Friday sermons, Sufi rituals, etc. – mosques were also important places of sociability. For many residents of Jeddah, the neighbourhood mosque was the primary place to meet friends and acquaintances (Sijeeni 1995: 152–61; Ṭarābulsī 2008: 304). In the evening after prayer, men would sit together chatting and exchanging news in front of the mosque or in other open spaces in the streets. Some of these spaces, called *barḥa* (pl. *barḥāt*), were just a widening of the street, large enough to set up a *mirkāz*, a group of benches for the men to sit on (Figure 2.5). The larger ones, like Barḥat al-ʿAidarūs in al-Yaman quarter, extended over the facades of several houses. Children used to play on a *barḥa* close to their home while their fathers, grandfathers or uncles sitting in front of the house could keep an eye on them. On special occasions, such as weddings or the Eid festivals, music was played and a dance called *mizmār* was performed on the squares (Figure 2.6).[8] The *mizmār*, danced by men with wooden sticks, was seen as a competitive display of manhood, usually carried

Figure 2.6 A boy dancing in front of a group of children dressed up for the *ʿīd al-fiṭr* at the end of the fast of Ramadan, around 1900. Unknown photographer. © Leiden University Libraries, C.S. Hurgronje collection (Or. 12.288 M: 39).

out in a playful way but sometimes causing violent clashes between rival groups (Freitag 2016a). During the two main festivities in the Muslim calendar, the Eid al-Adha towards the end of the *ḥajj* and the Eid al-Fitr at the end of the fast of Ramadan, wings for children were set up in some of the larger squares.

In every city quarter, several cafes (*maqāhī*, sing. *maqhā*) offering coffee, tea and water pipes provided shaded areas for sitting down,

Figure 2.7 Coffee house next to the Dutch consulate. Photo: van Voorthuysen 1926. © Leiden University Libraries, C.S. Hurgronje collection (Or. 12.288 B: 26).

meeting friends and socialising (Figure 2.7). The cafes were furnished with high wooden seats and benches made of local materials such as *dūm*-tree, palm leaves and rope. Customers were for the most part regulars who all knew each other. They were often of the same profession and used these informal meetings at the end of their workday to discuss news and make collective decisions pertaining to their business (Manāʿ 2008: 45–50; Ṭarābulsī 2008: 196–202). Another large portion of a cafe's customers were residents of the neighbourhood. In his autobiography, ʿAbdullāh Manāʿ, a physician and journalist from Jeddah, states that he and his *shilla* (clique, or group of young men) visited Qahwat al-Yamānī in al-Baḥr quarter so frequently that for them it became 'a centre of our everyday life' (2008: 45). Women and children avoided the cafes. Like the daily gatherings in open squares, cafes were exclusively adult male spaces.

In historical photographs, men usually wear some sort of robe, or jacket and trousers. Most men, rich and poor alike, cover their head with a turban or cap. The only bare chest visible in any of the historical

Figure 2.8 Prison inmates, 1917. Photo: Raphaël Savignac. © École biblique et archéologique française de Jérusalem.

photographs available to me belongs to an inmate of the local prison (Figure 2.8). The picture was taken on 9 May 1917 by Raphaël Savignac, a Dominican brother who travelled with the French military expedition to Saudi Arabia during the First World War. It shows a prison guard and two convicts who sit on the floor in an excruciating position, their arms and legs bound by strong iron bars. In pictures of slaves from the collection of Christiaan Snouck Hurgronje, one can see knees exposed. All other men, from the esteemed pilgrimage guides to shippers, donkey drivers, and water sellers, do not reveal naked parts of their body apart from the lower legs and feet, hands and head.

Visible, but unseen: Women and public space

My description of public spaces in Jeddah has thus far left out women. As mentioned above, they are almost completely absent from historical photographs of the city's streets and markets in the late nineteenth and early twentieth century. There are only a few exceptions: Raphaël Savignac, the Dominican brother, took a snapshot of two fully veiled women in the street as they passed by (Figure 2.9). The shaky image stands in sharp

Figure 2.9 Women in the street, 1917. Photo: Raphaël Savignac. © École biblique et archéologique française de Jérusalem.

contrast to Savignac's other photographs, suggesting that the picture was taken hastily, without a tripod. His travel journal reveals that he was aware of the fact that taking pictures of women was socially unacceptable.[9] A few similarly discreet point-and-shoot images of women were taken by Charles Winckelsen, also a Frenchman, who visited Jeddah in 1918, and some more can be found in the collection of Christiaan Snouck Hurgronje, which spans the period from the mid-1880s to the 1930s (Freitag 2016b). The only women who look into the camera without hesitation or distress are black Africans from clearly poor social backgrounds. In one picture by Winckelsen, a young, barefoot woman dressed in rags, carrying a baby and a basket, can be seen; in another, a young woman with a baby on her back sits next to some fishing boats at the port, her dress revealing her shoulders, arms and the upper part of her back (Figure 2.10). A third picture, also by Winckelsen, shows a barefoot black woman with a baby leaning to a wall, her breast exposed.[10] Some pictures of crowds taken from a distance are also available, with the photographers being able to operate unnoticed. With the exception of a few vendors of water, agricultural produce or homemade food, women do not feature (Figures 2.3, 2.4).[11] The almost complete absence of women

Figure 2.10 Poor woman of African origin with a baby in the harbour, 1918. Photo: Charles Winckelsen. © bpk / Ministère de la Culture – Médiathèque du Patrimoine, Dist. RMN-Grand Palais.

in the latter pictures in particular indicates that women not only avoided to be photographed, but also to be seen in public.

A Ḥijāzī saying confirms this impression, stating that, 'A woman leaves her house twice: she leaves her father's house when she is married, and [she] leaves her husband's house when she is buried.' The author who cites this saying, Hisham Jomah, limits its scope, adding: 'Women went out to visit relatives and parents but not for any sort of participation in public functions or entertainment' (Jomah 1992: 231). Ideally speaking, in early twentieth-century Jeddah a woman's place was inside the house, not outside (Altorki 1986: 55). The street was a place occupied by men, to be avoided by women of any but the lowest social strata.

Women from well-to-do families would not go to the market because shopkeepers or men sitting in the streets could have recognised them (Sijeeni 1995: 149). If their families could afford a servant or a slave, women would have him buy what they needed. Shopkeepers would also come to affluent households upon request, to allow women to choose from a selection of goods (Alireza 2002: 66–7). However, as mentioned by Hisham Jomah, women often left their homes in order to visit neighbours, friends and relatives, attend weddings and other festivities, or to go to the cemetery to pay their respects to the deceased (Didier 1857: 133; al-Shahrani 1992: 55). But whereas men spent much of their time lingering in the streets, women were only supposed to traverse public spaces, not to participate in the activities occurring there.

A distinction drawn by the ethnographer Michael Gilsenan (2008: chapter 8), between being seen and being visible, helps to explain women's limited presence in, but not complete absence from, the public realm. Gilsenan (2008: 171–2) observes that women walking down one of the narrow paths in the Lebanese village where he conducted his fieldwork in the 1970s are 'in the literal sense of the word visible. But they are not "seen". ... Men walk down the middle, women cling to the sides and walk fast. Neither gives any sign of seeing the other at all. The women are socially and for all practical purposes invisible' (Gilsenan 2008: 172). A very similar practice was common in Jeddah, as reported by Hisham Jomah (1992: 198), Mohammad al-Shahrani (1992: 55) and ʿAbbās al-Faḍlī (2010: 13). Adhering to this rule was not so much a matter of religiousness, as of social standing (cf. al-Rasheed 2013: 53–4). The two poor women with their children photographed by Winckelsen do not cover their faces, and one of them even has a naked shoulder. Their visibility indicated the low status of these women. Women at the other end of the social scale, such as the veiled ladies in Savignac's snapshot, avoided being seen. Being photographed, even fully veiled, represented being seen, and this was intolerable to them.

Hisham Jomah describes the close link between women and home in the Ḥijāz in somewhat idealising terms. Most of a woman's time, he writes, 'was devoted to the family, and in what remained she was allowed no scope for any other vocation (even if maids or servants were employed). Her sphere was wholly in the home. It was her workshop, her vehicle of expression, but was never thought of as a confinement' (Jomah 1992: 230–1). He does not mention that a considerable number of families were not able to conform to this ideal but depended on a woman's income to make ends meet. ʿAbdullāh Manāʿ's mother, for example, began working as a seamstress after her husband's death. Even his grandmother had to earn some money to support the widow with her two sons. In one of the rooms of the family home she established a school for young girls whom she taught reading, writing and the Quran (Manāʿ 2008: 21–23, 33). Women working in orphanages, doing laundry for other families or vending food in order to augment a scarce family income were quite common (Ṭarābulsī 2008: 308; al-Faḍlī 2010: 54).

If a woman was compelled to earn money, work inside the house was of higher esteem than any business in the street. Manāʿ (2008: 23) reports that, in times of severe financial straits, his grandmother sent him to a benevolent supporter of the family, who gave the child some money in return for a handful of empty bottles. As Manāʿ remembers it, this was an embarrassing experience, in spite of his young age. But it helped the family survive without making it necessary for the women to leave the house in order to earn money. A generation earlier, Manāʿ's family had been better off: his grandfather, captain on a *sanbūk* in the harbour of Jeddah, owned two houses in Ḥārat al-Baḥr, several boats and a few slaves (Manāʿ 2008: 21–2).[12] By avoiding any occupation that involved exposure to the public, Manāʿ's mother and grandmother maintained the social distinction of the family in spite of their poverty. Rather than leaving the house and having to interact with men outside the family, they would rely on male relatives if necessary. If an adult male was not available, a child could serve as a messenger. In his memoirs, Manāʿ (2011: 37–40) recounts the story of a man refusing to pay his dues to the author's mother. The widow sends her juvenile son to a man of some rank named Sulaymān Abū Dawūd, a friend of her deceased husband's, in order to ask for help. Sulaymān promises to settle the problem and tells the boy to visit the cheater the following Friday. Manāʿ does what he is told, collects the money and brings it home. As a widow, Manāʿ's mother was obviously able to fight for her rights and manage her economic affairs, which normally fell within the remit of a husband's duties. Yet she did so by communicating through a chain of male agents, thus avoiding direct contact with a man to whom she was unrelated.

The social practice of women avoiding being seen also required men to actively avoid seeing women. In his memoirs from al-Nuzla al-Yamaniyya, a former village to the southeast of Jeddah, al-Faḍlī (2010: 13) recounts how men in al-Nuzla, as well as in Jeddah, looked in another direction when a woman passed by, so as not to disturb her. It was a matter of good conduct to feign not seeing a passing woman. Al-Shahrani relates this practice to a religious demand articulated in 'Sūrat al-Nūr' in the Quran:

> Say to the believing men that they should lower their gaze and guard their modesty: that will make for greater purity for them: and God is well acquainted with all that they do. And say to the believing women that they should lower their gaze and guard their modesty; that they should not display their beauty and ornaments except

> what (must ordinarily) appear thereof; that they should draw their veils over their bosoms and not display their beauty except to their husbands, their fathers ...
>
> (Quran 24:30–1, quoted in al-Shahrani 1992: 55).[13]

An annual women's carnival constitutes an exception from the general picture sketched out here, in which women were a rare sight in the streets of Jeddah. During the *ḥajj* season, when the streets of Jeddah were empty of men because they either temporarily worked in Mecca or performed the pilgrimage themselves, women dressed as men paraded through the city, playing drums and performing dances. For the four nights of the al-Qays carnival, those men remaining in the city risked becoming subject to mock songs or even a beating when they got in the parading women's way (Freitag 2014). The al-Qays festival indicates that the concept of gender segregation did not generate a stable topography of permanently male or female places. Rather, it demanded that both men and women be constantly attentive to the rule that contact between unrelated men and women should be avoided, in the streets and, as we will see in the next section, inside homes.

Residential architecture: One building, multiple functions

While the streets and the market were, with the exception of the al-Qays festival, places occupied by men and avoided by women of a certain social standing, the houses, especially the upper floors, were associated with women and families. As I will show in the following pages, this did not entail a fixed spatial division between a male public sphere and a female private domain. Whereas women were excluded from male spaces of encounter outdoors, they convened inside the home and not outside to exchange news, discuss important affairs collectively, argue about right or wrong and celebrate. The home was hence not a strictly private space, nor was it reserved for women and family alone. As the centre of male social and commercial activity, the ground floors of houses in Jeddah were in fact designed to allow for the presence of unrelated men and strangers, unlike houses found in Syria, for example. How, then, was gender segregation achieved inside the house? Is it appropriate, after all, to speak of a division between the public and the private in Jeddah in the first half of the twentieth century? And if so, what role did architecture play in maintaining the border between these spheres?

Most of the day, the front door of a residential building served as a symbolic threshold rather than as a physical barrier (Jomah 1992: 179–81, 229). The front door was often left open but few people who were not invited would attempt to enter the house. Marking the transition from the street to the interior of the house, the entrance was often emphasised with green colour applied to some of its features – the door, lintel or arch. Visitors would utter religious formulas of blessing upon crossing the threshold, such as '*mā shā ʾ Allāh* (God's will be done)' (Jomah 1992: 179–81).

Many houses, especially the larger ones, had two entrances, one for men and their male guests and one for women (Jomah 1992: 61, 194; al-Shahrani 1992: 53). Entering a house via the main entrance, visitors found themselves in a reception hall, the *dihlīz*, with wooden benches attached to the walls. Next to the entrance hall was the *maq ʿad*, that is the office and reception area of the head of the family (Figure 2.11). From his *maq ʿad* the patriarch could watch over the entry and the way to the staircase. On the ground floor of larger houses there were other rooms beside the *maq ʿad* which could be used to receive guests, or as storerooms, or as servants' sleeping quarters (Pesce 1976: 118; Bokhari 1978: 183–4).

Figure 2.11 Ground floor office in the Dutch consulate in a typical old building, around 1900. Unknown photographer. © Leiden University Libraries, C.S. Hurgronje collection (Or. 26.365: 6).

Ground floors in the bazaar area accommodated retail shops. Unlike the *maqʿad* in a house in a residential quarter, a shop in a multi-storey building in the *sūq* was normally disconnected from the upper floors (Krause 1991: 53–6). During *ḥajj* season, rooms on the lower levels of residential buildings were rented to pilgrims (Anṣārī 1972: 183; Burckhardt 1829: 11; Rathjens and Wissmann 1947: 80–1). Some families temporarily gave up entire buildings or apartments on the lower floors of multi-storey houses to take in pilgrims. This practice was facilitated by the absence of many men during the *ḥajj*. For the duration of the *ḥajj*, the women, children and elderly people remaining in Jeddah withdrew to the upper floors of their houses or moved to the homes of relatives (Fadan 1983: 152–3; Manāʿ 2008: 19–20).

During evening hours, control of the entrance was transferred from the *maqʿad* inside to the *mirkāz* (gathering place) in front of the house (Figure 2.12. See al-Shahrani 1992: 55–6). The *mirkāz* consisted of sets of benches, most of which were made out of wood, while others

Figure 2.12 A *mirkāz* next to an entrance and another one in an open space in front of a row of houses, around 1900. Unknown photographer. © Leiden University Libraries, C.S. Hurgronje collection (Or. 12.288 J: 28).

were part of the masonry of the building (Bokhari 1978: 175; Krause 1991: 50; Ṭarābulsī 2008: 202). Sometimes referred to as an extension of the living room (*majlis*) in the street (Bokhari 1978: 175), these benches helped to maintain gender segregation: while male family members and their friends met in front of the house, women were able to socialise in the upstairs *majlis* (Jomah 1992: 61, 67, 193; al-Shahrani 1992: 55–6, 63–4). At a certain age, young men began to spend the evening hours sitting at their father's side in his *mirkāz*, thus integrating into his network of friends. The *mirkāz* was seemingly open to everyone, but it was normally occupied by a group of regular visitors. For outsiders it would have felt inappropriate to take a seat among them. Although situated in the street, the *mirkāz* legally belonged to the owner of the house, because in Islamic law the immediate surroundings of the house, called *al-finā'*, count as the homeowner's private property (Bokhari 1978: 175; al-Hathloul 1996: 94–102; Krause 1991: 50; Mortada 2003: 115).

Wealthy homeowners used their *maq'ad* or downstairs *dīwān/majlis* to receive guests on a regular basis, in some cases daily, thus providing another kind of platform of exchange for men. Particular salons (*nādī ijtimā'ī*, pl. *nawādī ijtimā'iyya*), for example the ones of Sulaymān Qābil and ʿAbdullāh Ṣaghīr, were known to be regularly attended by eminent people – rich merchants and local notables. Others were dedicated to young men, who came there to chat and play dominoes. In every salon, guests were offered coffee, tea and water pipes, and in some even dinner, all at the host's expense (Manāʿ 2011: 84, 107–8, 142; Ṭarābulsī 2008: 265). Even prior to the establishment of the first electricity company in Jeddah in 1950/1 (Anṣārī 1982: 35), radios were set up and films were screened in the *majlis* of houses with individual power plants, for example in the Surratī house in al-Shām quarter (Manāʿ 2008: 41–2; 2011: 106–7).[14] According to ʿAbdullāh Manāʿ's memories of the 1950s, the *maqā'id* of houses such as the Surratī house, the Nāẓir house, the Bā Nāja house, the Lārī house, the Tūnisī house and the Shams house provided a forum for 'a complete social network of men and male youths of a quarter to meet and gossip, explore the news of the day, and play games' (2011: 107–8). The neighbourhood representative, known as *shaykh al-ḥāra* or *ʿumda*, occupied a special position within this network. The *ʿumda* was responsible for security in his quarter and mediated between families or individuals in cases of dispute. Therefore, his office was open to everyone who needed help or advice. Important neighbourhood affairs were discussed in his *maq'ad* by elders of the quarter or people concerned (Freitag 2016a; Manāʿ 2011: 184; Ṭarābulsī 2008: 180–1). In sum, the ground floors of houses in Jeddah were open to guests and visitors who did not belong to the families residing in the buildings.

Whereas the entrance door constituted a symbolic threshold between the street and the house, an effective physical division between the reception hall and office on the ground floor and the residential space on the upper floor was achieved by a stairwell. Usually situated at the rear of the house, the stairwell led all the way up to the roof. Doors separating the stairs from each upstairs apartment regulated physical and visual access to the living rooms (Jomah 1992: 85, 89; King 1998: 50). While climbing up or down stairs, a man had to make himself conspicuous in order to avoid contact with female residents or visitors who were not *maḥram*, i.e. close relatives. He would say '*ṭarīq, ṭarīq* [make way]!' or '*yallā, ṭarīq* [hurry up, make way]!', for example (personal communication with a former resident of an old building in Jeddah; see also Alireza 2002: 63; Jomah 1992: 199; al-Faḍlī 2010: 13–14).

Every upper floor contained one or more separate apartments, each of which was inhabited by a segment of the extended family. The residence pattern was patrilocal; that is, a married couple usually lived together with the husband's family. In the patrilocal home in Jeddah, every married son shared an apartment with his wife and children (Altorki 1986: 30–2; Bokhari 1978: 184; Jomah 1992: 66). When a family grew and the building could no longer accommodate its members, it was often enlarged by constructing another apartment on top of the house, which was cheaper than acquiring another plot of land or a new building (Jomah 1992: 156–8). Sometimes neighbours negotiated an agreement which allowed an expanding family to build on top of a smaller building next door, resulting in horizontal extensions of an upper floor. Wealthy families bought larger homes or constructed ground-floor annexes and separate buildings to accommodate growing numbers of households within an extended family.

Each apartment in a typical residential building in Jeddah contained at least one large, prestigious reception room, the *majlis*. It was normally situated on the cooler side of the house and was airier than the other rooms due to large latticed bay windows, called *rūshān* (pl. *rawāshīn*). The *majlis* was therefore a preferred living room and sleeping place. In addition, the apartments contained one or more smaller family rooms, called *ṣuffa* and *mu'akhkhir*, a kitchen and a toilet (Bokhari 1978: 184; Jomah 1992: 66; Ṭarābulsī 2008: 110). The rooms were not strictly limited to specific functions, but could serve various purposes at different times and occasions, such as eating, sleeping, household chores and receiving guests. Heavy, immobile furniture was rare in the first decades of the twentieth century. People sat on cushions on the floor or in the alcove of a *rūshān* and they slept on mattresses that were spread out in the evening and rolled up again and put aside in the morning (Fadan 1983: 148–51; Jomah 1992: 88; al-Mutawea 1987: 71–2).

Although the upper floors were normally the place where a family resided, the *majlis* was also used to receive visitors. During informal calls on neighbours, relatives and friends, or on the occasion of formal visits known as *wuʿūd*, the family's living quarters were regularly used to host female guests. For women, who were not supposed to meet and gather outside, access to the upper floors of other people's houses was less restricted than for men (Jomah 1992: 193). Compared to women, men used an upstairs *majlis* to entertain guests relatively seldom because the presence of male visitors limited the freedom of movement of female family members. The rules of gender segregation required that family members of the opposite sex withdrew to different sections of the house when visitors were present (Jomah 1992: 199). Although men had other places to socialise, either downstairs or outside the home, trusted male guests were occasionally invited into the family domain as an indication of their closeness to the family. After having come to an agreement over a marriage, for example, a man was often allowed entry to the upper floors of his future wife's family home (Jomah 1992: 175). In addition, particularly honourable guests were entertained upstairs.

ʿAbdullāh Manāʿ, again, provides us with an example of this practice. He remembers a dinner party that took place in the house where he lived with his mother and members of the extended family. As secretary of a local football team, his uncle, who lived on the third floor, had invited team members for dinner (Manāʿ 2008: 61). Due to the presence of the guests, the third floor became a space temporarily limited to men. As a child of 12 or 13 years, ʿAbdullāh Manāʿ was still associated more closely with the female sphere than with the social world of men (Manāʿ 2008: 19, 31). The poor boy was considered too young to join the dinner party and was not allowed to walk up to, nor greet or even look at the admired football stars.

The rooftops were used as terraces (*khārijāt*, sing. *khārija or khārja*). They offered space to do household work, such as laundry and cooking, to gather and sleep during the hot summer months (Manāʿ 2008: 19–20), and for children to play. Protected from view with the help of perforated exterior walls or wooden fences, the terraces allowed residents, especially women, to be outside but within the domestic sphere (Eyuce n.d.: 27–9; Jomah 1992: 71–2).

In a comparative study of historical and contemporary houses in the Ḥijāz conducted in the early 1980s, a team of building researchers of King Abdulaziz University (KAU) Jeddah measured the proportion of openings in the facades of, among others, 14 old houses in the city. They found out that, on average, only one third (34 per cent) of the front of old buildings was constructed of solid stone (Eyuce n.d.: Appendices III–IV). Two thirds of a facade remained virtually open, covered only by splendidly ornate wooden lattices that were air-, light-, and sound-permeable and offered views (Figures 1.3, 1.5, 2.12). The wooden constructions of bay windows, referred to as *rūshān*, protruded about 60 cm into the street. Adding 60–80 cm for the thickness of the wall, the alcoves were approximately 1.20–1.40 m deep and over 2 m wide (Eyuce n.d.: 111–14; Greenlaw 1995: 21; Jomah 1992: 64). Before technological innovations rendered the *rūshān* useless, it fulfilled a variety of functions. It illuminated the interior without letting direct sunlight heat up the rooms, as screens and lattices shielded the large opening in the facade. Wind could enter the house through the unglazed opening and ascend the staircases to escape, allowing for a pleasant draft. Covered with carpets and cushions, a *rūshān* was a comfortable place to sit in or to sleep in at night. Furthermore, the lattices made it possible to look out of the house and even talk to people in the street or in the *rūshān* next door without being seen, which was particularly important for women (Bokhari 1978: 176, 180–1, 187–8; Eyuce n.d.: 34–9, 75–80; Fadan 1983: 56, 59; Jomah 1992: 54–5, 91–2). Hidden like this, mothers could supervise their children in the street without leaving the house themselves (al-Shahrani 1992: 52). ʿAbdullāh Manāʿ (2011: 153–4) recounts an anecdote which demonstrates the sound-permeability of the *rūshān*. In Manāʿ's childhood, his neighbour, together with his son, would entertain children of the quarter with a puppet theatre in the open square in front of the house. At night, sitting in his own *rūshān*, Manāʿ could hear the father teaching his son puppet plays in the *rūshān* next door.

Together with the staircases at the rear of the house and, if available, the separate entrances, the latticed openings in a wall provided the local answer to the religious demand that women and unrelated (non-*maḥram*) men should avoid visual contact. At the same time, they allowed the house's inhabitants to communicate with the outside world. A person standing or sitting in the alcove of a *rūshān* had one foot inside the house and one in the street. The *rūshān* allowed a woman to stay dressed according to the rules of the house – i.e. she did not have to wear a veil – while she observed the activities outside and supervised her children in the street. To some extent, the *rūshān* can be regarded as an extension of the living room into the street, just like the benches of a *mirkāz* in front of the house. And as much as the streets were primarily occupied by men, so that women avoided being seen outside, the upper floors of houses were the places where women socialised, which required that male visitors and family members alike were particularly attentive and did not disturb them there.

Theoretical reflections (1): The problem of translation

The *rūshān*, the *mirkāz* and the roof terrace enabled the inhabitants of a house to use the surfaces of the walls as floors, thus dissolving the phenomenological border between inside and outside. In addition, people associated with the outside world were allowed to enter the *dihlīz* and the *maqʿad* on the ground floor. Neighbours, customers, traders and pilgrims lodging downstairs transformed the ground floor into an almost public space. The reception of guests in the upstairs *majlis* further connected domestic space with the external world. Obviously, the residential house in Jeddah was not conceived as a strictly private space.

Does this mean that using the terms 'privacy' and 'private/public space' in a study of social life in Jeddah would be inappropriate? Trying to prevent a reading of my material that hinges on Western notions of publicness and privacy, I have so far largely avoided these terms in my description of Jeddah in the first half of the twentieth century. In favour of an account that is closer to the way the city's inhabitants spoke about their own built environment, I have turned to local terminology instead. Anthropologists and historians of the Middle East familiar with the political theory of the concepts of public and private sometimes find it difficult to apply these categories to societies where, at first glance, they do not seem to apply. Moreover, they feel uncomfortable with the apparently Eurocentric idea of transferring concepts deeply rooted in Western political thought to Middle Eastern societies – an act which risks failing to acknowledge the particularity of these societies.

There has not always been such reluctance to transfer these terms to a non-European context. Until recently, geographers and historians dedicated to the task of identifying structural similarities between cities in the Islamic world claimed that a clear separation of the private domestic sphere from the public realm was a key characteristic of the 'Islamic City' (see most recently Ammann 2004; Wirth 2000). A critical discussion of the Islamic City paradigm is provided in chapter 4. Suffice it to say here that such an unambiguous distinction cannot be maintained for

Jeddah, and since the 1980s it has repeatedly been challenged for other cities as well.[15]

Responding to a tendency in anthropology to apply Pierre Bourdieu's (1979) model of the Algerian Kabyle house,[16] which also involves a gendered private/public divide, to other contexts across the Middle East, Gabriele vom Bruck published an article entitled 'A House Turned Inside Out: Inhabiting Space in a Yemeni City' (1997). Based on her own fieldwork in Northern Yemen, mostly in the Yemeni capital Sanaa, vom Bruck casts doubt on the general validity of Bourdieu's dichotomous model. In Northern Yemeni tower houses she discovered principles of spatial arrangement of social life which contradicted Bourdieu's findings. As vom Bruck maintains, 'rather than being rigidly compartmentalized, the meanings attached to the spatial domains of the house shift in accordance with the categories of people who occupy them' (1997: 166). In other words, rules of behaviour depend less on whether people meet inside or outside the house, or in a specific part of the house, than on the social categories they belong to, such as male, female, *maḥram*, non-*maḥram*, trusted friend, stranger, old or young, high or low social status. In this respect, her interpretation seems to apply to early twentieth-century Jeddah as well.

Her observations lead vom Bruck to the conclusion that boundaries between the public and the private spheres in Northern Yemen 'are inherently unstable, and they shift both inside and outside the house in accordance with the categories of people moving in space' (vom Bruck 1997: 144). On that account, she not only calls the applicability of Bourdieu's model outside Algeria into question (vom Bruck 1997: 152, 166) but also rejects the use of the terms 'public' and 'private' in a cultural context such as the one she studies:[17]

> In the case I examine certain behavioural codes operate in all spatial domains – 'inside' and 'outside' – and they are always contextual. Whether they are observed or not depends on factors such as the categories of people who act within them and the moral evaluation of specific types of practice. Therefore, the 'public'/'private' terminology carries little analytical weight.
>
> (vom Bruck 1997: 143)

Similarly, Suad Joseph argues that '[t]he public/private is an imagined divide which enables critical moves in law and social arrangements impacting citizenship, but does not correspond neatly with the lived experience of daily life in any state, Western or Southern' (1997: 76).[18]

However, the problem that lies at the core of these scholars' reservations about these categories disappears if we do not equate public and private space with inside and outside or with physically defined localities, such as the house, street or marketplace. I want to suggest instead that we conceive of these spaces as variable products of social practice involving both people and artefacts. According to Martina Löw (2001: 153–7) and Doreen Massey (2005: 9–12, 119, 131–2), people do not move *in* space, as vom Bruck puts it, but rather belong to the elements that constitute space. This means, for example, that walls, doors, curtains etc. are not enough to turn a building into a private space. It could just as well be used as an office or for the assembly of a political party. In order for it to become a private space, whether continuously or temporarily, people have to use it as such, that is, keep other people out to remain undisturbed, screen certain bodily appearances and activities from view, do what they only want to do alone or with a limited number of persons with whom they share an intimate bond. On the other hand, a public does not necessarily assemble 'in public'. The political circles of bourgeois men, literary salons and charity organisations of women prominent in eighteenth- and nineteenth-century Europe convened in the reception rooms of private homes. In spite of their location, these gatherings are often regarded as archetypes of a public sphere (cf. Habermas 1989; Ryan 1992; Fraser 1992: 113–18).

In physical terms, the boundaries of private space in early to mid-twentieth-century Jeddah, just as in Sanaa in the 1990s, were not fixed and cannot be localised easily because of the relatively high openness of buildings to strangers and the varying functions of rooms. With regard to the social dimension of space, however, the boundaries between public and private were well defined and, as far as the sources suggest, strictly respected. As we have seen, precise rules of who was allowed access to places and people at specific times of the day existed, and visual, verbal and physical contact was highly regulated according to these rules with the aid of architectural elements, clothes and social practice. The boundaries were drawn first and foremost in relation to the human body and depended on social status as well as on gender. By saying this, I do not mean to associate men with the public and women with the private sphere. Rather, my objective is to explore mutually exclusive gendered publics as well as conceptions of privacy that varied between men and women of different social strata.

Another reason for vom Bruck's rejection of the categories 'public' and 'private' is that there are no Arabic terms corresponding directly to them (vom Bruck 1997: 143–4). Yet architects, urban planners and building archaeologists from Saudi Arabia as well as several of my non-specialist interlocutors are surprisingly at ease with these concepts. Either using the English term 'privacy' or the Arabic translation of it, *khuṣūṣiyya* – a neologism based on the adjective *khāṣṣ* (in private property; particular) – they frequently describe privacy protection as a key principle in building design, urban layout and rules of behaviour in Jeddah and other Saudi cities (most recently: Gazzaz and Gazzaz 2019). They devote journal articles and theses to the question of how the relationship between public and private space has changed in their city or in Saudi Arabia in general over the course of the twentieth century. Most of these texts, some of them published, others unpublished, date to the 1980s and 1990s, a few of them to the 2000s.[19] Prior to the 1980s, and hence also in the period discussed in this chapter, the concepts of public and private space have to be considered as largely unknown in Jeddah.

It is interesting to note that Saudi urbanists nevertheless consider privacy to be a genuinely Islamic concept. Moreover, they regard the urban structure and architecture in the old town of Jeddah – that is, in early twentieth-century Jeddah – as ideal in terms of Muslim conceptions of privacy and public space. In his doctoral thesis Fahad Mohammed al-Mutawea, for example, dedicates 14 pages to the subject of privacy in Islam (1987: 55–69). He claims that 'Islam … has given much attention to the privacy of the family and the house, and the inside of the house is regarded as a sacred place which can be entered only by permission' (al-Mutawea 1987: 56). Mohammed Eben Saleh speaks of a 'religious and cultural imperative of privacy' (2002: 516). He declares that 'violating this privacy can be considered a crime in the Islamic sense' (Eben Saleh 2002: 516). To give another example, Tawfiq Abu-Gazzeh published an article on the topic of 'Privacy as the Basis of Architectural Planning in the Islamic Culture of Saudi Arabia' (1996). In another article the same author asserts that, '[a]ccording to Islamic teachings, human behavior should be committed to respecting privacy' (Abu-Gazzeh 1994: 56).

Abu-Gazzeh (1994) and other Saudi architects and urban planners maintain that private, semi-public and public spaces in the historical city of Jeddah were arranged according to Islamic principles. In their writings, they explore the 'Impact of Islam on the built environment' (al-Mutawea 1987: chapter 2.2) or 'The Formation of the Muslim Urban Community and the Traditional Muslim City' (Sijeeni 1995: chapter 2). The teachings of Islam, they argue, led to the emergence of a gradual transition from the private realm over various forms of semi-private or semi-public spaces to the more or less anonymous, public arena of the bazaar and the mosque.[20]

In order to substantiate the claim that the idea of privacy is deeply rooted in Islam, these authors quote from, or make reference to, the Quran and Hadith (the collection of sayings of the prophet Muhammad). They often refer to verses in 'Sūrat al-Nūr' 24:30–1, which I have already cited above (with reference to al-Shahrani 1992: 55), as well as another verse from the same sura (24:27): 'O ye who believe enter no house other than your own, until you have asked permission and saluted those in them' (e.g. Abu-Gazzeh 1996: 96; Jomah 1992: 197; Mortada 2003: 78–9; al-Mutawea 1987: 56; al-Nafea' 2005: 48, 52). Quotations from the Hadith suggest that the prophet disapproved of anyone 'who looks into a house without the occupants' permission', justifying even severe physical punishment of 'intruders' (al-Mutawea 1987: 56; al-Nafea' 2005: 48, 56–7). The 'hierarchy of open spaces' – a phrase often used to label the varying degrees of accessibility of spaces in the city – is explained with sayings of the Prophet such as: 'Avoid sitting in thoroughfares … but if you insist then you should respect the rights of thoroughfares … Avoid staring, do not create harm. Salute back to those who salute you, bid to honour and forbid dishonour' (Abu-Gazzeh 1994: 56; Mortada 2003: 83; al-Shahrani 1992: 55). Such rules of behaviour in public, the architects and urban planners argue, shaped the appearance and the location of *dihlīz, maq'ad* and *mirkāz*.

In sum, for all these authors, the terminology of 'public' and 'private' does carry analytical weight, in contrast to vom Bruck's conclusion quoted above. Although the terms are not used in the sense of a binary division between a public and a private domain, the concepts are useful for them to articulate the changes they observed in the environment of their hometown or country of origin. Taking these voices seriously – that is, listening to the residents' own stories of cultural change in their hometown and not dismissing their use of the categories 'public' and 'private' as false adaptations – offers the opportunity to compare basic principles of social coexistence in Jeddah and other places, or in Jeddah in different periods. Moreover, relating the description of various places and institutions in Jeddah to the abstract and more general categories of 'public' and 'private' allows one to study the local particularities of spatial organisation and to contextualise them within a wider frame of reference.

Since the authors quoted here already belong to a generation later than the one they write about, we are faced with a discourse that claims to reconstruct social practices and collective enunciations of the past. My attempt to analyse the conception of public and private space in Jeddah in the early twentieth century necessarily relies on these discursive reconstructions. That being said, my own reconstruction of the past through non-contemporary sources need not be entirely disconnected from what residents of Jeddah experienced as their own reality. It is only important to note at this point that a substantial part of the information on which I base my account has been filtered by a layer of discourse with a marked tendency to idealise the past. A detailed discussion of the project behind this idealising discourse can be found in chapter 4, and its repercussions for the architecture of public and private spaces in Jeddah are dealt with in chapters 5 and 6.

One question raised by vom Bruck, among other researchers, remains to be answered: Are there any Arabic concepts corresponding to the terms 'public' and 'private'? In order to situate the material from Jeddah presented here in the broader cultural and linguistic horizon, I will discuss this question in the next section.

Theoretical reflections (2): Approaches to public and private space in Arab-Muslim societies

A linguistic approach to notions of public and private space in Arabic has been presented by Ludwig Ammann (2004) in an article ambitiously titled 'Privatsphäre und Öffentlichkeit in der muslimischen Zivilisation' ('Privacy and the Public Sphere in Muslim Civilization'). Ammann shows that Arabic expressions based on the roots *ʾ-m-m*, *ʿ-m-m*, *j-m-ʿ* and *j-m-h-r* are close to Western concepts of the public sphere, which he defines as an 'autonomous, open sphere of debate about the common good, situated between the official sphere of the state and the private realm' (Ammann 2004: 75). Among the derivatives of these roots are terms and concepts like *umma* (community, nation), *ʿāmm* (common, general; accessible to all), *jamāʿa* (community, congregation), *ijmāʿ al-umma* (the consensus of the Muslim community) and *jumhūriyya* (republic, audience) (Ammann 2004: 80–3). Ammann (2004: 84–91) compares the meaning of 'privacy' to expressions derived from the Arabic roots *kh-ṣ-ṣ*, *ḥ-r-m*, *ḥ-j-b* and *s-t-r*. Derivatives of *kh-ṣ-ṣ* centre around individuality and private property, for example *khāṣṣ* = 1. special, particular, 2. in private property. Words derived from *ḥ-r-m* are related to the vulnerability of bodies and places, for example *ḥaram* = sacred space; *ḥarām* = forbidden, religious taboo; *ḥurma* = 1. integrity of the human body, 2. woman; *ḥarīm* = 1. the interior of a building, 2. the sphere of women. The protection, covering and veiling of what is denoted by these terms is referred to by *ḥajaba* or *satara*, for example, derivatives of *ḥ-j-b* and *s-t-r* which translate as covering, screening, veiling or blocking. Ammann emphasises the religious dimension of the Arabic–Islamic concept of privacy, because the *sharīʿa*, which Muslims regard as sacred law since it is based on the rulings of the Quran and the traditions of the Prophet, protects the integrity of the human body (*ḥurma*) and the interior of the house (*ḥaram*) as well as the space of the women (*ḥarīm*) (Ammann 2004: 84–91, referring to Krawietz 1991: 278–80). If we define private space as a sphere to which outsiders have only limited access, a space that is withdrawn from the public and of no concern to a wider group of people, a space that is regarded as vulnerable and in need of protection by means of social norms, codified rules of behaviour and physical boundaries, we find all these aspects embraced by the Arabic semantic fields suggested by Ammann.[21]

Michael Cook (2000) was, to my knowledge, the first scholar to have produced a brief English account of notions of privacy in the Quran and Hadith. In a short passage in his long book on *Commanding Right and Forbidding Wrong in Islamic Thought*, Cook (2000: 80–2) mentions three different but complementary principles which jointly correspond to Western concepts of privacy. One centres around the prohibition of spying (*tajassus*), the second restricts actions that would dishonour a Muslim and the third secures the integrity of the home and protects it from intrusion. Owing to the overall subject of his study, Cook is primarily interested in respect for privacy as a principle that places a limit on the exhortation to believers to forbid wrong (*al-nahy ʿan al-munkar*). A similar, yet more comprehensive study of legal sources related to Muslim conceptions of privacy has been presented by Mohammad Hashim Kamali (2008: chapter 3) in a book entitled *The Right to Life, Security, Privacy and Ownership in Islam*. Apart from the themes addressed by Cook, Kamali deals with legal protection of private correspondence and confidential conversation as well as instructions in the Quran and the Sunna not to conceal other people's nakedness, weaknesses and failings. Both Cook and Kamali provide an overview of the legal foundations on which Muslim conceptions of privacy are built, thus corroborating the claim made by Saudi architects that values corresponding to Western notions of privacy are embedded in an Islamic tradition. The question that remains, however, is how these values, rules and regulations are dealt with in a particular historical context.

This question has been addressed in an article by Eli Alshech (2004). Defining privacy briefly as the recognition and safeguarding of 'a person's need for a sphere immune from intrusion' (2004: 293), Alshech examines how Sunni scholars in the classical period of Islam interpreted the Quranic verses:

> Oh you who believe! Do not enter houses other than your own, until you have asked permission (*tasta᾽nisū*) and greeted (*tusallimū*) those in them: that is best for you, in order that you may remember. If you find no one in the house, enter not until permission is given to you, if you are asked to go back, go back, that makes for greater purity for yourselves (*azkā lakum*), and God knows well all that you do. It is no fault on your part to enter buildings not used for living (*ghayr maskūn*), which serve some (other) use for you, and God has knowledge of what you reveal and what you conceal.
>
> (Quran 24: 27–9, quoted in Alshech 2004: 294)

He discusses how authoritative scholars from the seventh to the thirteenth centuries (CE, i.e. first to seventh centuries AH) addressed the question of what exactly is to be protected from intrusion – houses occupied by people, specific groups of people themselves or people's personal affairs, including their bodies, letters and conduct, be they inside a house or elsewhere. He shows that in the first two centuries of Islam, exegetes tended to defend a private sphere defined in terms of property rights and occupancy of buildings, whereas legal scholars from the third/ninth century on offered protection of private affairs independent of places, buildings and property rights. In contrast to their early classical antecedents, these scholars did not conceive of the house as such as an inviolable zone. It was rather people's private affairs inside the domestic sphere which mattered. Alshech's approach, which puts an emphasis on exegetical texts and legal rulings, does not reveal much about the changing modes of producing and protecting private space by means of physical boundaries and rules of behaviour. Nevertheless, his analysis clearly demonstrates that the verses in the Quran cited as fundamental to the establishment of an Islamic legal category of privacy have been interpreted in different ways at different times and that the conception of private space is subject to negotiation and change.

One of the rare case studies dedicated to the topic of privacy in an Islamic urban context has been conducted by Abraham Marcus (1986). In his inspiring article, he examines attitudes, norms and legal rulings related to 'modesty, sexual morality, civility, respect, honor, and other prized values' granting people a personal sphere of limited access for outsiders (Marcus 1986: 167). Marcus's study is based on rich archival sources produced by Aleppo's Islamic law (*sharīʿa*) court in the mid-eighteenth century. A comparable corpus of material was not available to me. Still, Marcus's approach provides useful analytical tools for my own work on Jeddah. Firstly, Marcus differentiates between the ideals of privacy which prevailed in Aleppo and the varying degrees to which townspeople of different financial and social backgrounds were able to meet them or to prioritise other values and social obligations (1986: 170–4). Secondly, he distinguishes between physical privacy and the privacy of information. He notes that the latter enjoyed far less legal protection and was only seen as an issue when knowledge of personal affairs threatened to cause severe damage to a family's reputation (1986: 167, 174–8). By contrast, much attention in terms of legal and physical protection was given to bodily and domestic privacy (1986: 167–74), an observation that seems to hold true for early twentieth-century Jeddah as well. Marcus shows surprisingly little consideration for gender differences. In dealing with a society that creates sharp distinctions between the sexes, the question of how different notions of privacy applied to men and women certainly deserves more examination.

With regard to the public sphere, Armando Salvatore (2007) has explored institutions analogous to modern notions of publicness in different pre-modern societies, among them the early Islamic community. His aim is to develop a transcultural concept of the public sphere based on Habermas's theory of communicative action. With the exception of *j-m-h-r/jumhūriyya*, Salvatore (2007: 140–1, 155–65) elaborates on the same concepts as Ammann, namely *maṣlaḥa ʿāmma* (common good/public weal), and *ijmāʿ al-umma* (the consensus of the community of believers). He does not fail to note that, in practice, the idea of a unified will of the Muslim community remained an unachievable ideal (2007: 141). This observation leads him to analyse institutions dedicated to practical reasoning about *maṣlaḥa ʿāmma*, including the four Sunni legal schools (*madhahib*, sing. *madhhab*), Sufi brotherhoods (*ṭuruq*, sing. *ṭariqa*), guilds, and pious endowments (*awqāf*, sing. *waqf*) in different stages of the early Islamic period (2007: 150–5). Salvatore convincingly extends Habermas's model of the public sphere to an Islamic context, challenging the liberal-secular assumption that religion can and should be separated from the public sphere. The idea that religious beliefs, Islamic, Catholic or other, cannot be confined to the private realm and do not contradict the notion of a public sphere is intrinsic to his approach. Yet, like Habermas, he neither pays attention to any forms of exclusion from the institutions of the public sphere under scrutiny, nor does he take the role of women into account (for such criticism of Habermas, see e.g. Benhabib 1992a;

Fraser 1992; Ryan 1992). His argument implicitly supports the impression that any sort of public in Muslim societies was restricted to men. The same can be said about other publications with a similar objective, for example the volume edited by Hoexter, Eisenstadt and Levtzion (2002), which I do not summarise here for the sake of brevity.

The inherent gender blindness of these accounts is surprising in so far as feminist scholars of the Middle East since the 1980s have shown that women in various Muslim contexts were organised in formal and informal networks, had a rich public life and were not powerless at all (e.g. Abu-Lughod 1986, 1990; Chatty and Rabo 1997; Hale 1986; Hegland 1986; Joseph 1983; Peteet 1986). For twentieth-century Jeddah, for example, Altorki (1986) has shown that, although women were not organised in guilds or convents and did not occupy powerful offices such as that of a judge, they did have networks and regular gatherings quite similar to those of men. It would be a severe mistake to believe that the rules of social coexistence were not reproduced and renegotiated within women's networks, discussions and decisions as well.

Women, however, are not the only category of people who do not feature in many analyses of Muslim publics. Critical studies in masculinity (e.g. Ghoussoub and Sinclair-Webb 2000) have drawn attention to the fact that not all men have the same access to power. Even in a patriarchal society there are some types of women who are more powerful than certain categories of men. Research following this line of thought is often informed by the concept of hegemonic masculinity developed by Tim Carrigan, Bob Connell and John Lee (1985; see also Connell and Messerschmidt 2005; for a critique, see Demetriou 2001; Amar 2011). It is not my intention here to define what kind of men embodied hegemonic masculinity in Jeddah in the first half of the twentieth century, but rather to ask who precisely had and who did not have access to various publics in Jeddah. A second question I want to raise is whether subjects excluded from those publics had the opportunity to constitute their own subaltern publics.

At the beginning of this chapter, I mapped the architectural framework of sociability in early twentieth-century Jeddah. I have subsequently argued that the categories of 'public' and 'private' are fruitful concepts for an analysis of the spatial arrangement of social life in a place like Jeddah, and I have elaborated on the premises upon which the use of these terms should build. In the remainder of this chapter I will connect the historiographic material to the theoretical discussion provided thereafter. The aim is to inquire into the local conception of public and private space in Jeddah in the first half of the twentieth century, focusing on the material manifestations of and social practices related to these concepts. The analysis of private and public spaces will serve as a starting point for the trajectories I explore in the following chapters.

Privacy in an open house

Particularly illuminating with regard to the question of how privacy was previously constructed in Jeddah in terms of architecture and social practice is the Ph.D. thesis of Hisham Jomah (1992). It is based primarily on oral history, and therefore actually says more about the early twentieth than the eighteenth and nineteenth centuries and is hence illuminating for the period investigated in this chapter. A sub-chapter is dedicated to the topic of 'Privacy in the traditional Ḥedjāzī house'.[22] Of particular importance in his analysis is the concept of *ḥaram*. The upper floors of a building in Jeddah were referred to using this term, which Jomah in this context translates as 'the most private quarters' of a house. The *ḥaram* was, as Jomah explains, 'restricted to the men of the house and to the female members of the family. It was considered critically improper for other men to enter these areas' (1992: 175). Jomah draws attention to the connection between the word *ḥaram* and the holy city of Mecca, thus alluding to the religious connotations of this term: 'the *ḥaram* or inviolable zone which was first known in prehistoric Arabia to distinguish Makkah from other places became the term used to distinguish the most private quarters of the family in the Ḥedjāzī house' (1992: 179). At a later point, he asserts that '[t]he sacredness of the Arab/Muslim house or *ḥaram* (inviolable-zone) derives from the presence of women (*ḥarīm*) within its walls' (1992: 234).

As Eli Alshech (2004) convincingly argues, this generalising statement is hardly true for all periods and places in the Arab-Muslim world. In view of Jomah's sources, which consist mainly of qualitative interviews with some of the last master builders in the old city of Jeddah alive at his time of writing, we can assume that his remarks are part of the discourse of around 1990 which linked local architecture and social practice of the early twentieth century to a specific interpretation of religious doctrine and moral standards. In the terminology of Deleuze and Guattari (1987: 504), Jomah's explanation reflects on the connection between a particular 'machinic assemblage' – the Ḥijāzī house – and 'collective enunciations' (i.e. religious concepts etc.) that are subject to change. The concept of privacy played an important role in Saudi architectural discourse of the 1980s and 1990s, as I will show in more detail in chapter 4. There I will also discuss the societal and political context of the discourse itself. What is of interest at this point is that Saudi architects and urban planners more or less univocally suggest that shielding household members, particularly females, from the view of outsiders was integral to the idea of privacy in Jeddah and other cities in the Ḥijāz (Abu-Gazzeh 1994: 56; Jomah 1992: 189, 195–6; Mortada 1992: 226–45; al-Mutawea 1987: 56).

In view of the relatively high openness of the buildings to strangers, a combination of architectural structures and social practice kept the movement of visitors from interfering with the family space (*ḥaram*) and unrelated men from disturbing the privacy of women (*ḥarīm*; cf. Jomah 1992: 300). This interplay between artefacts and everyday practice constitutes what can be called the Ḥijāzī assemblage of privacy. Architectural elements included separate entrances, ground floors above street level, the design of the stairwell and screened and latticed windows. Furthermore, roof terraces and windows were positioned in such a way that residents were neither able to look into their neighbours' houses nor be seen by their neighbours (Abu-Gazzeh 1994: 55–6; Jomah 1992: 134–5, 195–6; al-Mutawea 1987: 62). According to al-Mutawea (1987: 57–8) the house was separated into two spheres: rooms where male guests who were considered to be non-*maḥram* and in principle entitled to marry female members of the family were received; and areas reserved for family, especially women and their guests, as well as male relatives considered to be *maḥram*, that is not entitled to marry a female family member. Jomah notes several exceptions to this gender division within the house. Men were often allowed entrance to the more private upper parts of their future father-in-law's house. In addition, the upstairs *majlis* could, as mentioned above, temporarily be turned into a space of exclusively male visitors (Jomah 1992: 193, 199). The division of the upper floors into separate sections with multi-functional living rooms enabled the reception of guests, who brought the social conditions of public space into the home, while privacy was maintained in other parts of the house.

Everyday practices protecting private space included social control, such as control of the house entrance and passage to the stairs by the head of the family from his *maqʿad* (office) or from the *mirkāz*. As we have seen, private space was neither congruent with the boundaries of the house nor fixed to a space within the house. Yet numerous rules of behaviour determined who had access to places and specific categories of people at particular times of the day. Rules which ensured that the private sphere was not violated included that women avoided being seen in public, that visitors knocked on the door before entering a house and men made themselves heard while climbing the stairs. Jomah describes how the relationship between family and guest determined where the guest was received: 'the closer one was to the family occupying the house, the deeper and the higher one was allowed inside it' (1992: 175). Following this rule, the host signalled whether or not a threshold was allowed to be crossed and where the guest should settle. Coughing or making similar sounds at the doorstep, for example, alerted female household members of the need to evacuate the *majlis* and indicated to the visitor that he was to be admitted into the respective room as soon as it was vacant (Jomah 1992: 192). Children and family members falling into the category of *maḥram* often communicated between male visitors and female household members. Even within the extended family, different rules of interaction applied depending on the respective kinship relationship between a male and a female family member. In the presence of her grandfathers, her father, her brothers, her sons, her grandsons and her own husband, a woman did not wear the veil, but she was usually veiled before grown-up male in-laws (Altorki 1986: 36).

Within the home, privacy could have variable meanings. For Marianne Alireza, an American woman married to a Saudi, who spent the years between 1945 and 1957 in Jeddah, this was quite unusual. In her memoirs she writes:

> If we had privacy it was a changing state with different definitions at different times – qualified as single or conjugal privacy, a privacy among various combinations of souls inhabiting the house; or it could be called privacy when we all came at one time in a gathering of all men, women, children within the compound, sitting together, eating together, talking together, playing together. Sometimes, of course, we seemed at such times more like a club that meets once a month with nothing better to do than read the minutes of the last meeting, but that was no doubt because of the way we rotated in different circles most of the day and only came together to share the oneness of family when other activities let us.
>
> (Alireza 2002: 151–2)

Alireza lived together with her husband's extended family in a newly built home of the early 1940s. Although the building was constructed out of new materials – concrete and glass – the social custom she describes in this passage seems to be the same as the one practised in the old town. A conjugal couple in an old building used to have some privacy because of architecturally separated residential units on each floor, but limits to a couple's and, even more so, to an individual's privacy were set by shared entrances, a shared stairwell and shared roof terraces. In addition, collective activities of either men or women of different generations and sometimes, as mentioned by Alireza, of the entire household took precedence over individual or conjugal seclusion. Hardly any household member enjoyed unrestricted freedom of movement. Women, and to a lesser extent men of the younger generation, were not allowed to leave the house without permission. A married woman had to ask her husband or her mother-in-law for permission if she wanted to go out to make visits or attend celebrations at a friend's home. For young men, rules were less strict, but they were expected to be at home at certain times of the day (Altorki 1986: 33–4, 55). Women were sometimes able to circumvent the obligation to seek permission and went out without their husband's knowledge. A husband's authority was thus never total (Altorki 1986: 55–6, 61). Nevertheless, the overall impression prevails that individual autonomy, especially of women, was fairly restricted.

The walls and gratings of the residential building in Jeddah and the social practice connected to it protected first and foremost the privacy of the extended family as a whole. Privacy was not defined as the autonomous sphere of an individual, but rather as a collective space sheltering members of a household from visual and physical contact with strangers. The categories of people present in a setting, not the architecture itself, determined whether a space was considered to be private or public. A combination of architectural elements and social practice helped secure the boundaries between public and private spaces, which were set differently at different times. Always dependent on the relationship between people present in a place, the limits of private space were maintained both inside and outside the house. While much emphasis was placed on shielding bodies from view and on the regulation of physical access to people, the permeability of walls to sound did not seem to pose a problem. The close proximity of neighbouring houses and the large latticed openings in the facades hardly prevented the spread of sounds between buildings or from a building to the street.

All the authors dealing with the topic of privacy in the Ḥijāz tend to ignore the fact that a significant number of men and women were excluded from the rules and norms described thus far, either because they could not afford a lifestyle that conformed to the ideals of privacy or because they were denied the right to maintain a personal private space. According to the travel report by Heinrich von Maltzan, travellers seeking 'inexpensive lodgings and lewd temptations' had to go to the settlements of huts outside the city gates, where prostitution was 'exceedingly well represented' (von Maltzan 1873: 47). Prostitutes apparently received customers in their own dwellings (see also Burckhardt 1829: 9). Not only were these women visible in public to a greater degree than women of higher social standing, but their homes were also not conceived as shelters protecting inhabitants from the view of outsiders. Furthermore, prostitutes were not able to follow the rules of the integrity of the body (*al-ḥurma*) as defined by Islamic law (Krawietz 1991).

A second group of people for whom the general rules of privacy did not apply were slaves. Enslaved men and women usually lived in the houses of their owners, but their sleeping quarters, purportedly on the ground floors (Bokhari 1978: 183–4; Pesce 1976: 118), are not marked in any of the ground plans of old houses produced by architects and building archaeologists since the 1980s. Rooms on the ground floor are labelled *diwān/majlis/maqʿad, dihlīz* or entrance hall, and *khazzāna* or storage, for example. This is not just because the existence of slaves was omitted by these authors. Slaves simply did not have a space of their own. Although none of the rooms – except for the *maqʿad* of the household's patriarch – were reserved for any single family member, slaves must have been intruded upon very regularly, because their lodgings were not protected by the rules of behaviour that regulated access to free men and women.

The rules of gender segregation demanded that slaves recruited to help with household chores in order to reduce the workload of free women had to be female (Altorki 1986: 31). Whereas male servants were not supposed to see their mistresses, female slaves were not hidden from their masters' sight. Considering slaves as property, the law allowed slaveholders to have sex with them, even without their consent (Toledano 1998: 72–3; Toledano 2007: 83–7, 101). Writing about slavery in the Ottoman Middle East, Ehud Toledano reminds us of the fact that the legal conditions for married women were not very different – neither in the Ottoman Empire nor in other pre-modern societies, where arranged marriage was common and conjugal rape not prohibited (2007: 83–4, 167). In contrast to married women who were subject to sexual abuse and ill-treatment, however, slaves, who were deported from their place of origin, could not take refuge with their own family. Measured against the values and norms discussed above, the privacy of prostitutes and slaves in Jeddah was severely curtailed or even completely lacking. The scarcity of information about both groups does not allow me to evaluate if they nevertheless had their own notions and niches of privacy.

The ability to define a personal private sphere and protect it from visual and physical intrusion certainly depended on social status and wealth. Households ranking between the poles of severely disadvantaged people, such as slaves, prostitutes and beggars, on the one hand, and owners of large mansions containing separate apartments for several segments of an extended family on the other, compromised, or upheld, ideals of privacy to varying degrees. The fact that it was socially acceptable for women of poor families to sell food at the local market, for example, indicates that family wellbeing was given priority over the local ideal of personal privacy.

Exposure of female family members was avoided as far as a household could afford it. The veiling of body, hair and face generally allowed women to move from one place to another, but they ideally did not engage with and become part of the public realm by having physical or visual contact with men in the street. Such contact posed a threat to a woman's privacy and, since men were considered guardians of their wives and unmarried daughters, to her entire family's reputation (Altorki 1986: 67; al-Shahrani 1992: 55, 58). A woman of any but the lowest social class therefore limited her own physical presence in public as much as possible. In the case of ʿAbdullāh Manāʿ's family, asking for and receiving financial support from benevolent sponsors was considered less shameful than any activity contributing to the family income which would have involved a female family member being visible in public and having contact with non-*maḥram* men. The maintenance and protection of a private sphere can thus be regarded as having defined a person's, especially a woman's, social distinction (Bourdieu 1984).

The architects and urban planners writing about the issue of privacy in Jeddah emphasise the protection of female private space with the help of architecture and social practice, but they say little about men. This corresponds to the overall pattern in Islamic jurisprudence (*fiqh*) which, as Birgit Krawietz (2016) observes, is much more attentive to the female than to the male body. With reference to the sociologist Michael Meuser (2005; Meuser and Lautmann 1997), Krawietz contends that, in Muslim and non-Muslim cultures, it is mainly the female who is perceived as a sexual body. Furthermore, women tend to be regarded as the particular which deserves more attention than the universal male. The silence of the urbanists with respect to male privacy makes it far more difficult to reconstruct the conception of male as opposed to female private space in Jeddah, but it does not mean that men did not enjoy the blessings of a sphere that was protected from intrusion either legally or by means of social conventions, nor were they exempt from social obligations to maintain their own or to respect other men's and women's privacy.

The principle that no one was allowed to enter a house without asking permission, together with the convention that a woman had to inform her husband or father about her comings and goings, as well as the position of *mirkāz* and *maqʿad*, ensured that chiefly male members of a household had control over who entered and left the home. At the same time, they were also expected to be in control, and were held responsible, if the privacy of female household members was intruded on or not safeguarded. Moreover, as highlighted above, men were required to respect women's privacy by not looking at or talking to them in the streets, not meeting them outside the house and not entering rooms occupied by women, as well as alerting female household members while climbing the stairs. Stairwells, apartment doors and latticed windows sheltered men as much as women in the upstairs apartments from view and from the physical intrusion of outsiders. In fact, rules regarding the concealment of the body from view, based on a rather strict notion of shameful nudity (*ʿawra*), existed for men too (Lange 2012). The only naked parts of the male body that could regularly be seen in public were the hands, lower legs, the head and sometimes the arms. The special garment of pilgrims also occasionally revealed parts of a man's upper torso. Unlike many other cities in the Middle East, public bath-houses did not exist in Jeddah. Even within families and same-sex groups, men in Jeddah probably covered the penis, testicles and rectum, as this is a widespread rule among Muslims (Krawietz 2016). For prisoners and, again, slaves, rules were different. Their clothes often revealed knees and chest – parts of the body that other men usually covered. As their dress had little to do with free choice, it seems appropriate to say that they were denied the right to comply with the general standards of nudity and thus, once more, deprived of the privilege of privacy.

Strong publics, weak publics and public space

Just as the rights and opportunities of slaves, prostitutes and the poor to define a personal space and protect it from intrusion were limited, so was their access to formalised publics. A slave or servant may have been present in the gathering of men in the *mirkāz* or of women in the *majlis*. However, with a few exceptions of slaves who made careers as assistants to rich merchants (Pétriat 2016: 169–75), or as favoured concubines who became accepted members of their masters' family and subsequently of the community at large (Manāʿ 2008: 19–21), under-privileged subalterns were not supposed to participate in discussions taking place during such meetings. They also did not have a voice in collective decision-making processes, such as the election of an *ʿumda* or the leader of a guild. Needless to say, slaves and prostitutes were not organised in guilds.[23]

Subalterns were not the only group of people who were excluded from public spaces and institutions. Explicitly public places, such as a *mirkāz*, cafes, open squares during festivities and even market streets in Jeddah were not open to everyone in the same way. Women, as we have seen, were excluded from many places of encounter in public. Men, on the other hand, were not allowed to enter a room in which their mothers, sisters or wives met with relatives and friends. Precise ideas about who was allowed to enter, pass through or stay at a specific place and who was or was not supposed to be seen there determined the social composition of every space in the city.

This does not mean that genuinely public space did not exist in Jeddah in the early twentieth century, nor that women did not have any public life. Sociologists, anthropologists and geographers have shown that access to any kind of public is limited, never open to everyone (e.g. Benhabib 1992b: 75–9; Stolleis 2004: 167–8; Wilson 1992). They suggest that the public sphere, like any other space, is regulated by explicit and implicit rules. As an outcome of competitive processes and negotiation, these rules are determined by social differences (see e.g. Ardener 1993; Fraser 1992: 112–21). Therefore, according to Massey (2005: 152–3), for example, public space is always shaped by unequal power relations and exclusion. In Jeddah, the principle of gender segregation caused the emergence of mutually exclusive gendered public spaces. Having said that, I do not want to deny the patriarchal character of Ḥijāzī society.[24] In early twentieth-century Jeddah, it meant, among other things, that all public offices were occupied by men, who thus dominated important institutions and controlled decisions pertaining to the common weal (*maṣlaḥa ʿāmma*). A woman had the right to see the *ʿumda* in his office, but she could not become an *ʿumda* herself. The governor of the city, the cleric, the judiciary, as well as the leaders of guilds, Sufi convents and pious endowments had to be men.

Women were in principle precluded from almost all decisions reaching beyond the domain of the family or the household. But the patriarchal society did not prevent them from forming their own publics, nor were those female publics powerless. Nancy Fraser (1992: 132–6) labels publics possessing the capacity of decision-making as 'strong' publics. 'Weak' publics, in contrast, are defined by her as circles of debate lacking such power. They can nevertheless be crucial in shaping people's opinion, or influencing decisions relating to the common interest, and as such have a political dimension. This idea was further elaborated on by Michael Warner (2002), who inquired into publics that exist, or come into being, through the circulation of texts, spoken or written, and images: theatre audiences, readers of books, articles or newspapers, crowds listening to speeches and sermons, viewers of TV shows. Charles Hirschkind's (2006) study of what he labels Islamic counterpublics (a term borrowed from Fraser and Warner and adapted to an Islamic context) provides an illuminating example of how such publics can change the overall social landscape.[25] Likewise, feminist scholars of the Middle East have argued that Muslim women in various historical contexts, while being excluded from so-called 'strong' publics, were and are organised in formal and informal networks. The alliances forged within these networks and the activities they engage in often have reverberations in the community at large (e.g. Chatty and Rabo 1997; Nelson 1974; Stolleis 2004).

Slaves were also not living in isolation from their social environment (Toledano 2007: 70). They had contact with other people, both enslaved and free, and in cases of severe maltreatment and abuse they were sometimes capable of organising resistance. Toledano (2007: 65–6) gives an account of an incident involving 17 slaves who sought refuge in a British ship lying at anchor in the harbour of Jeddah in March 1879. Although we do not have any traces of the precise circumstances under which these people were able to meet and plan their escape, the example shows that slaves were able to connect with each other, exchange news, discuss strategies to improve their working conditions or to abscond, and organise mutual support. British and, to a lesser extent, French consular reports repeatedly mention cases of slaves seeking refuge at the European consulates to escape their masters. These reports sometimes allude to a concerted strategy of the absconders, similar to that of the 17 slaves mentioned by Toledano.[26] These cases indicate that subalterns were able to constitute their own publics.

The example also indicates that not every male public in Jeddah was a 'strong' public and that not every man was equally involved in public decisions concerning, for instance, the living and working conditions of slaves, let alone the existence of slavery in general. Social hierarchies in the Ḥijāz, which made a distinction between highly esteemed families (*ʿawāʾil*) and ordinary people, masters and slaves, rich and poor, old and young, as well as professions of high and low regard, determined a man's influence and his likelihood of attaining powerful offices (cf. Manāʿ 2008: chapters 1, 2; Yamani 2004). Furthermore, the regular meetings of men in the *mirkāz* or the *maqʿad* fulfilled functions quite similar to the gatherings of women in the upstairs *majlis*: sociability, exchange of news, opinion formation – and not necessarily decision-making. But all decisions pertaining to the common good were made by men or exclusively male publics (Altorki 1986: 23–5; for an example of such a male public, see Freitag 2015a). The distinction between 'strong' and 'weak' publics offers a way to address power asymmetry between men and women without reproducing the stereotype that associates men in Middle Eastern societies with the public sphere, on the one hand, and women with a domestic private sphere of no political importance.

The mutual dependence of husband and wife on information about the sphere of the opposite sex is, again, vividly depicted by Marianne Alireza:

> We women depended on the men to keep us informed of all such little stories. I look back on how much a husband and wife (perhaps Ali and I more than other couples because we could have been more aware of the separation of the sexes) learned about events in the other's circles. Ali told me things that happened in that part of his life where I had no entree, and I would tell him of events in mine and thus we shared what was not experienced together. … Besides the chit-chat concerning local happenings there was an enormous amount of information, anecdotes, and history that I gleaned about Ali's own family to recount to him later. He hated to admit it, but he learned a lot from me that he had never known before.
>
> (Alireza 2002: 155–6)

Particularly the institution of *wuʿūd*, or formal social visits between women, can be considered a form of 'weak' female public in Jeddah. The guests to such a meeting were usually entertained in the *majlis* of the mother or of her new daughter-in-law. As a demonstration of unity and amity between members of the household, every woman in the family was expected to be present on the day of the *wuʿūd*. Consequently, social networks were never limited to only one generation. As they grew up, members of the younger generation were automatically integrated. *Wuʿūd* and other, less formal meetings of women inside the home were held to exchange news and to organise support for anyone who needed it. Social norms were reproduced and negotiated. Furthermore, female social networks in Jeddah played, and still play today, though to a lesser degree, an important role in finding suitable marriage partners for family members (Altorki 1986: 24–5, 32, chapter 5).[27] It is a well-known fact that the question of who marries whom can have far-reaching economic and political consequences – in the tribal society of the Arabian Peninsula as much as elsewhere. Women's conversations may have differed from those of men, but their knowledge of family affairs, their social networks and their ability to arrange marriages were also politically relevant. While men sat in front of the house discussing local politics, economic and neighbourhood affairs, their mothers, wives and sisters in the upstairs *majlis* negotiated marriages and organised material and mental succour in times of hardship and distress. Like the men's regular gatherings, the women's get-togethers helped forge alliances which had an effect on the dynamics and the coherence of the entire community (cf. Nelson 1974).

Just like any other female space in Jeddah, women's spaces of sociability had to be protected from the visual intrusion of non-*maḥram* men. Expressed in terms of publicness and privacy, this observation seems perhaps like a paradox: female publics were concealed behind the walls and screens of residential buildings to preserve the privacy of the women involved. Yet if we think about the clothes we wear when we leave our home, this phenomenon may appear familiar. Layers of cloth conceal our private parts when we enter the public realm. Maintaining our privacy with the aid of clothes is a precondition for our being public. In Jeddah, where women were not supposed to be seen by men outside the family, the architecture of the residential building which protected women's privacy, allowed them to constitute publics. Since women's privacy was at stake, non-*maḥram* men were forbidden from entering rooms in which they had settled to chat and exchange news.

Men therefore often met outside the home. The location of male public gatherings was chosen according to the principle that women should be able to pass by undisturbed. A *mirkāz* was normally located in an open square or at a widening part of the street, not in a narrow thoroughfare. The fact that these spaces were within the visible range of outsiders rendered them taboo for women. In comparison to female spaces of sociability, access to male publics was regulated to a lesser extent with the help of architecture. Even entry to the *dihlīz* and the *maqʿad* inside the house was not obstructed by any effective physical barrier. The symbolic value of the threshold indicates that limits to male spaces of encounter were set rather by social conventions.

Conclusion

As we have seen, rules of, and access to, both privacy and public spaces in Jeddah in the first half of the twentieth century depended on gender, class and other criteria defining a person's social status. Privacy was not understood as the autonomous space of an individual but as a vulnerable sphere with the human body at its core. Furthermore, privacy was thought of collectively, that is, as the protected sphere of an extended family. Inappropriate behaviour of an individual family member – such as public exposure of a woman – put the entire family's reputation at risk. Gendered conceptions of nudity (*ʿawra*) determined the way men and women dressed and which parts of their bodies were to be concealed from whom. Publicly revealing one's arms and upper torso, knees and, as far as women were concerned, the hair and face was a sign of low social distinction. Of particular concern was the visibility of women, but not every household could afford a lifestyle that complied with the ideals of female privacy. Depending on their family's financial capacities and social distinction, women compromised these ideals to varying degrees. The extent to which a person's body was publicly exposed thus marked his or her social position. Slaves, prostitutes and prisoners did not enjoy the privilege of personal privacy, at least not in terms of integrity of the body (*ḥurma*).

Because concealing the body from the sight of outsiders was intrinsic to the conception of privacy in Jeddah, the architecture was designed to provide visual protection. Physical access to the home was chiefly regulated by social control, which was enabled by locally specific architectural solutions. A combination of architectural elements and rules of behaviour in the house kept the circulation of men separate from the non-*maḥram* women visiting or living in the same building. In spite of very strict rules of privacy protection that were derived from a specific interpretation of Islamic law, as various authors from Jeddah quoted here have argued, the home was not a private space per se. Most residential buildings did not only serve domestic functions, but were also used for commercial and representative purposes. Since gender segregation had to be maintained in almost every situation, mutually exclusive gendered public spaces existed. While specific aspects of male public life were regularly hosted on the ground floors and sometimes in the upstairs apartments, women normally constituted their own publics on the upper floors, protected from view by walls and lattices. Maintenance of their privacy with the aid of architecture and rules of gender segregation was a precondition for their public activities.

Men also met outside the home, in cafes, in open squares, in front of the mosque or by a house's entrance. Women were ideally not to be visible in public, but they were able to move from one place to another. Separating male from female public activities and allowing women to traverse public space without being seen demanded of both women and men a constant awareness of the categories of people present in a given place, inside the house and outside. Gender segregation thus did not only restrict the movements of women, but of men as well.

However, the point I wish to make is not that men and women were actually treated equally and had the same rights and opportunities. As I have shown, male and female publics were not only spatially divided, but they could also have different qualities, labelled here as 'strong' and 'weak' publics. Representative offices and the power to make decisions pertaining to the common weal were limited to men – that is to say, to men of a certain social standing. The participation of women, men of low social status and even slaves in so-called 'weak' publics, however, could also have political and economic consequences for the community at large. The public spheres of men and women in Jeddah were thus mutually exclusive and, since the information circulated in these gendered publics was different but relevant to all, they were interdependent.

Notes

1. Because of the coral reef in the bay of Jeddah, larger ships could not enter the harbour. Until 1951, when the first pier extending into deeper waters was constructed, ships had to anchor at a distance of 2.5 to 4.5 km from the port. Passengers and goods were brought into the harbour by smaller vessels, locally referred to as *sanbūk, ṣandal* or *lansh* (from the English 'launch'). A large number of workers was involved in recording the imported goods on the merchant ships, transferring them to small boats, navigating cargo and passengers to the port and discharging the boats at the pier (Manāʿ 2011: 50–5, 140–1; Rathjens and von Wissmann 1947: 76; Ṭarābulsī 2008: 152–9, 169). Ṭarābulsī (2008: 153) estimates that 300 such boats were in use in the first half of the twentieth century.
2. According to Ṭarābulsī (2008: 235), the street was named after Sulaiman Qābil, mayor (*raʾīs al-baladiyya*) in the Hashemite era, who bought the street, electrified it and built offices on top of existing shops.
3. According to Manāʿ (2011: 143–4), Sūq al-ʿAlawī is named after al-Sayyid Abū Bakr al-ʿAlawī, a descendant of the prophet Muhammad who is buried in the neighbourhood.
4. Examples of these buildings, known as *wakāla, khān* or *qaysariyya* in Arabic, have been preserved in different parts of the old city. They are no longer in use today, but one can still recognise them by their typical structure. They consist of several separate rooms on one or two floors arranged around a common courtyard.
5. According to Ṭarābulsī (2008: 251–4), the first hotels in the city – the Kandara Hotel, the Basātīn or Garden Hotel and the Kandara Palace Hotel – were opened after the Saudi conquest, but probably not before the 1940s (cf. Sanger 1954: 4–6). The names of these hotels indicate that they were situated outside the city gates: al-Kandara is the district – at that time still a suburb – where the first airport was built in 1946 (Ṭarābulsī 2008: 618). In the old town hotels were established in former residential houses or in new buildings from the 1950s onwards (Ṭarābulsī 2008: 253; Manāʿ 2008: 47, 51; 2011: 96).
6. In a map by Carl Rathjens and Hermann von Wissmann (1947: 77), two German geographers who visited Jeddah in 1927, Sūq al-ʿAlawī is clearly indicated as the city's main market area and passage from the harbour to the Mecca Gate in the east.
7. Built under governor Bakr Pasha in 1724–5, the mosque was famous for its leaning minaret. The entire structure was torn down in 1978 (Ṭarābulsī 2008: 205).
8. For descriptions of this practice, see al-Shahrani 1992: 52–58; Ṭarābulsī 2008: 190–95, Manāʿ 2008: 37–43; Manāʿ 2011: 82–85, 105–6, 137–38, 181, 193–95.

9. In his travel journal Savignac remarks that, at Eve's Tomb outside the city walls, he saw two women who did not seem to bother about him taking their picture (Savignac 1917: 7 May; I thank Jean-Michel de Tarragon for sharing Savignac's unpublished journal with me). His remark indicates that he was surprised that they did not evade his picture taking, which he saw as an exception proving the rule.
10. All three pictures were taken by Charles Winckelsen in 1918. They are available through the website of the French Ministry of Culture's Médiathèque de l'architecture et du patrimoine (https://www.photo.rmn.fr/archive/16-590374-2C6NU0AERH46B.html, https://www.photo.rmn.fr/archive/08-500544-2C6NU0JDOSVW.html, http://www2.culture.gouv.fr/public/mistral/memoire_fr?ACTION=CHERCHER&FIELD_1=REF&VALUE_1=APOS000880, accessed 12 April 2019).
11. Burckhardt (1829: 31) noticed women in the street selling bread, and Ṭarābulsī (2008: 248, 308) mentions a few women selling beans and other cooked meals in Sūq al-Nūriyya in al-Yaman quarter.
12. The family of shippers was struck first by misfortune because of the opening of the first harbour pier in 1950/1 which allowed direct unloading of vessels, leading to the unemployment of men like Manāʿ's father (Manāʿ 2011: 50–7). Secondly, the death of the father shortly afterwards left the family without a male breadwinner.
13. The verse continues: '... their husbands' fathers, their sons, their husbands' sons, their brothers or their brothers' sons, or their sisters' sons, or their women, or the slaves whom their right hands possess, or male servants free of physical needs, or small children who have no sense of the shame of sex; and that they should not strike their feet in order to draw attention to their hidden ornaments'. This part is not quoted by al-Shahrani.
14. According to Ṭarābulsī (2008: 235, 236), the houses of the Jukhdār and Qābil families were the first houses to have electricity produced by private generators, probably in the 1920s. Already in the Hashemite era (1916–25), the entire Qābil street was electrified. In the 1940s, power plants of the Surratī, the Bā Ghaffār and the Abū Zanāda families supplied several houses in the city with electricity (Manāʿ 2008: 41; 2011: 106).
15. A summary of the critical debate on the Islamic City paradigm with regard to its presuppositions about public and private space in relation to gender has been presented by Friederike Stolleis (2004: 13–19).
16. Bourdieu supports the assumption of a gendered private/public divide in his famous essay 'The Kabyle House or the World Reversed' (1979). Following a strictly structuralist approach, Bourdieu depicts the Kabyle house, and Kabyle society as a whole, as being organised in terms of dual oppositions. He associates the sphere of Kabyle women with the interior of the house and the private domain, which he contrasts with a male public sphere located outside the house.
17. Gabriele vom Bruck remarks that 'Space comes into being through practice; cultural meanings thus invoked are principally unstable and contextual' (vom Bruck 1997: 166). Nevertheless, she rejects the use of the terms 'public' and 'private' space in the Yemeni context because there they do not correspond to outside and inside, market and home. This implies that a distinction between public and private can meaningfully be drawn. After all, vom Bruck does not refrain from frequently using this terminology herself.
18. Suad Joseph contends that the 'public/private divide' simplifies social activity in such a way that male domination is normalised, naturalised or glossed over, although she also recapitulates an earlier strand of feminist scholarship that employs the categories of public and private to criticise patriarchal structures (Joseph 1997: 74–6, 88).
19. The authors I refer to here, and will discuss in more detail later, are Abu-Gazzeh (1994, 1996), Eben Saleh (2002), Fadan (1983), al-Hathloul (1996), Jomah (1992), Mortada (1992), al-Mutawea (1987), al-Nafea' (2005), al-Shahrani (1992) and Sijeeni (1995).
20. Among the authors employing this concept in the context of cities in Saudi Arabia are Abu-Gazzeh (1994: 56), al-Mutawea (1987: 40–1), Eyuce n.d.: 56, Sijeeni (1995: 74, 140), al-Shahrani (1992: 47–8) and Mortada (2003: 83–5). Fahad al-Mutawea, for example, writes: 'As domestic life calls for full privacy which requires maximum segregation from outside activities[,] at the same time, moslems ... are encouraged and required to participate fully in public community life where there is lack of privacy. Such relations ... resulted in compromise between the extreme privacy for the man of the family in the house, to the reverse in public life through the development of spatial organisation. The concept of sequences in spatial organi-

sation are quite clear on two scales; the domestic scale and the community scale' (al-Mutawea 1987: 58).

21. Whereas Ammann provides a very useful linguistic analysis, his approach is problematic in that he claims to write about 'Muslim Civilization' as if he was dealing with a closed and static entity. His analysis deals with neither local differences nor changes in Muslim conceptions of privacy and the public sphere. Moreover, he does not even suggest that local and temporal varieties have ever existed. On the contrary, he combines Quranic exegesis with eclectic quotations of medieval authorities on Islamic jurisprudence, pre-Islamic Arabic etymology, and geographical knowledge produced in studies of contemporary cities in Morocco, Turkey, Iran and other countries. This leads to the impression that a universal Muslim culture in opposition to 'the West' produced uniform and stable definitions of privacy and the public sphere. However, Ammann's article is meant to provide an overview, and it is indeed a useful starting point for investigations into specific local interpretations of the concepts he outlines.
22. Unlike other authors I refer to (with the exception of Ammann 2004), Jomah touches on the problem of translating the English term 'privacy' into Arabic. He points out that no single Arabic word is completely equivalent to the English term, but several local expressions reflecting aspects of it 'were used in similar contexts' (Jomah 1992: 190). He suggests comparing the concept of privacy to the Arabic concepts of *ʿār* (1. the part of a person's body which is not supposed to be exposed to others; 2. shame), *ʾarḍ* (land, area, territory) and *ḥaram* (1. sacred space, 2. a place in the house forbidden to outsiders). The phrase *iḥfaẓ ʿārak* (literally translated, 'keep your honour') was, according to Jomah, used as an appeal 'to defend or protect one's private things or honour like the female of the house', similar to the English expression 'maintain your privacy' (1992: 190).
23. On guilds in the Ḥijāz, see Ochsenwald (1984: 113–15).
24. On patriarchy in Middle Eastern societies in general, see e.g. Kandiyoti (1996) and Joseph (2000); for Saudi Arabia, see al-Rasheed (2013: chapter 1).
25. In opposition to the Egyptian state and hence without access to political decision-making, these Islamic counterpublics made extensive use of cassette-recorded sermons to share their thoughts and ideas about ethical self-improvement and pious living, thus influencing the political climate contributing to what is known as the Islamic Revival (Hirschkind 2006).
26. I owe this observation to Philippe Pétriat.
27. For similar institutions of formal social visits between women in Mocha, Yemen, see Um (2009: 143); for Damascus, see Stolleis (2004).

3
The transformation of urban space in the early oil era, 1950s and 1960s

> The Jedda airport seemed even more crowded than Cairo's had been. Our party became another shuffling unit in the shifting mass with every race on earth represented. Each party was making its way toward the long line waiting to go through Customs. Before reaching Customs, each Hajj party was assigned a *Mutawaf*, who would be responsible for transferring that party from Jedda to Mecca. Some pilgrims cried 'Labbayka!' Others, sometimes large groups, were chanting in unison a prayer that will translate, 'I submit to no one but Thee, O Allah, I submit to no one but Thee. I submit to Thee because Thou hast no partner. All praise and blessings come from Thee, and Thou art alone in Thy Kingdom'.
>
> (Malcolm X 2001: 437)

This is how Malcolm X, African-American civil rights activist, Muslim convert and one of approximately 260,000 foreign pilgrims who joined the pilgrimage to Mecca in 1964 (Long 1979: 129), remembers his arrival in Jeddah. His autobiography was originally published one year later in 1965. It is one of few sources offering a personal view of the city at that time – a period of radical transformation. The fact that large crowds of pilgrims now arrived in Jeddah by aeroplane, while fewer and fewer people came by boat, is an example of the changes which, in sum, profoundly affected also the constitution of public and private spaces.

During the two decades prior to Malcolm X's visit, Jeddah had witnessed a rapid expansion and infrastructural modernisation, beginning with the demolition of the city wall in 1947. Revenues of the Saudi state increased significantly after the Second World War, as the production of crude and refined oil in Saudi Arabia grew continually. This enabled the government to invest in several major urban developments. From 1947, a new water supply system known as al-ʿAyn al-ʿAzīziyya piped water over a distance of 64 km from Wadi Fatima to Jeddah. It secured the city's entire demand for fresh water for the following two decades (Anṣārī 1972; Bokhari 1978: 121, 279; Duncan 1987: 97–8; Idārat al-ʿAyn al-ʿAzīziyya n.d.). In 1951, the first seaport pier was opened, allowing ships to unload cargo and passengers to embark and disembark directly at the mole. Sailing dhows that transferred goods and people from ships anchoring at sea to the harbour and vice versa thus became obsolete. Throughout the 1950s, the harbour was expanded several times. The airport, operating since 1945, was enlarged in order to handle the increasing number of pilgrims arriving by air. The Saudi Ministry of Foreign Affairs was erected to the north of the old city centre in 1952 and 1953. From the mid-1950s several new streets were built, most importantly the first ring road connecting al-Baghdādiyya district, the airport, al-Khozam Palace and the seaport. Existing streets, such as the Mecca and Medina roads, were tarmacked. A large oil refinery behind the seaport to the south of Jeddah and a concrete factory in the north were inaugurated in 1956. Telephone networks were established in the same year.[1] The first mass accommodation for pilgrims was built close to the seaport in 1950. A similar complex was constructed at the airport in 1958, and a third one for African pilgrims to the south of the city in 1953/4. These so-called pilgrims' cities (*mudun al-ḥujjāj*) were frequently enlarged in the following years due to an ever increasing number of pilgrims (Figure 3.1). Initially there were dormitories for 5,000 people in the pilgrims' city at the seaport,

Figure 3.1 Mass accommodation for pilgrims at the old airport. Photo: © Stefan Maneval 2012.

over 2,000 in the one at the airport, and another 2,000 in the complex for African pilgrims. In 1974 they provided accommodation for a total of approximately 60,000 pilgrims (Anṣārī 1972: 183–91; Idārat al-ʿAyn al-ʿAzīziyya n.d.: 101–22).

Developments such as these changed the way travellers as well as permanent or temporary residents perceived the city. Furthermore, new building materials and house types, new facilities and employment opportunities as well as increasing flows of people moving to or passing through Jeddah profoundly transformed the conditions of social coexistence. My intention in this chapter is to explore how, as a consequence of these transformations, the material framework of public and private spaces changed. I will trace these changes by starting, as in the previous chapter, with the perspective of a traveller in Jeddah – this time not an imaginary one but a historical figure. Malcolm X's account provides valuable insights into how a pilgrim experienced his stay in Jeddah after some of the major transformations had taken place. Next, I move on to the experience of Jeddah's residents, first with regard to the transformation of urban space and then to residential architecture. I want to argue that, although notions of public and private space that prevailed in previous decades were not replaced by new ones in the course of a few years, important changes in the relationship between and the conceptions of these spheres were initiated in the first decades of the oil era.

Malcolm X in Jeddah

Malcolm had planned to travel from the airport in Jeddah directly to Mecca, but at customs his American passport aroused suspicion. The customs officer wanted the *maḥkama sharʿiyya*, the Islamic court, to check if he was actually a Muslim, a prerequisite for entering Mecca. For that reason, Malcolm was forced to spend a night in the pilgrims' city next to the airport (Figure 3.1). He gives a vivid description of the facilities:

> Right outside the airport was a mosque, and above the airport was a huge, dormitory-like building, four tiers high. It was semi-dark, not long before dawn, and planes were regularly taking off and landing, their landing lights sweeping the runways, or their wing and tail lights blinking in the sky. Pilgrims from Ghana, Indonesia, Japan and Russia, to mention some, were moving to and from the dormitory where I was being taken. I don't believe that motion picture cameras ever have filmed a human spectacle more colorful than

my eyes took in. We reached the dormitory and began climbing, up to the fourth, top, tier, passing members of every race on earth. Chinese, Indonesians, Afghanistanians. Many, not yet changed into the *Ihram* garb, still wore their national dress. It was like pages out of the *National Geographic* magazine.

> My guide, on the fourth tier, gestured me into a compartment that contained about fifteen people. Most lay curled on their rugs, asleep. I could tell that some were women, covered head and foot. An old Russian Muslim and his wife were not asleep. They stared frankly at me. Two Egyptian Muslims and a Persian roused and also stared as my guide moved us over into a corner.
>
> (Malcolm X 2001: 439)

As the *maḥkama* was closed the next day, a Friday, Malcolm had to stay in the pilgrims' city another day. He obviously did not leave the compound, but spent the time practising the prayer posture in his compartment, conversing with other English-speaking pilgrims, attending prayer in the adjacent mosque and having his meals in the courtyard (Malcolm X 2001: 438–43). His roommates and many other pilgrims also do not seem to have left the compound very often. He watched them eating, chatting, praying and sleeping in their compartment or in the courtyard:

> These Muslims prayed on their rugs there in the compartment. Then they spread a table-cloth over the rug and ate, so the rug became the dining-room. Removing the dishes and cloth, they sat on the rug – a living-room. Then they curl up and sleep on the rug – a bedroom.
>
> (Malcolm X 2001: 440)

In principle, pilgrims did not have to leave the pilgrims' city at all before they continued on their journey to Mecca. All the required services were offered on the premises: there were restaurants, shops, money changers, banks, health services, offices of pilgrimage guides (*muṭawwifūn*, sing. *muṭawwif*), a mosque, a police station, a customs office and passport services, as well as branches of several ministries and government agencies concerned in some way with the pilgrimage (Anṣārī 1972: 185–90; Idārat al-ʿAyn al-ʿAzīziyya n.d.: 101, 111, 118–19). Everyone in the pilgrims' cities was either on their way to Mecca or working to make the pilgrimage possible.

Before the introduction of mass accommodation, the situation was quite different. As indicated in the previous chapter, many pilgrims were accommodated on the ground floors of residential houses. Some even slept in the streets. ʿAbdullāh Manāʿ describes these changes from the perspective of a native inhabitant of Jeddah:

> The pilgrims spent their days happily and contentedly in Jeddah's residential quarters (*ḥārāt*), until, in the late 70s and early 80s of the Hijra [around 1960], the two pilgrims' cities for pilgrims travelling by sea and by air were constructed. Step by step, the pilgrims were separated from the city of Jeddah, its inhabitants and its life.
> (Manāʿ 2008: 76, my translation)

The author clearly sees the opening of the first mass accommodation as the beginning of a process leading to the more or less complete cutting off of the pilgrims from the city of Jeddah. Already in 1964, Malcolm X does not seem to set foot in the city centre, even after leaving the pilgrims' city on the evening of his second day in Jeddah. Remembering the introduction to an influential person he had been given in New York, Malcolm makes a phone call, and is immediately picked up and driven to the home of his new acquaintance, Dr Azzam. Early in the morning, he is taken to a luxury hotel in the city centre, the Jeddah Palace, where he spends a few hours sleeping. Over the course of the next two days, he moves between the hotel and the home of Dr Azzam, visits the Hajj Committee Court to secure authorisation for travel to Mecca, and finally leaves Jeddah – all by car (Malcolm X 2001: 444–9). He finds himself in the city of Jeddah, but he only observes it from the window of a car or from his hotel room.

I do not mean to suggest that what Malcolm experienced was the rule. His influential contacts and his prominent name ensured that he received extraordinary attention, culminating in a personal audience with Prince Fayṣal, later King of Saudi Arabia (Malcolm X 2001: 462–3). Not every pilgrim circumvented the city to the same degree as Malcolm did. Malcolm himself reports that, from his hotel room, he watched the streets of the ancient Red Sea city, 'filled with the incoming pilgrims from all over the world' (2001: 447). Neither did all of these pilgrims stay in one of the pilgrims' cities. These facilities were only capable of taking in approximately 10–20 per cent of the annual total of 140,000 to 180,000 pilgrims travelling to Mecca between 1957 and 1962 (Lewis 2012). Other pilgrims stayed in one of the numerous new hotels or, just as previously, in accommodation provided by their respective *muṭawwif* (pilgrimage guide) or in the streets.

Yet, at this point in Jeddah's history, Malcolm's experience had become possible, and it was becoming more normal for pilgrims to see hardly anything of the city. Again, ʿAbdullāh Manāʿ comments on this development with regret:

> Then, all the rules, instructions and worries caused the pilgrims to gallop. They are allowed to stay 24 hours in the city. Buses are waiting for them in order to take those arriving early to Medina and those arriving late directly to Mecca, as if Jeddah did not want them or could not take them in. Although the opposite is the case.
>
> (Manāʿ 2008: 76–7, my translation)

Spatial differentiation

The mass accommodation for pilgrims contributed to the gradual separation of the pilgrims from the city. In addition, it provided plenty of new job opportunities for the inhabitants of Jeddah (Anṣārī 1972: 187–90). In this respect, the pilgrims' cities were part of a wider phenomenon. Large numbers of jobs were created by the oil refinery, the concrete factory, the growing state apparatus, new hotels, shopping centres, schools, hospitals, the construction industry and so on. Within 20 years, the number of employees of the al-ʿAyn al-ʿAzīziyya water supply system grew to 1,200. Some of these jobs, such as that of a pilgrimage guide, were not entirely new, but the workplace changed. Previously, a *muṭawwif* used to receive customers in his own house. Now he had his office on the premises of the pilgrims' city, for example.

The construction of infrastructure and the creation of new jobs in Jeddah in the first decades of the oil era was thus accompanied by an increasing degree of spatial differentiation, experienced by both pilgrims and the local population. Of course, many residents of Jeddah kept their occupation and their workplace in the house where their families lived. Others had always had a job outside the home, for example masons, fishermen or dock workers. The combination of work and domestic life under one roof, which had previously been so common in Jeddah, however, became rarer, as all new jobs were situated in external workplaces (see Fadan 1983: 69–76).

At the same time, the new residential architecture reduced the possibility of working at home. Houses constructed out of concrete in an ad hoc manner by migrant workers in the late 1940s and throughout the 1950s usually consisted of no more than one or two rooms and sometimes a courtyard. In the 1950s, the first apartment buildings were built. By 1970, they made up a large proportion of residential units in the new neighbourhoods of Jeddah. Both the ad hoc buildings and the modern apartments were designed to serve exclusively domestic functions. They were either too small to contain offices and other kinds of workrooms, or their floor plans did not fulfil the required division between family life on the one hand and employees, customers etc. on the other hand, as had been the case in old houses. The same can be said about the detached single-family houses of wealthier families, who began to settle in the north of Jeddah, particularly along the Medina Road in al-Ruways and al-Sharafiyya districts, from the 1950s onwards. Although larger than other types of new buildings, these 'villas', as they were called, were also not used for commercial purposes, nor were they rented out to pilgrims (see Sijeeni 1995: 155, 161–2; Yamani 2000: 94).

The new architecture in this era was constructed out of concrete. Instead of wooden lattices, the windows now had panes. *Rūshāns* (latticed oriel windows) disappeared and were sometimes replaced by open balconies (Figure 3.2). The majority of the new buildings were of rather poor quality. The building materials were not suitable for the climatic conditions (Bokhari 1978: 279–80). The thin concrete walls did not insulate the interior against heat in the same way as the massive limestone

Figure 3.2 Concrete building, constructed around 1960, in al-Hindāwiyya. Photo: © Stefan Maneval 2011.

blocks used in the old buildings, and the windowpanes prevented air from circulating. Even when windows were open, the cooling draft was far less effective, since the apartments, one- or two-storey buildings and villas did not have stairwells similar to the old tower houses, where the warm air could ascend to the roof. The systematic electrification of the city, starting in 1950/1, enabled well-to-do families to install ceiling fans, electric lights and refrigerators. Air conditioners, still rare in the 1950s, became more common in the 1960s (Anṣārī 1982: 35; Bokhari 1978: 121, 279; Sanger 1954: 14).

In their writings and in personal conversations, architects and urban planners from Jeddah emphasise that the architecture constructed in Jeddah in the 1950s and 1960s was designed by foreigners who were not familiar with the local architectural traditions and sociocultural norms. Following this narrative, professionals, not necessarily architects, from Egypt, Lebanon and other mostly Mediterranean countries imported architectural solutions without paying attention to the climatic conditions and way of life in the Red Sea city. One of the early chroniclers of the urban development of Jeddah, Abdullah Bokhari, comments on the work of these expatriates as follows:

> The pseudo-architects who arrived and practiced in Jeddah in the early 1950s neither valued nor maintained the old because they could not understand it, they did not adapt the new to the old because they had no sense of either, and they could not properly apply the new building materials to satisfy the esthetic and the functional wants of Jeddah's society. In the absence of any professional regulatory and supervisory body they created a cacophony of architecture, oblivious to the social values as well as to the principles of function, esthetics and climatic requirements.
>
> (Bokhari 1978: 280)

Bokhari and other observers sharing his criticisms do not forget to mention that the inhabitants of Jeddah readily adapted to the new settings. Chiefly migrant workers and members of the younger generation moved to new neighbourhoods. Saudi urbanists in the 1980s and 1990s held that fascination with the modern, Western lifestyle led people to abandon what they now considered as old-fashioned: the buildings in the old town, life within the framework of the extended family, strong neighbourhood ties and, moreover, the moral principles manifested in the traditional architecture (see chapter 4).

A modern lifestyle was certainly not the only motivation for leaving the old town and settling in another district. Asked about his father's motivation for leaving the old town and moving to a new building in the 1960s, one of my interlocutors mentioned the social status connected to a modern home and the lack of space in the old house. Inhabited by an extended family, often spanning three or four generations, the old buildings were often rather crowded (personal communication, January 2009; see also Fadan 1983: 310). Adult sons had also previously moved house when they got married if there was not enough space for their wife and children in their father's house. By the middle of the twentieth century, the densely populated area of the old town was covered with buildings. Unable to build new houses in the city centre, the only opportunity for many families to expand was to move to a new neighbourhood.

An increasing number of cars and, from the mid-1950s onwards, an expanding telephone network helped family members who did not live under the same roof any longer to stay in touch with one another (Anṣārī 1982: 36–7; Sanger 1954: 14; Ṭarābulsī 2008: 615–16). It was also common practice among those who had moved to the suburbs to visit friends and relatives in the old town. Men who moved to the suburbs with their families often continued spending the evening hours in their respective *mirkāz* in the old town to the end of their life (personal communication, January 2009). During fieldwork in 2009 and 2012, I still found three such circles of men who kept meeting in the old town although most of them were living in different districts. One of these groups regularly gathered in a room on the ground floor of an old building, probably the former *maqʿad*. It was now equipped with an air conditioner, a television and a glass door, so that passers-by could see the men inside. The other two circles used a group of benches in the streets to spend evenings together, just as in former times.

In the new neighbourhoods of the 1950s and 1960s, similar spaces seem to have been rare. In his thesis about leisure and recreation patterns and their relationship to open space and landscape design in Jeddah, Mohammad Ali al-Shahrani (1992: 77) states that areas in front of new homes were occupied by cars, and no one gathered close to the house any more. Public squares such as the *barḥāt* (sing. *barḥa*) in the old town could hardly be found in the densely built-up areas of unplanned settlements like al-Sabīl and al-Kandara. In districts where wealthier families lived in single-family houses, such as al-Sharafiyya and al-ʿAmmāriyya, walls surrounding the buildings isolated courtyards, or *aḥwāsh* (sing. *ḥawsh*), from the street. The streets in these areas were mainly used for

Figure 3.3 A lane in al-Kandara district. Photo: © Stefan Maneval 2011.

transportation. Undeveloped plots of land between buildings were used by youths to play football. Open spaces for men to meet, sit together, chat, sip tea or coffee and watch their children playing were much fewer than in the old town. Children playing in the streets of the old town were watched over either by men in the *mirkāz* or by women from the windows of the *rūshān*. The new architecture, in contrast, often did not enable the supervision of children playing outside (Figure 3.3). As a result, children spent more time indoors and were a less common sight in the streets, especially in neighbourhoods with regular street patterns where the amount of traffic was higher (al-Shahrani 1992: 76–87).

Nevertheless, in retrospective interviews conducted by Tariq Sijeeni (1995: 153–6, 161–2), residents from al-Kandara district judged the social life and community ties in their neighbourhood in the 1950s and 1960s as very good. Having lived in al-Kandara for 30 years at the time of the interview, one of Sijeeni's interlocutors states that, in the past, he knew 'at least 30 families in the area' (1995: 155). He reports:

> We used to exchange visits and meet in the late afternoon in front of the local mosque. All the residents (were) families … . Today I know two people only and our social relationship is formal. In the past, people's behaviour was decent and friendly, you would not

> find anyone making noise or looking into your house. Today most people do not care about the area.
>
> (Sijeeni 1995: 155)

This resident is not the only one to complain that, from the 1970s onwards, a massive influx of new immigrants brought about more anonymity and looser neighbourhood ties. Still, many residents of unplanned settlements of the 1950s and 1960s, such as al-Kandara, al-Nuzla al-Yamāniyya and al-Hindāwiyya, perceive the social network in their own district as better than in more recently developed neighbourhoods. Sijeeni quotes another resident from al-Kandara district as stating:

> The contemporary districts are clean, spacious, and much better than here in terms of organization and planning and (building) materials .... The houses are designed in a variety of cubical shapes with many different colors, and amenities. But from the sociocultural standpoint Al-Kandarah is superior.
>
> (Sijeeni 1995: 155)

Although spaces like the *mirkāz* were fewer, streets in unplanned settlements of the 1950s and 1960s did not simply cease to be places of encounter. On the contrary, residents often appreciated the vibrant street life in these neighbourhoods (Sijeeni 1995: 143, 154, 162). The places of sociability in these areas, however, were different from those in the old town. Restaurants and shops, the first department stores, garden cafes and *jīlātī*s (gelati – ice cream parlours) situated in these districts, attracted customers from all parts of the city. Consequently, more cars and pedestrians frequented the streets. New cafes were located either in or near commercial centres, or on the fringes of the expanding city. A large proportion of the residents of these districts were migrant labourers from foreign countries or other parts of Saudi Arabia who came as single males and lived in very simple dwellings, sometimes sharing a room with other migrants. Without a family to care for, these men spent the evenings after work in the streets, cafes and restaurants (see Manāʿ 2008: 50–3; al-Shahrani 1992: 78–81).

The cases discussed thus far suggest that the changes in the built environment that occurred in the first decades of the oil era were connected to new forms of sociability. The following section offers a closer look at the residential architecture of this period. My exploration is guided by the question of how the new architecture was interrelated with changing notions of public and private space.

New residential architecture

A clear division between inside and outside distinguished the new buildings from the traditional architecture more than anything else. In contrast to the permeable facades of old buildings, the thin concrete walls and windowpanes of new buildings cut off the interiors of houses from their surroundings. Spaces on the border of the house which characterised the buildings in the old town of Jeddah, such as the *rūshān*, the *khārija* (walled terrace, pl. *khārijāt*) or the masoned benches of the *mirkāz*, were no longer built. Furthermore, rooms that were open to the public, like the *dihlīz* and the *maqʿad* on the ground floor of the old buildings, were not included in new residential architecture. Social activities that had formerly been centred on one of these rooms now had to take place either within the family domain or outside the house.

Both foreigners and Saudis who moved to new apartments with their families often did not have a separate room to receive guests at home. Space was particularly limited in the one- or two-room houses constructed in an ad hoc manner (Figure 3.4). While women living in a small home entertained friends and relatives in the living room, the primary places for men to meet friends, relatives and colleagues were outside the home, such as in the local mosque or new cafes.

Figure 3.4 Small residential units constructed on an ad hoc basis in al-Thaghr district. Photo: © Stefan Maneval 2010.

Figure 3.5 Apartment building, constructed around 1960, to the northeast of the old town: Yasemin's home when she grew up. Photo: © Stefan Maneval 2011.

In larger apartments or single-family houses, a reception room allowed families to receive guests and, if necessary, to maintain gender segregation at the same time. The reception room (*majlis* or *ṣālūn*) was usually used by men. In many Saudi households, it was the only room, apart from the bathroom, a male guest was allowed to enter. Female guests were permitted to enter the family domain. Depending on their relationship to the host, that is *maḥram* or non-*maḥram*, this could imply that male members of the household temporarily had to avoid rooms occupied by women.[2] In old buildings, the situation had been similar. Yet one reception room could not replace the various functions of *dihlīz*, *maqʿad* and *mirkāz* entirely. In the past, according to Hisham Jomah, 'the closer one was to the family occupying the house, the deeper and the higher one was allowed inside' (1992: 175). The host decided and signalled to the guest which threshold he was allowed to pass through and where to stay (Jomah 1992: 192). In most new buildings, by contrast, the only option for receiving male guests was in the *majlis*. The host now had to decide whether the relationship to a potential visitor was close enough to let him enter his house. All other friends and acquaintances had to be met outside. Whereas the residential architecture had previously provided the framework for many activities associated with male publics, the new buildings were largely reduced to female publics and domestic functions.

Women were more isolated from the outside world than previously, in spite of the fact that many new houses had open balconies instead of latticed windows. In apartment buildings, household chores such as laundry and cooking, which were formerly done on *khārijāt*, now had to take place indoors. Compared to the alcove of a *rūshān*, the balcony of a house from the 1950s or 1960s was much more exposed to the public. A woman in a *rūshān* was able to see and communicate with people in the street, but she was still inside the house and did not have to wear a veil. A person on a balcony, on the other hand, was visible from the street. Since women were not supposed to be seen, let alone to linger in public, it was considered inappropriate for them to sit on a balcony. As a consequence, many Saudi families did not use their balconies at all (Jomah 1992: 43; Yamani 2000: 92–7; Mortada 1992: 234).

An exception to this rule was provided by one of my interlocutors, Yasemin, a woman who was born in Jeddah around 1950. In her youth, she had lived with her family on the seventh floor of a new upscale apartment building to the northeast of the old town (Figure 3.5). The building had captured my attention even before I interviewed Yasemin and learned that she had previously lived in it. The eight-storey structure is still a landmark in the area due to its imposing height and its curved northwest corner. On each level except for the ground and top floors, a generous balcony of several metres extends over this corner. In my interview with Yasemin, she recalled how she and her sisters, all in their teens, used to sit on the balcony and watch people in the street. They were allowed to do so because their parents considered the distance from the seventh floor to the street as sufficient to render the girls invisible. Yet upper-floor balconies in apartments which did not face any other building were rare. When Yasemin's family moved to a new single-family home in al-ʿAzīziyya district, they did not use the balcony there because it faced the street and they could be seen by passers-by (interview, 29 March 2011).

Zuhayr, one of my informants, had moved from the old town to a new building in al-Nuzla al-Yamāniyya in the 1960s. I asked him what was different in the new neighbourhood, and he mentioned cars, many foreigners, trees in the streets and the sight of girls on balconies. When I asked how much use was actually made of the open balconies constructed at that time, he reported that they were frequently used by the migrant population, but not so much by native Saudis. To my interlocutor, it was of secondary importance whether the girls he observed were daughters of Saudis or of foreigners. The mere fact that girls could be glimpsed was excitingly novel to the boy coming of age (personal communication, January 2009).

Sources documenting how residents of Jeddah experienced the changes in everyday life brought about by the transformation of the built environment in the 1950s and 1960s are rare. The female perspective is particularly under-represented. Architecture and urban planning are exclusively male disciplines at King Abdulaziz University Jeddah and predominantly male fields of employment in Saudi Arabia. Studies in these disciplines dealing with the period under investigation in this chapter have been produced only by men (Abu-Gazzeh 1994; Bokhari 1978; Fadan 1983; Jomah 1992; al-Shahrani 1992; Sijeeni 1995). Some of the authors conducted qualitative interviews to collect data. For reasons of gender segregation, all their interlocutors were male. I myself did not manage to interview more than one woman who had lived in Jeddah in the 1950s and 1960s (Yasemin). The autobiographical texts which I have quoted thus far were all written by men, too (Faḍlī 2010; Malcolm X 2001; Manāʿ 2008, 2011; Ṭarābulsī 2008). The only autobiographical account dealing with this period published by a female author is the book *At the Drop of a Veil*, already mentioned in the previous chapter (Alireza 2002). In 1943 the American author Marianne Alireza married a wealthy Saudi expatriate, Ali Alireza, and adopted his name. Two years later the couple moved to Jeddah, where Ali's extended family lived in a recently finished villa in al-Ruways district to the north of the old town. Marianne Alireza spent the next 12 years in Saudi Arabia. Subtitled *The True Story of an American Woman's Years in a Saudi Arabian Harem*, the memoirs were published in 1971. Prominent in her account is the feeling of being locked in together with other women:

> It had been easy to say I would accept the need to be veiled, but I had not been prepared for the confinement I felt as we lived each day within room walls, within house walls, within garden walls. … I felt so cooped up that I could hardly stand it, and I found it hard to believe that there was really no out-of-the-house place to go.
>
> Men with men, and women with women, that was the way it was, and unaccustomed as I was to the social segregation of the sexes, I fussed and fumed about it. …
>
> Any release from the house, even temporary, was welcome, and from the time dear Uncle Yousuf started his day, and mine, calling mightily for his manservant ('Ya Awad, Ya Awaaaad!') until the time I crawled onto my stone bed to sleep, I pondered and ached for my lost freedom. Never, never again would I take it for granted.

> We had activities, of course, which were useful and gratifying, companionable and fun. … But freedom is special. It is the element mixed with everyday duties and pleasures that makes the whole tolerable and enjoyable, and in Arabia, we lacked freedom. We women sewed, cared for our children, cooked up a pot of something now and then, made jam, talked, played games and wrote letters, but we were not free to come and go. Visiting offered an outlet, but it just meant exchanging the confines of our own rooms for the confines of those of some other lady. A male had to get us a car, a male had to drive us, and in between, cloaked and veiled from the time we left our door until we reached the upstairs parlor of whomever we were visiting, we had no contact with anyone or anything.
>
> (Alireza 2002: 60–2)

Describing her first impressions of her new life in Saudi Arabia, Alireza does not conceal the fact that she writes from a Western perspective. She was well aware of the fact that she suffered more under the impression of being 'cooped up' than the Saudi women she lived together with because, as an American, she was used to a different life and severely missed her 'lost freedom'. Neither Alireza's memoirs nor any other source available to me from that time contains first-hand information from Saudi women. It is thus impossible to evaluate how they perceived the environment in which they lived as well as the architectural and socio-economic changes they witnessed. Yet Alireza's account does provide some valuable insights into female everyday practices in the Ḥijāz in the late 1940s and the 1950s.

The activities women engaged in, as described by Alireza, seem to have been the same as in previous decades: household tasks, rearing of children, meeting and conversing with other women. The fact that Marianne and her female in-laws travelled to visit other women by car, however, can be considered a novelty of that time, even if some cars already existed in Jeddah before the Second World War. In the old city, distances between houses had never been too long to walk. In the late 1940s, cars were still a privilege of the elite, but rising average incomes soon enabled more and more people to buy a car. The expansion of the city made motor vehicles more desirable, if not necessary. Owing to the absence of an effective system of public transport, private cars soon became the primary means of transportation in Jeddah. In 1971, approximately 55 per cent of all households owned a vehicle – a relatively high figure considering that 25 years earlier cars were hardly available at all (see Duncan 1987: 94–5, 201, 314). The dependence on a car and a driver minimised women's opportunities to leave the house on their own, as Alireza painfully observed. Even though her Arab in-laws may not have felt the same way about this restriction as a Californian expatriate, the presence of Saudi women in public was reduced by it (see also Altorki 1986: 38). Studies dealing with the social life of women in Jeddah have all focused on Saudi women, and on women of the elite in particular. To my knowledge, no study covering the 1950s and 1960s explores the perspective of the growing migrant community. I can only presume that women belonging to expatriate communities were less confined to their homes.

Other events indicate that reduced visibility in public is not to be equated with fewer opportunities to engage in public life. The opening of the first private girls' school in Jeddah in 1957 and the introduction of girls' state schools in Saudi Arabia in 1960 offered formal, non-religious education for a limited number of privileged girls (al-Rasheed 2013: 88–9). The schools were non-religious in the sense that, in contrast to Quran schools, non-religious subjects were taught. Yet religion was, and still is, an integral part of the curriculum of state schools (see Prokop 2003, 2005). In 1970, the literacy rate among women was still as low as 2 per cent. That of men was also not very high, approximately 15 per cent. But the number of girls enrolled in schools that year, 135,000 as compared to 412,000 boys out of a population of approximately 6 million, shows that the trend was slowly shifting towards greater acceptance of girls' education (al-Rasheed 2013: 95–6). This would open up opportunities to participate in new forms of publics for a future generation of women.

In the passage quoted above, Alireza actually describes her experience in the family's summer house in Taif, a nearby town in the mountains of the Ḥijāz. I have chosen this excerpt because it reflects the consequences of motor transport for the relationship of women to the world outside the home. In the late 1940s, life in the Alireza family's newly built house in Jeddah's al-Ruways district was quite similar to the life lived in an old building as depicted in the previous chapter: An extended family was living together in the same house; the presence of male visitors temporarily forbade female family members from entering certain spaces; women regularly paid visits to friends and relatives, whom they met indoors, usually upstairs, whereas men gathered outside; women avoided streets as much as possible. Comparing her own situation in the old building in Taif with that in the new home in al-Ruways, Alireza, much to her relief, notes some differences: 'Our life was still centered in and around the home but at least we could see through real glass windows, look at the Red Sea in front of us, see the mountains behind us, and have the pleasure of walking in our yard in relative freedom' (Alireza 2002: 99).

Windowpanes and gardens or courtyards around the new single-family houses insulated the buildings from their surroundings and made interacting with neighbours or relatives in the streets impossible (see Eyuce n.d.: 139–40). On the other hand, the enclosed garden was a novelty at that time, which allowed the Alireza family to spend time outside the house without being visible. Outside, but not in public, the garden fulfilled similar functions to those of *khārijāt* in old buildings. In the Alireza family's new villa, and in some other large single-family houses, such terraces were available. The majority of new buildings, however, had neither a *khārija* that was protected from view nor a private garden. While the male residents of average new houses and apartments were, as mentioned above, away from home most of the day, their wives, unmarried daughters and young children of both sexes spent more time indoors.

The entire extended family of the Alirezas moved to the new home in al-Ruways district. All members of an extended family moving house together would soon become exceptional. Most new single-family homes and apartments were designed to accommodate nuclear families of young Saudis or migrant labourers. Gradually, more nuclear families of the younger generation moved to one of the new suburbs, leaving parents, grandparents and other family members in the old town or in another new building.[3] In 1957 Marianne Alireza and her husband Ali made plans to build their own single-family home. For Marianne, the dream of her own Arabian home ended while still in the planning stages, as her husband divorced her that same year. We can only assume that the divorce did not prevent Ali from moving into the new building with his second wife. Ali's brother was already living in a separate building with his second wife at that time. The story is paradigmatic: an extended family successively splits into smaller units which move into separate homes either within a larger family compound or scattered in different parts of the city.

Houses large enough for an extended family, or family compounds consisting of a couple of independent residential units arranged around a common courtyard, were an exception (Eyuce n.d.: 39). Even if they lived together on the same walled plot of land, contact between married couples and their parents, usually the husbands' parents, was reduced by the use of separate entrances. The anthropologist Soraya Altorki (1986: 21–2, 33–4) has shown that, as a result of the greater distance between segments of an extended family, husbands and wives spent more time together, while less time came to be spent with family members of different generations. The changing relationship between conjugal couples and their parents was accompanied by a new understanding of private space. Altorki quotes an old lady as saying:

> When young girls get married, they make it a condition to live alone. ... A girl wants to move out because she wants to feel that she is the mistress of her new home. They want the liberty to go and come without notifying their mothers-in-law, which they would have to do if they lived in the same house.... In the past, the husband's mother was the mistress of the house. Now the young girl wants this position herself.
>
> (Altorki 1986: 33–4)

Another informant quoted by Altorki, a man who lives in a compound of buildings together with his married son, explains:

> These days, young people want to live their lives their own way, which is different from ours. Unless one can provide them with this privacy, they'll leave [the father's house]. I have my married son live with me because I do not interfere in his family's life. Each can come and go as he pleases and do whatever he likes in his house.
>
> (Altorki 1986: 33)

The first quotation provides an example of the social control to which a married woman living together with her husband's extended family had previously been – but no longer was – subject. Traditionally she was obliged to inform her mother-in-law of her comings and goings. The second statement is particularly interesting because of its explicit mention of the term 'privacy'. What is striking about the use of the term by this informant is that the privacy he refers to is defended by conjugal couples against their own parents. In the old buildings, shared entrances and stairwells, greater interaction between family members of different generations and the social obligation of seeking permission to leave the house had limited the freedom of movement and the autonomy of individual household members, particularly of women, and even more so of women of the younger generation. From the 1950s onwards, a desire for autonomy from one's parents began to grow among the younger generation. This offers yet another explanation for the great success of nuclear family homes in Jeddah, even though they were initially constructed almost exclusively by foreign architects. The new homes designed for nuclear families satisfied a growing desire for more independence. Spatial distance and architectural barriers between segments of an extended family limited the opportunities for a married son's parents to control and interfere with the affairs of the conjugal couple of a younger generation. The collective privacy of the extended family in the patrilocal home with its strong focus on the protection of females from the view of male strangers made way for more privacy of the conjugal couple. While protection from the sight of outsiders still played a prominent role, the younger generation increasingly defined privacy as a sphere of non-interference which had to be defended even against one's own parents or parents-in-law.

While their autonomy from the parental generation grew and their conjugal relationships gained importance, women of the younger generation became less involved in networks of relatives and friends, particularly of their parents' friends. Altorki even asserts that a 'gradual substitution of one set of relationships (conjugal) for another (friendship)' took place (1986: 22). I do not believe that this shift has ever been fully achieved. Drawing on my own observations in recent years, I believe that friendship networks were transformed rather than replaced. Networks extending over several generations, which had been established and maintained in institutions such as *wuʿūd*, became less important as young women did not participate in their mother-in-laws' meetings as much as before. The same can be said about men growing up in districts where the *mirkāz*, as both an architectural phenomenon and a social institution, did not exist: young men were not integrated into their father's network of friends as easily as before, because they did not spend the evening hours next to him in the *mirkāz* any more. Yet the younger generation established their own forms of sociability, as will be discussed in chapters 5 and 6.

The overall impression gained from these observations is that the residential building became a more private space, whereas public activities, especially those of men, were resettled in the streets and in other places outside the home. An opposite trend seems to have occurred in at least one aspect. Mark Sedgwick (1997) describes how Sufis reacted to the banning of Sufi rituals in public under Saudi rule. His observations from the 1980s lead Sedgwick to assume that Sufis in the Ḥijāz continued to regularly conduct *dhikr* rituals and *mawlid al-nabī* celebrations in private homes. The Saudi state, promoting virtue and forbidding vice in public, understood and still understands itself as respecting privacy. Heterodox rituals were prohibited in mosques and *zāwiyas*, but not interfered with as long as they remained invisible (Sedgwick 1997: 360–7). The fact that Sufi rituals moved from public spaces to private homes did not turn them into private affairs. The gatherings of the brotherhoods, which brought together men who were connected by a shared belief system, remained institutions of public life even though their position in society was somewhat weakened. The gatherings temporarily turned the residential building into a public space. Increased seclusion of the home as well as an understanding of it as a sphere of non-interference supported this development.

Conclusion

Although friendship networks spanning two or more generations may have lost some importance as architectural and sociocultural frameworks changed, they certainly did not dissolve completely. Similarly, other trends explored in this chapter neither came to an end within the time-span covered thus far, nor did they encompass the entire populace. I have concentrated here on crossroads, prerequisites and harbingers of change. I do not mean to argue that every institution, every element and every space in Jeddah changed according to the patterns described here within a mere 25 years. The actual processes of transformation lasted for several decades. Some of them still continue today, and many will probably never encompass the entire population of Jeddah. But in the first two or three decades after the Second World War, profound changes in the built environment of Jeddah were initiated, and this both led to and reflected a changing relationship between public and private space. To conclude this chapter, I briefly summarise the trends and changes initiated in the 1950s and 1960s.

One of these trends can be labelled as spatial differentiation. The multiple functions fulfilled by residential architecture in earlier times – work, education of children, accommodation of pilgrims and reception of guests, in addition to domestic life – were gradually dispersed and relocated to places with more specific purposes. This process was caused, on the one hand, by the new infrastructure built during this time – mass accommodation for pilgrims, department stores, hospitals, office buildings, hotels, new public and private schools, factories etc. The large number of external workplaces created by these facilities and services led to the division of work and domestic life – one of the most decisive aspects of spatial differentiation occurring during this period. On the other hand, most of the new residential architecture was designed to serve only domestic purposes. As a consequence, the home lost many of its public functions and became a place almost exclusively dedicated to family life.

Because of a clear division between inside and outside, activities that had been situated between these spheres in the old buildings now had to take place either completely indoors or further away from home. Whereas male commercial, recreational and social activities tended to move to external places – external workplaces, cafes, streets – women and children spent more time inside the home or other interiors, such as cars. A second trend can thus be described as spatial polarisation: privacy was increasingly identified with the home, which became a more family-oriented, intimate and female space. Public spaces, on the other hand, were to a greater degree associated with the outside world, except for female publics, which were still constituted primarily inside homes. In the new neighbourhoods of Jeddah, a growing number of cars and lack of spaces to sit and socialise in public increased movement in the streets while at the same time making them more anonymous. With the proliferation of cars, the presence of women in the streets, at least of Saudi women, was reduced.

Another major tendency was the growing importance of the nuclear family and the conjugal relationship. The majority of new homes were built to accommodate nuclear families, and larger family compounds divided units of an extended family more effectively than Jeddah's old buildings had. The great acceptance of, and adaptation to, the new residential architecture was accompanied by a different notion of privacy. The autonomy of conjugal couples of the younger generation vis-à-vis their parents strengthened. Privacy was now understood as a sphere of independence and non-interference in the affairs of the nuclear family. As the distance between segments of an extended family increased, publics involving family members of different generations became less important.

The trends I have analysed in this chapter were subject to harsh criticism in the decades that followed. The critical discourse on the urban development of Jeddah in the oil era is the subject of the next chapter.

Notes

1. The developments summarised here are reported by Anṣārī (1982: 36–7), Bokhari (1978: 281–5), Duncan (1987: 44, 96, 137), al-Ḥārithī (2003/4: 237) and Ṭarābulsī (2008: 155, 626).
2. This practice was reported to me by Yasemin, who, as a teenager, used to live in a large apartment building in al-Baghdādiyya district with her family in the 1960s (interview, 29 March 2011). The same arrangement is also mentioned by al-Shahrani (1992: 83–4).
3. This process is recounted by numerous authors from Jeddah, such as Fadan (1983: 75–7), al-Shahrani (1992: 80–4), Sijeeni (1995: 81) and Altorki (1986: 21–2).

4

Architecture and religious reform: Architectural discourse from the 1970s to the 1990s

The enormous wealth that swept Saudi Arabia with the high price of oil in the 1970s soon had an effect on the urban environment of Jeddah. The Real Estate Development Fund, created in 1974, allowed more people to build their own homes. It encouraged in particular the construction of single-family units (Bokhari 1978: 334–6). While the general types and forms of the new buildings were similar to those of previous decades and evolved relatively slowly, building materials, decoration and finishing became more elaborate. Already in 1978, five years after the overnight quintupling of oil prices, Abdulla Bokhari observed:

> [T]he large sudden wealth which fell into the hands of the middle-class has had an extremely negative effect on the quality of architecture, and the built environment. A large portion of this middle-class *nouveau riche* were architecturally naive, and esthetically insensitive individuals, whose involvement in lavish spending on building resulted in ostentatious, gaudy architecture, in which stylistic modern features were allowed to become an end.... The contemporary residential architecture became in the hands of the unguided wealthy middle class a strange fusion of forms from different architectural styles and periods, indiscriminately combined in exotic shapes which belong nowhere.... Much of the new residential architecture in the city reflects bizarre features, trying to emulate flashy Western style architecture, while some of the architectural forms cast doubt on the seriousness or clear headedness of their designers. In many cases one senses that some architects went through a great

deal of gymnastics in order to produce an incomprehensible type of architecture, no doubt at great expense to their clients. It is also depressing to witness such ubiquitous undisciplined architecture in the new urban scene of a city that previously produced elegant and dignified local architecture with much lesser means.

(Bokhari 1978: 345–6)

This passage is not only an articulation of dissatisfaction with the aesthetics of the new architecture. It also expresses the author's alienation from his hometown by the spread of new building styles. The author appears to be especially disquieted by the fact that some of the new buildings reference Western architectural styles, or that Western architects were commissioned to build houses in so-called Islamic styles and even to build mosques (Bokhari 1978: 346–52). The overall fear behind this criticism seems to be the loss of identity, as the author's comparison between these newer forms and the 'elegant and dignified local architecture' of previous times in the last sentence of the quotation suggests.

Bokhari was one of the first observers who voiced this kind of criticism of architecture and urban development in the oil era, but he was not alone. In their writings – unpublished theses, journal articles and a few monographs – many Saudi architects and urban planners echo Bokhari's anxieties. During the 1980s and 1990s, however, they became concerned not only about loss of cultural identity in general but that contemporary architecture and urban design contravened the rulings of Islam in particular. This chapter deals with these concerns as well as the societal context in which they thrived.

Bokhari's 1978 study, and a Ph.D. thesis written by Tariq Sijeeni in 1995, are the earliest and latest texts in a body of nine included in my analysis. Apart from one journal article, the body of texts consists of unpublished studies on architecture and urban development in Jeddah, seven Ph.D. theses and one working paper. I discovered them in the library of the Faculty of Environmental Design of King Abdulaziz University. Since the article was published in an international journal and the Ph.D. theses were all submitted at American or British universities, all texts are in English. The availability of these texts for students in Jeddah is an important factor: the thoughts developed by the respective authors were not only in principle accessible to thousands of readers interested in the field but, as numerous cross-references indicate, they were circulated among future generations of architects and urban planners – those who would later design homes in Jeddah or plan the further development of the city.

My analysis in this chapter begins with a critical summary of a Ph.D. thesis submitted in 1983 by Yousef Fadan, which deals with the architectural development in Saudi Arabia in the oil era in a paradigmatic way. Fadan saw architectural development in that era as embedded in a disquieting transformation of society. I go on to demonstrate that other authors shared Fadan's concerns and followed strikingly similar lines of argument. Principles of social coexistence that play a vital role in the constitution of public and private spaces occupy a central position in their texts. My discussion of these is followed by a section dedicated to the religious revival movement in Saudi Arabia in the 1980s and 1990s, a movement which also occurred in similar forms in other Muslim contexts. I argue that there are salient parallels between the criticism voiced by architects and urban planners and wider public debate on religious renewal. The final section of this chapter explores frames of reference deployed by authors who were engaged in critical debate on architecture and urban development in the oil era, as well as their suggestions as to how the problems they diagnose should be remedied. Since this debate was not limited to Jeddah, I include in this part authors who write about architecture and urban planning in Saudi Arabia in general. By doing so, I intend to highlight the scope of this discourse, as well as to lay the groundwork for my argument in the next chapter, in which I analyse the impact of this discourse on residential architecture and the construction of private and public spaces.

Islamic architectural criticism: A case study

In his Ph.D. thesis, 'The Development of Contemporary Housing in Saudi Arabia (1950–1983)', submitted at MIT in 1983, Yousef Fadan introduces the hypothesis of his study with the following words:

> Radical and hastily executed development plans and an attraction to Western life-styles have drawn Saudi attention away from developing a clear and concise understanding of the evolution of a traditional living environment.... This has further prevented the society from maintaining the valuable characteristics of the traditional residential environment and cultural heritage. The result is a completely foreign physical residential environment transplanted into the country.
>
> (Fadan 1983: 15)

Rather than merely repeating Bokhari (1978), whose thesis, quoted above, is listed among Fadan's references, these lines take the criticism one step further. The random adoption of Western architecture and lifestyle leads, in the eyes of Fadan, not just to an incoherent, ridiculous-looking cityscape. It also draws Saudis away from their own traditions and ultimately results in a loss of cultural values:

> Physical development on foreign models was not seriously questioned by the local elite which permitted the establishment of exotic architectural styles within the physical environment of Saudi society, while allowing the conventional building practices with their attendant values to be lost.
>
> (Fadan 1983: 11)

Fadan then documents a history of Saudi urban planning in the oil era that deviates considerably from official Saudi and American accounts. Twenty-four years before Robert Vitalis, claiming to be the first scholar to cast light on the darker chapters of the Arabian-American Oil Company (ARAMCO; see Vitalis 2007: x), blamed the Americans for having implemented a Jim Crow system in the ARAMCO camps, Fadan criticised the company for having provided luxury villas for American employees, housing of relatively poor quality for non-American expatriate workers from Italy, India, Pakistan, Lebanon, Sudan, Palestine, etc., and 'army-style dormitory barracks' without access to running water for Saudi workers (Fadan 1983: 105–10). Fadan then compares the unequal living conditions in the oil camps to social hierarchies manifested in housing developments for government employees constructed in Riyadh after 1953. He asserts that these two earliest examples of mass housing projects in Saudi Arabia served in the following decades as prototypes for modern residential architecture in all Saudi cities (Fadan 1983: 188–92).

Although Yousef Fadan's and Robert Vitalis's studies share many parallels, they are written from different perspectives. Whereas the former clearly writes about Saudi Arabia, the latter declares that his inquiry into 'Mythmaking on the Saudi Oil Frontier' is actually a book about the United States (Vitalis 2007: xxxvi). It may be due to this approach that ordinary Saudis appear in Vitalis's account first of all as victims: they suffered from ARAMCO's racist policy, exploitative working conditions and cruel treatment of protesters. Their only weapon – striking – eventually proved ineffective, since it only led to new forms of exploitation. For example, the company provided interest-free loans instead of better housing, so that Saudis were lured into houses they did not want to have in places where they did not want to live, and were incapable of changing their situation. In contrast, while not denying the ambiguous influence of ARAMCO's employment and housing policies, Yousef Fadan positions Saudi society in a more active role:

> Through advice and consultation, ARAMCO heavily influenced a non-communist development policy which seeks to generate popular enthusiasm and admiration for the modern Western world. … [B]oth individuals and society accepted, almost without hesitation, exotic and physically as well as culturally unsuitable forms of residential units. Along with these new housing forms, the Government authorities also adopted new legal and administrative instruments to control the building of these new environments and their perpetuation.
>
> (Fadan 1983: 159)

He refers to his own experience to corroborate this point:

> It took me more than a decade to realize that the admiration and fantasies I held for the modern villa were partially the result of an image engraved in my mind during the many visits to Jeddah of ARAMCO's mobile exhibits. The display of villas built through the company's home ownership program magnified such fantasies of attaining the promising modern life.
>
> (Fadan 1983: 179)

Important values lost in the course of this collective process of abandoning local traditions and adopting the modern Western way of life include, according to Fadan, appreciation and maintenance of one's neighbourhood community, strong family ties, the protection of privacy and an egalitarian concept of society (1983: 307–17). With regard to the last of these principles, Fadan notes that:

> Equality among Muslims is not only the principle of Ikhowan (the brotherhood) of the 1920s, but it is an Islamic way of life. It is clearly manifested in two of the five pillars of Islam, the Hajj (pilgrimage): during which every Hajji (pilgrim) wears simple white clothing. The rich and the poor, king and peasant, are all indistinguishable, all are equal. [Secondly, t]he fasting during Ramadan is not intended to make people suffer from hunger. Rather the philosophy of fasting is not only to remind the rich that there are people who do not have

> food to eat, but also to stress equality among all Muslims, in which no adult Muslim is exempt from this religious observance.
>
> Islam consequently prohibits strictly any act that shows any sign of arrogance. Such social behavior has been condemned in many verses in the Quran and Hadith. The thirteenth Hadith is an example: … 'None of you (truly) believes until he wishes for his brother what he wishes for himself'.
>
> (Fadan 1983: 316–17)

Fadan (1983: 299) claims that the architecture constructed in Saudi Arabia from the beginning of the oil era conflicts with the Islamic principle of equality among members of the Muslim community. The chapter covering what Fadan considers to be shortcomings in the contemporary architecture of the 1980s – the chapter before his conclusion – ends with a reassessment of Ḥijāzī residential architecture (Fadan 1983: 323–38). Fadan depicts the century-old building tradition in pre-oil Mecca as an ideal case of openness to innovation without loss of social values.

As I have shown in my second chapter, severe discrepancies between the dwellings of rich and poor people in Jeddah already existed in the pre-oil era. In his description of traditional residential architecture in the Arabian Peninsula and his case study of the Ḥijāzī house, however, Fadan does not mention social differences, African slaves, prostitutes or villages of huts constructed by the poor, who were expelled from the walled city area. He does not interpret different degrees of architectural decoration in old buildings as markers of social distinction. Instead, he praises the rich variety of style (Fadan 1983: 337). The blind spots in Fadan's analysis reveal his biased view of the old times. For him, the old was good although people were ready to abandon it as soon as new building techniques and house forms were introduced in the country. And the new is bad because it 'will result in social disintegration' (Fadan 1983: 299) and fails to comply with the precepts of Islam.

I have summarised Fadan's thesis here in some detail because it epitomises the way Saudi architects and urban planners of his generation wrote about the transformation of their own cities. Regardless of the specific topic they investigated, from leisure places (al-Shahrani 1992) to housing for university staff (al-Mutawea 1987), and whether they focused on the past (e.g. Jomah 1992; Abu-Gazzeh 1994) or the present (e.g. Mortada 1992; Sijeeni 1995), their argument follows a similar pattern. They compare the contemporary with the traditional, and they all have a strong preference for the latter. They all agree that what had been abandoned in the previous decades were not simply old buildings, but social ties, moral values and, above all, a way of life that accorded with religion. They indicate the same, or strikingly similar, principles and concepts to substantiate this assumption. And they criticise society for its susceptibility to 'Westernisation', which allows such social transformation to take place.

I am not arguing that the authors I refer to have all parroted each other, nor that their work is without any merits. They have collected valuable data on diverse topics, documented opinions, knowledge and processes which otherwise would have been forgotten, and formulated criticism with which significant parts of Saudi society obviously concurred at that time. Much of my own knowledge of the history of urban planning and architecture in Jeddah and Saudi Arabia is based on their writings. This is one reason why, at this point, I find it necessary to illuminate the underlying assumptions of their work. Another reason is that I want to show that they partook in a wider discourse of Islamic Revival and that the widespread popularity of that discourse provided fertile ground for their ideas. Before I turn to the public debate on religious reform, I elaborate in the following section on three key issues addressed in some way or another by all Saudi urbanists in my archive: the weakening of social ties, the loss of privacy and so-called Westernisation of society.

Social connectedness

'Today, as a result of the recent arrangement of the built environment, community activities are lacking and social ties are diminishing', remarks Tawfiq Abu-Gazzeh (1994: 58). Likewise, Tariq Sijeeni remarks:

> The spiritual ties of extended family life in traditional residential clusters were stretched and broken, intimate relationships between neighbors in traditional communities disintegrated, and alienation and isolation became dominant social problems in the new communities of Jeddah.
>
> (Sijeeni 1995: 81)

Both Abu-Gazzeh and Sijeeni sum up in one sentence a judgement developed over many pages by almost all authors in my sample. They focus particularly on two forms of social ties purportedly on the wane: extended family and neighbourhood bonds. Although the title of his thesis is 'The Traditional Process of Producing a House in Arabia during the 18th and 19th Centuries', Hisham Jomah (1992), for example, comments on an alleged deterioration of family ties in the second half of the twentieth century.[1] He first describes how 'private life ... was family-centred in Ḥedjāz', with the members of an extended family residing in the same building, only to remark that 'today this intensive family closeness has been somewhat dispersed. The imitation of the Western lifestyle by modern Saudis has not only weakened the family ties, but also made it no longer the prime focus of loyalty' (Jomah 1992: 35–6). The narrative he presents is very similar to Fadan's, as summarised above: attracted by the modern, progressive lifestyle promised by the new buildings, all equipped with air-conditioners, people did not immediately notice the social changes that went along with this different kind of architecture. Designed for nuclear families, 'these homes meant the separation of the extended family and consequently far greater isolation of the women, young children and the elderly' (Jomah 1992: 43). Jomah's description of this process is infused with nostalgia and moral judgement, as he goes on to say (1992: 43, emphasis in the original):

> And so, the traditional houses where the whole family once shared their evening meal, and where the children and old people had a particularly happy life, were left to decay with their age-old owners. The old who had a position of considerable prestige in the extended family ... were reduced to *once-a-month* visitors.

With regard to neighbourhood bonds, Abu-Gazzeh, for example, recounts a corresponding story.[2] He first explains that, 'Islam urges Muslims to be good neighbors. Mohammed explained that "Neighborhood extends to 40 houses in all directions"' (Abu-Gazzeh 1994: 55). After describing how this and other Islamic principles were lived up to in Jeddah in the pre-oil era, he turns to the present, lamenting that 'the possibility for person-to-person interaction in the environment has decreased as a result of increased distances between residential buildings. Thus, the inherited Muslim norm of commitment and belonging, a concept that is strongly supported by Islamic religion, has suffered' (Abu-Gazzeh 1994: 58).[3]

Sijeeni, whose study is based on qualitative interviews with 30 residents of different types of neighbourhoods in Jeddah – the old city, districts dating from the 1950s and 1960s, and a contemporary neighbourhood of single-family units – shows that many people share the experience of weakening social bonds in the course of the expansion of the city. To be more precise, many male Saudi nationals aged 35 to 65 do (Sijeeni 1995: 137). Women's voices are absent in Sijeeni's sample as well as in my sample of authors, and so are the voices of the hundreds of thousands of immigrants living in Jeddah. This means that those who participate in the discourse, shaping its particular assumptions, only represent a tiny minority. It is not entirely unlikely that other groups of people – elders, or women, for example – would concur with this minority. But the opposite may be true as well, especially since the trend of moving from the old city to homes for nuclear families continued.

The male Saudi experts engaged in the discourse on architecture and urban development of the 1980s and 1990s do not simply voice their subjective opinions. They construct a normative argument. This is salient in Fadan's comments cited above on the egalitarian society promoted by Islam, and in Abu-Gazzeh's reference to the neglect of local traditions and, in particular, 'Muslim' norms, as well as in the quotations of other authors cited thus far. All authors in my sample are wary that society is moving in a wrong direction. Fadan warns that the processes he observes lead to 'social disintegration' and 'isolated nuclear famil[ies]' (Fadan 1983: 299, 310). And Mortada dedicates chapter 7 of his thesis, in its entirety, to exploring 'the violation of the traditional social and physical principles of Islam' (Mortada 1992: 275). Among the principles violated, according to him, are 'Making the House a Source of Strong Neighbourliness', 'Extended Family' and 'Strong Family Ties'. He further prognosticates that less involvement in 'family and society affairs' along with a deteriorating 'sense of community and co-operation' will 'affect the solidarity of the entire society' (Mortada 1992: 143–4). He reports that 'many of the new Saudi generation suffer from an emptiness of soul and a distorted perception of life' because 'the psychological impact of modernity has been so deep' (Mortada 1992: 144). As a consequence, 'they escape to other individuals (friends) who share with them this feeling and waste time by such superficial activities as card playing' (Mortada 1992: 144). Poor boys.

As is evident in the multitude of quotations I have provided thus far, all the authors I refer to describe the recent transformation of the urban community as a process of decay. Narratives of decline are always unbalanced. They tend to overlook deviations from rules and norms, injustices and other miseries of the past. And although they may be right in asserting the decline of a specific historic phenomenon, they often fail to recognise new formations replacing lost ones. During my visits to Jeddah, I got to know three informal networks of men, the first two consisting of business contacts, friends and distant relatives, the third one of friends and acquaintances who were all converts to Shiite Islam. To each of these networks I was introduced by an individual who took an interest in my research. Most of the time my informants did not arrange meetings to establish contact between me and someone else. Rather, they would invite me to join them whenever they paid a visit to any of their acquaintances who might have information for me. And they paid a visit to a number of acquaintances almost every night. Whenever I accepted an invitation I ended up spending the night from approximately 9 p.m. to well past midnight driving or walking from one place to another, sipping tea in downtown offices or cafes, visiting the workplaces of clients, clients-to-be or distant cousins, having dinner at restaurants and, in the case of some well-off Shiite converts, sitting around on couches in opulent living rooms. Neighbours were indeed not included in any of these networks, but members of the extended family were. What is most important, however, is the fact that these networks bear witness to new social ties, forged in different places and architectural settings, and maintained with new means of communication and transport such as mobile phones and cars. None of the urbanists enquires into the emergence and functions of such new social networks. Brief allusions to them are made in a purely derogatory way, as in the case of Mortada's card players. Nor does any of the authors discussed here seriously engage with the motivation of the younger generation for giving up life within the framework of the extended family, in neighbourhoods where everyone knew – and observed the comings and goings of – everyone else. Living with less social control and more individual privacy, as a sphere of personal freedom and non-interference also from family members, seems to have had a strong appeal for the younger generation, not just air conditioners and the lure of a modern home and lifestyle.

Privacy

> The traditional Moslem environment controlled the mobility, thus limited the movement, controlled behaviour and created hierarchical domains of privacy. The winding and cul-de-sac streets satisfy some cultural and environmental needs, such as security, privacy and shade. The modern western planning concepts and standards, which had been widely applied in Jeddah, maximized movement and accessibility; thus destroying the privacy (a major cultural need) and adding to the severity of an already harsh environment.
> (al-Shahrani 1992: 281)

The narrative of decline is also made use of with respect to privacy, as this quotation indicates. Again, this involves blind spots and inconsistencies. A particularly telling example in this respect is Fahad Mohammed al-Mutawea (1987), who is especially concerned about insufficient privacy in new homes. I have previously quoted from his thesis in the context of the question of privacy in Islam (chapter 2). The core of his thesis is a questionnaire-based quantitative survey of the newly built university housing, conducted in the mid-1980s. From his analysis of 87 questionnaires answered by university staff residing in on-campus housing compounds, al-Mutawea arrives at the conclusion that:

> [P]rivacy within the family domain is less maintained. That is due to the treatment of windows where there is no screen to prevent overlooking and direct visual contact from adjacent buildings. Unless window blinds are used … family privacy would be lost.… [T]he terraces have no function at all. If occupants tended to use them as an area for relaxation, their privacy would be lost and also their neighbours' privacy would be destroyed. This would not be acceptable morally, as well as culturally.… In order to avoid these social and environmental problems, the terraces should be enclosed.
>
> (al-Mutawea 1987: 184–6)

It is worth mentioning that al-Mutawea's evaluation is, more than anything else, an expression of his own opinion. It is not supported by his own statistical data. Contrary to al-Mutawea's conclusion, the majority (52 per cent) of his respondents had answered the question 'How effective is the privacy generally inside the flat?' with 'good'. One-third (34 per cent) considered the protection of privacy inside apartments to be fair, ranging midway between good and bad on a questionnaire offering just three options. Only 14 per cent were actually dissatisfied (al-Mutawea 1987: 146). This outcome obviously contradicted al-Mutawea's view and expectations in such a strong way that he simply reinterpreted it:

> The response to the socio-cultural issues, although the overall result is fair, especially to the issue of privacy and to the flats' adaptability to family growth, should have been bad. However, it is my impression that if the evaluation scale was more elaborated, for instance, the grade of 1–10 then the majority might be bad rather than fair.
>
> (al-Mutawea 1987: 159)

His assertion that privacy in new homes is not adequately protected is thus based on speculative interpretation of quantitative data which suggest a different conclusion.

However doubtful al-Mutawea's interpretation may be, many architects and town planners were of the same opinion. Although, as al-Mutawea's survey indicates, not all residents of Jeddah, let alone a majority, shared their standpoint, the studies conducted by Abu-Gazzeh (1996), Eyuce (n.d.), Fadan (1983), Jomah (1992), Mortada (1992) and Sijeeni (1995) offer valuable insights into how these experts and other male Saudi nationals aged 35–65 conceived of privacy and envisioned its relationship to residential architecture in the 1980s and 1990s. A particularly fruitful source of information, in this regard, is Hisham Mortada's unpublished Ph.D. thesis. The discussion of how the traditional Islamic principle of 'Site Visual Privacy' is violated in the contemporary architecture of Jeddah extends over several pages (Mortada 1992: 226–45).[4] Balconies, windows and entrances of single-family houses and apartments are viewed as particularly precarious. To protect visual privacy when entering the home, Mortada recommends a 'transitional space', that is, a walled entrance area screening the inner parts of the home (Mortada 1992: 242–5).[5] He complains that most contemporary residential buildings do not provide such an 'airlock'. Particularly problematic, in his opinion, are 'apartment buildings where the central staircase is shared by all residents, and once the apartment door is opened, the interior is immediately open to the view of users of the staircase or hallway' (Mortada 1992: 242–5). Mortada is not just concerned about violation of privacy by neighbours and passers-by due to inadequate architectural protection of privacy. Even guests can threaten the privacy of the family, first and foremost male guests. Entering the house or using the bathroom, they might catch sight of female family members unless these stay in the kitchen or living room.[6] It is important to note here that in the past, houses also did not have a clear architectural division between guest areas and the family domain. Gender segregation was, as mentioned in chapter 2, often achieved by the temporary avoidance of certain rooms by either men or women while guests of the opposite sex were visiting. This phenomenon is used as an example by Jomah (1992: 193, 199) of the simple solutions of the past which allowed people in Jeddah to live in accordance with Islam. When it comes to contemporary architecture, however, authors such as Mortada and al-Mutawea (1987: 146) complain that the lack of internal physical boundaries violates Islamic privacy requirements and causes inconveniences for residents, particularly for women.

Mortada reports that residents who were concerned about 'visual intrusion' of visitors into the family domain, and especially about male guests catching glimpses of female members of the household, altered the building according to their needs. Demolishing interior walls or constructing new ones are cited as common steps taken to keep guests and family members of the opposite sex separated (Mortada 1992: 239–42; cf. al-Mutawea 1987: 141–6). Furthermore, Mortada complains about lack of 'acoustic privacy' (1992: 245). Concrete walls of only 15–20 cm, thin roofs and single-pane windows and balconies, according to Mortada, allow sounds to travel between neighbouring villas and apartments, to the annoyance of many residents. Sound-permeability of walls dividing rooms inside the home itself is also regarded as a problem (1992: 245).

Jomah (1992: 36), as he argues that the ideal of privacy is deeply rooted in Islam, supports the criticism articulated in greater detail by al-Mutawea and Mortada. In contrast to most of his contemporary critics, however, he notes that privacy is not simply neglected in recent architecture. He recognises that the very conception of privacy is subject to change. He suggests that the privacy of the individual has become more important than the notion of a collective private sphere of an entire family. In the course of this process of individualisation, social control and practices serving to protect privacy in the home have been replaced by physical barriers.[7] Although Jomah is clearly in favour of the social mechanisms of privacy protection in the past, he hints at the opportunities which contemporary changes may offer to individuals: more freedom and independence, more choice in respect of clothing, social interaction and lifestyle, and more diversity.[8] Nevertheless, his final verdict is as negative as it remains vague and unspecific:

> The separation between the age groups in modern cities have [sic] resulted in major social and psychological problems that were not experienced traditionally. Amongst these are the loss of status of the elderly, severing the traditional process of transmitted knowledge from one generation to the other, the loss of moral and behaviour standards and the discontinuity of culture altogether.
>
> (Jomah 1992: 341)

It is interesting to contrast the opinions expressed by scholars such as al-Mutawea, Mortada and Jomah with that of Bokhari. Writing approximately 10–15 years earlier, Bokhari is no less critical of the transformation of his city. He, too, complains that contemporary architecture has 'lost all meaningful contact with the prevailing social spirit and consciousness' (Bokhari 1978: 344). But he sees 'the citizens' exclusive concern for privacy over esthetics' as the major problem (1978: 348). In his view, the strong desire for privacy prevailing in Saudi society has resulted in 'introversion and isolation inside high boundary-walls' (1978:

354). In turn, '[t]he neglect of the role of the street has led to an obvious introversion of the citizens behind the high walls of their houses and, subsequently, to a gradual disappearance of the citizens' civic pride in their environment' (1978: 348). Bokhari's position demonstrates that the changes in the residential architecture of Jeddah in the oil era can also be evaluated differently. He is the only author who does not refer to moral judgements and religion to persuade his readers of his views. The focus of his criticism is on the architecture itself, whereas it seems that his younger colleagues' criticism is focused first and foremost on society. I will further explore this assumption in the following section.

Westernisation versus Islam

All the authors quoted here tend to regard Western lifestyles as a threat to the local culture and tradition. Moreover, in the view of all scholars except Bokhari, the values at stake are genuinely Islamic values. This is evident even in studies which are primarily concerned with technical aspects, such as the one by Eyuce (n.d.). Comparing openings and spatial organisation in old and new residential buildings, he contends that 'an appropriate hierarchical sequence from the most public to the most private' which 'has its origins in classical Islamic teachings' is no longer given in the contemporary cities of the Ḥijāz (Eyuce n.d.: 55–6).

In the case of Sijeeni's (1995) Ph.D. thesis, the religious dimension is manifest in the title, 'Contemporary Arabian City: Muslim *Ummah* in Sociocultural and Urban Design Context'. Sijeeni sets the Muslim *umma*, or community of believers, in binary opposition to an unspecified 'West':

> Throughout the fifties, the impact on young Jeddahwis of the incursion of Western business, which brought about increased contact with Westerners, as well as the expansion of formal education – inside the country as well as abroad – brought about the diminution of the Muslim *Ummah* and the steady adoption of Western life styles, particularly Western business practices and an orientation toward the Western-style nuclear family as opposed to the extended family of the Muslim community.
>
> (Sijeeni 1995: 71)

Westernisation, which to Sijeeni and other Saudi urbanists encompasses the adoption of Western architectural elements and building styles, a nuclear family framework, materialism and individualism, is seen as a contradiction to the conventions of Islam. Hisham Mortada, for example, contends that, 'Motivated by the example of Western culture, the modern Saudi life is oriented toward materialistic achievement', such as status, success and wealth. 'As a result of these new materialistic norms', he asserts, 'social interaction between people has declined' (Mortada 1992: 139). He quotes a book by Muhtar Holland (1988) to support his argument. In the opinion of Holland, 'a contemporary Muslim theorist' (Mortada 1992: 139),[9] 'The new type of social relationships, which are almost typical everywhere in the globe result in alienation, personality disturbance, emotional distress and empty lives. Whatever the close social relationships are, they are far from the affection and the warm and brotherhood that Islam has called for' (Holland 1988: 7, quoted in Mortada 1992: 139–42).

As is apparent, Sijeeni, Mortada and others assess the quality of architecture not only on aesthetic grounds, as Bokhari did before them. Nor are they particularly concerned about functionality, sustainability or other possible principles, except one: the decisive factor for them is whether the buildings enable or hinder an Islamic way of life. Al-Mutawea, for example, discusses '[t]he impact of Islam on the built environment' (1987: 39–70) only to argue that Islamic principles such as respect towards parents, hospitality, strong neighbourhood ties and privacy had been neglected to a grave extent in the decades before his time of writing.[10] Hisham Mortada (1992) follows the same logic. He asserts that, in a city predominantly inhabited by Muslims, Islamic law should govern housing design and building processes, and Muslims, not Western experts unfamiliar with Islamic law, should be in charge of urban planning.[11] Finally, Hisham Jomah concludes: 'In the process of liberating themselves from the ties of family and tradition, the modern Ḥedjāzīes seem to have also liberated themselves from religion and its bonding, presumably to be more receptive of changes and adoptive of non-native lifestyles' (1992: 330).[12] 'What is needed in Ḥedjāz today', in his opinion, 'is a revival of Islamic values, a renewal of faith in the teachings of Islam, to assure the next generations of clients and architects that only adherence to traditional values and religious teachings can provide the answers to their problems' (Jomah 1992: 386–7).

Islamic Revival

Conservative Muslim scholars, preachers and Islamic activists from the 1970s to the 1990s popularised a cultural climate demanding a return to the moral concepts of an idealised past, to the teachings of pious forefathers (*al-salaf al-ṣāliḥ*). The most radical expression of Islamic criticism occurred in 1979, when a few hundred religious extremists led by Juhaimān al-ʿUtaibī occupied the Grand Mosque in Mecca in order to draw attention to their discontent with the Saudi government. They viewed the ruling family as corrupt and oppressive and condemned it for cooperating with the United States. After three weeks, the occupation was ended by the Saudi authorities, causing bloodshed and killing within the sanctuary (Dekmejian 1994; Doumato 1992; Ochsenwald 1981; Okruhlik 2002).

While the radical activism of Juhaimān al-ʿUtaibī was observed sceptically by the majority of Saudis, a movement known as *al-ṣaḥwa al-islāmiyya*, Islamic awakening, grew quite strong. The advocates of this movement, known as *shuyūkh al-ṣaḥwa*, were religious scholars and eloquent preachers who disseminated their criticism of the Saudi government, of Western-style consumption and an alleged weakening of moral standards in books, pamphlets and tape-recorded sermons. Their writings and cassette sermons were circulated, copied and embraced by large parts of Saudi society. The *ṣaḥwa* had been active throughout the 1980s, but it was against the background of the Gulf War in 1990–1 that they rose to prominence. Responding to the Iraqi invasion of Kuwait and fearing that Saddam Hussein might attack the Kingdom, the Saudi government called on the United States to station troops in the country in August 1990. The presence of a non-Muslim army inside the Land of the Two Holy Shrines (*al-ḥaramayn*, i.e. Mecca and Medina), as well as the fact that the Saudi regime had to rely on foreign forces to protect the country, generated widespread discontent. Safar al-Ḥawālī and Salmān al-ʿAwda, the two eminent leaders of the *ṣaḥwa*, won public acclaim for openly criticising the policy of the Āl Saʿūd (see Fandy 1999a: chapters 2 and 3; Jones 2003; Lacroix 2011; Teitelbaum 2000). In a taped lecture from 1991, sheikh Safar al-Ḥawālī claimed:

> It is not the world against Iraq. It is the West against Islam.... [I]f Iraq has occupied Kuwait, then America has occupied Saudi Arabia. The real enemy is not Iraq. It is the West.... While Iraq was the enemy of the hour, America and the West were the enemies of Judgment Day.
>
> (al-Ḥawālī quoted in Teitelbaum 2000: 30)

In al-Ḥawālī's view, Operations Desert Shield and Desert Storm, as the US military operations were officially labelled, were only the tip of the iceberg. For him, 'the West' is 'the enemy'[13], and he is concerned about the Westernisation of Saudi society – or rather of Muslim culture in general. In view of a perceived 'retreat of Islamic values' he is wary of Western 'cultural and moral pollution' (al-Ḥawālī quoted in Fandy 1999a: 66, 86), and in particular of the influence of 'secularists' (*ʿilmāniyyūn*). The loss of Islamic identity is a recurrent theme, sometimes phrased prospectively as a warning addressed to the ruling family and the wider Saudi public alike,[14] and sometimes as a retrospective depiction of a process of alienation. In an article for the *ṣaḥwī* journal *al-Islah* (Islamic Reform), for example, Saʿd al-Faqīḥ remarks: 'What is un-Islamic dominated the social life, although it is contrary to what the society is all about, and what is good and Islamic receded in the society, contrary to the fact that it is rooted in the society and its people' (al-Faqīḥ quoted in Fandy 1999a: 160). Remedy is to be sought solely in the religion of Islam, especially in a return to the foundational texts of Islam and in the restoration of a pure and uncorrupted Islamic community. As Salmān al-ʿAwda stated in a taped sermon in 1991: '[F]or the unity of this land to be preserved, we have to return to fundamentals and reform our society.... This country can be only united under the Shariʿa with the Sunna and the Quran as our only reference' (al-ʿAwda quoted in Fandy 1999a: 95).

The fear of Westernisation and liberal tendencies in Saudi society, articulated by al-Ḥawālī, al-ʿAwda and other preachers of the *ṣaḥwa*, was not fostered by the presence of foreign troops alone. In September 1990, King Fahd launched a volunteer programme allowing women to work in civil defence and medical services, fuelling the hopes of Western-oriented women for more opportunities to participate in public life. In November 1990, a group of 49 Saudi women demonstrating for the right to drive paraded down a main street in Riyadh in their cars.[15] It is generally held that the policy of the Āl Saʿūd vis-à-vis the Gulf crisis and the women's volunteer programme gave the impetus for the demonstration in Riyadh, whose organisers anticipated a further opening of the country towards the West. The incident caused an outcry among the followers of the *ṣaḥwa*, manifested in a gathering of 10–30,000 people in front of the headquarters of the Council of Senior *ʿUlamāʾ* as well as in broadsides listing the names of the women involved in the demonstrations and denouncing them as whores (Fandy 1999a: 49–50; Lacroix 2011: 163–4, 226; al-Rasheed 2013: 129–30).

The women's demonstration was clamped down on, but in the same month, King Fahd declared that he intended to establish a consultative council (*majlis al-shūrā*) and launch political reforms. This encouraged a group of 43 liberal businessmen and intellectuals to submit a petition to the Saudi government in December 1990 listing 10 proposals for reform. Their proposals aimed at a cautious democratisation of the political system, but they also touched sensitive religious issues, such as the Committee for the Promotion of Virtue and Prevention of Vice, or religious police, the judicial system and the system of *iftāʾ*, i.e. the process of issuing religious rulings or fatwas (Teitelbaum 2000: 31–2; Dekmejian 2003).

A few months later, in May 1991, a group of conservative religious scholars responded by circulating their own petition. Entitled 'Letter of Demands' (*khiṭāb al-maṭālib*), it was sent to King Fahd with over 400 signatures. The one-page 'Letter' was followed by a more comprehensive document, the 'Memorandum of Advice' (*mudhakkirat al-naṣīḥa*), a booklet of 45 pages submitted to the king in the summer of 1992 (Lacroix 2011: 179–87; Teitelbaum 2000: 32–41).[16] In both texts, the Islamic reformers spoke out against usury, favouritism and nepotism, demanded the creation of a strong army capable of protecting 'the country and its holy places', reform of the media 'so that they serve Islam', true independence of the judiciary and reorientation of the foreign policy in a way that 'preserves the interests of the *umma*, far removed from alliances contrary to God's law' ('Letter of Demands', quoted in Lacroix 2011: 179–81; see also Fandy 1999a: 50–60, 159–61). The authors believed that the Islamic character of the Saudi state was in jeopardy and demanded that laws and administration be brought into conformity with Islamic law.

The Saudi government found itself under attack from multiple sides – the women's rights movement, the liberal-modernist reformers and the conservative Islamic opposition – and responded with restrictive measures. Members of the Committee for the Promotion of Virtue and Prevention of Vice halted the parade of women drivers and took participants to the police office. The women's and their husbands' passports were confiscated for several months, and those demonstrators who were employed as teachers lost their jobs. The Interior Ministry officially banned women from driving – previously the ban had only been an unofficial rule – and Shaykh ʿAbd al-ʿAzīz bin Bāz, in his function as the head of the Directorate of Islamic Research, Ruling, Propaganda and Guidance, issued a fatwa confirming that women should not be allowed to drive motor vehicles (Doumato 1992: 32).

The Āl Saʿūd sensed that the general atmosphere was in favour of conservative religious reform and that the liberal petitioners represented only a small Western-educated minority in the Kingdom. They also knew that the more serious threat to their legitimacy as the country's rulers came from the Islamists. Therefore the government adopted a dual policy of silencing leaders of the Islamic opposition while strengthening the religious establishment as well as loyal *ʿulamāʾ* and preachers. Numerous *shuyūkh al-ṣaḥwa* and hundreds of their supporters were imprisoned. Their leaders, among them Safar al-Ḥawālī and Salmān al-ʿAwda, were detained for several years. Others were barred from preaching or travelling, or dismissed from their positions as preachers, university teachers or judges. In addition, the government increased state control of religious institutions – universities, *awqāf*, mosques and charitable organisations – in order to reduce the influence of the *ṣaḥwa* in public life (Lacroix 2011: 202–11; Yamani 1996: 267). Simultaneously, Islamist scholars loyal to the regime and critical of the *ṣaḥwa* were empowered. Shaykh ʿAbd al-ʿAzīz bin Bāz and Dr ʿAbdullāh al-Turkī, two leading figures of the religious establishment, were appointed as ministers in July 1993. Ibn Bāz, who had officially justified the policy of the Saudi state during the Gulf War in a controversial fatwa, was assigned the position of Grand Mufti of the Kingdom, at the rank of minister, as well as being elevated to president of the Council of Senior *ʿUlamāʾ*. Al-Turkī, director of Imām Muḥammad bin Saʿūd Islamic University in Riyadh, became the head of the new Ministry of Islamic Affairs, Pious Endowments, Mission and Guidance. Others loyal Salafis were installed as university directors or faculty heads (Lacroix 2011: 209–21; Teitelbaum 2000: 101–3).[17]

In order to tame conservative religious critics questioning the Islamic character of the Saudi state, large sums of money were poured into religious institutions – first of all mosques and Wahhabi universities (Hamzawy 2008; Teitelbaum 2000: 101). The punishment of the women drivers also aimed at appeasing the large conservative constituency in the country. As Eleanor Doumato (1992; 1999) and Madawi al-Rasheed (2013: chapter 3) have shown, in times of crisis the Saudi regime often turns to gender politics to demonstrate its commitment to Islam. Against the background of the seizure of the Great Mosque in Mecca in 1979 and the '*ṣaḥwa* insurrection' (*intifāḍat al-ṣaḥwa*) during and after the Gulf War, the visibility of state piety became a matter of regime stability. The Committee for the Promotion of Virtue and Prevention of Vice increasingly enforced gender segregation, and the establishment *ʿulamāʾ* promoted the invisibility of women in public.[18] In the early 1990s, Shaykh Abū ʿAbdullāh ibn ʿUthaymīn, a member of the Council of Senior ʿUlamāʾ led by Ibn Bāz, not only condemned women driving themselves, but also expressed the opinion that they should not ride in a car alone with a hired driver (Doumato 1999: 579). In an article titled 'Women's Work is Quick Road to Adultery' published in June 1996 in the Saudi weekly journal *al-Muslimūn*, Ibn Bāz disapproved of women working outside the home on the grounds that this contradicts their natural state of being, and women mixing with men would open the way for adultery, thus wrecking morals and threatening 'Islamic society'.[19] *'Ulamā'* loyal to the state thus used the regulation of female behaviour and movement as a means of corroborating the Islamic legitimacy of the Āl Sa'ūd. Madawi al-Rasheed (2013: 111–12) mentions more than 30,000 fatwas on women produced by Saudi *'ulamā'*, the majority of which were issued from the 1980s onwards.

In addition, the Āl Sa'ūd stressed the religious foundations of the state in public statements and a series of new laws – a Basic Law of Governance (*al-niẓām al-asāsī li-l-ḥukm*), a *Shūrā* Council Law (*niẓām majlis al-shūrā*) and a Law of Provinces (*al-niẓām al-manātiq*). Already in September 1932, a few days after officially declaring himself King of Saudi Arabia, 'Abd al-'Azīz bin Sa'ūd had promised a basic law of governance for the first time. Each of 'Abd al-'Azīz's successors repeated the promise, but it was only because of pressure from petitions by both liberals and Islamists during the Gulf crisis that King Fahd finally promulgated the basic law of governance on 1 March 1992, alongside the two other laws. The 60 members of the first *Shūrā*, or Consultative, Council, were appointed by the king in August 1993 (al-Fahad 2005; al-Rasheed 1996; 2002: 172–5; Teitelbaum 2000: 99–100). The Basic Law is permeated by references to Quran, Sunna and Islamic law. As if to avoid mistaking it for the country's constitution, the first article proclaims: 'The Kingdom of Saudi Arabia is a sovereign Arab Islamic state with Islam as its religion; God's Book (the Quran) and the Sunnah of His Prophet ... are its constitution ...' (Basic Law of Governance, quoted in Vassiliev 2000: 466). King Fahd used the occasion of the implementation of the new laws to emphasise the religious nature of the state once more in a speech broadcast to the Saudi public on 2 March 1992. He reminded his audience of the close connection between religious reform initiated by Muḥammad bin 'Abd al-Wahhāb in the middle of the eighteenth century and the Saudi nation-building process. The Saudi state, according to the king, had always adhered to the teachings of Muḥammad bin 'Abd al-Wahhāb (see al-Rasheed 1996: 366–7). He even made use of Islamic rhetoric to justify the limits on political participation. Invoking widespread anti-Western resentments, King Fahd claimed that free elections were alien to Islamic beliefs and not suitable for a Muslim country like Saudi Arabia.[20] In sum, the new laws were aimed at placating liberals with what has been called 'Ornamental Constitutionalism' (al-Fahad 2005) and the Islamist opposition with Islamic rhetoric while actually changing as little as possible in the architecture of power in the Saudi state.

Whether or not this strategy was a success is disputable. The *ṣaḥwa* lost much of its influence in the second half of the 1990s. Simultaneously, a radicalisation of Islamists occurred, leading to the rise of 'global jihad' embodied first of all by the al-Qāʿida network and its prominent leader Usāma bin Lādin (Fandy 1999a: chapter 6; Lacroix 2011: 193–201, 238; Teitelbaum 2000: chapter 5). The liberals remained quiescent for approximately 10 years. An alliance of liberal and moderate Islamist reformers began approaching the ruling family again with petitions after 11 September 2001 and a series of jihadist terror attacks in Saudi Arabia in 2003 (Dekmejian 2003; al-Fahad 2005: 392–4; Lacroix 2004; Maneval 2010). As a consequence of the harsh treatment of the women involved in the driving demonstration, the women's rights movement refrained from spectacular activism for a time. They continued expressing their demands in newspaper articles, books and public discussions, however. After 9/11 and the 2003 bombings in Saudi Arabia, they were granted more opportunities for speaking up because the state wanted to counteract the image of Saudi Arabia as promoting an intolerant, 'backward' form of Islam and as an exporter of terrorism (al-Rasheed 2013: chapter 4; Le Renard 2008). The policy change did not deter women activists from forming a new Women to Drive movement which called on women to defy the ban on driving, posting videos of women driving in Saudi Arabia on YouTube (*Guardian* 2013), until the ban was finally lifted in June 2018.

The Saudi regime has proved stable until the present day without making significant concessions to any of the groups demanding political reform, neither with regard to civil rights, a transparent and more balanced distribution of the enormous wealth of the country, a division of powers or more political participation. The ruling family keeps a firm hold on the executive, the legislature and, to a large degree, the judiciary, but direct involvement in decision making and the distribution of material capital are not the only forms of power. In a Foucauldian sense, power is also manifested in the ability to set the parameters of a discourse, to influence people's thinking and social practice (Foucault 1972). What I aim to show with the above discussion of dissident movements and state reactions is that, throughout the 1980s and 1990s, conservative Islamic voices dominated public discourse on various facets of Saudi society, from foreign policy and the judicial system to gender roles and moral standards. In contrast to the visions of society articulated by religious reformers, the alternatives offered by liberals and women's rights activists at that time failed to gain the support of a larger section of society. The voices of the eloquent leaders of the Islamic Revival were, literally speaking, listened to by millions of Saudis. Copies of their tape-recorded sermons were produced in huge quantities, with single recordings disseminated through the circulation of up to an estimated several million copies (Fandy 1999b; Lacroix 2011: 140, 143–4; Teitelbaum 2000: 30).

Maha Malluh, a contemporary artist from Saudi Arabia, commented on the proliferation of Islamic cassettes with an installation of bread trays stocked with cassette tapes of conservative preachers (Figure 4.1). The artwork, shown in Jeddah in February 2012 in the first public exhibition of the Saudi artists' group Edge of Arabia inside Saudi Arabia,[21] carries the title 'Food for Thought' (Edge of Arabia 2012: 30–1). From a distance of some metres, one realises that the multi-coloured cassette tapes are assembled in such a way as to form words in Arabic script, one word in each tray. *Ḥarām*, *ʿayb* and *bāṭil*, they state, which means 'forbidden by Islamic law', 'shameful' and 'inappropriate' (Maneval 2012b). 'It's the food we were fed for the past 30 years', the artist explained to the London newspaper *The Times* (Whitworth 2012).

Like every good work of art, Maha Malluh's installation allows for more than just one reading – for example, one that ascribes a less passive role to the consumers of the cassette tapes. In an innovative study, Charles Hirschkind (2006) has shown that listening to sermon tapes involves much more than passive listening. In fact, the consumers of these cassettes regard their engagement with the sermons as an act of piety.[22] According to Hirschkind (2006: 9–10, 37–40, chapter 3), listening to a sermon is considered to have a therapeutic effect on the soul. It is believed to purify the heart and to strengthen the will, improving the listener's capacity to resist immoral temptations. Thus it leads to right

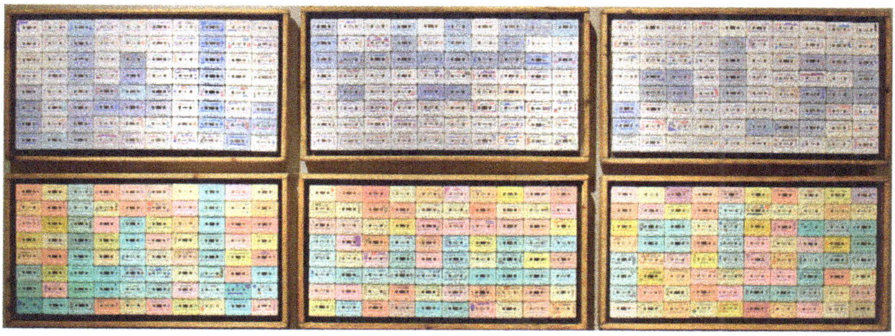

Figure 4.1 Maha Malluh's art installation 'Food for Thought' at the 2012 Edge of Arabia exhibition in Jeddah. Photo: © Stefan Maneval 2012.

behaviour and enables the listener to become a better Muslim. Featuring in a section of the 2012 exhibition labelled 'We need to talk about the past', Maha Malluh's baking trays reminded the beholder of a time when tape-recorded Islamic teachings sold like hot cakes, and conservative values, including strict notions of what is to be considered *ḥarām* or shameful, were embraced by a substantial portion of the Saudi populace. Her installation is an invitation to reflect upon the consequences of the high receptivity of the Saudi public to these ideas, and on the ways they survived even decades later.

I want to suggest that architecture, due to its tangibility, endurance and stabilising effects, contributed to the persistence of these ideas. Before I discuss how it did, in the following chapter, it is important to highlight the many parallels that can be found between the topics and strategies of argumentation in the conservative Islamic discourse on political and societal reform of the 1980s and 1990s and the discourse on architecture and urban development of that time. These parallels include complaints about declining moral values, criticism of continuous Westernisation which, in the eyes of preachers and architects alike, leads to the loss of Islamic identity, and a strong preoccupation with the public visibility of women, which is seen as a determining factor in the contest between 'Islam' and 'the West'. While Islamic reformers called for a return to the religious foundations laid out by pious forefathers (*al-salaf al-ṣāliḥ*), Saudi architects and town planners of the same era advocated a reorientation in environmental design inspired by the buildings and neighbourhoods of the Old Town. In the next section I will show that, instead of a return to the Golden Age of Islam – the lifetime of the prophet Muḥammad and the early caliphate – they romanticised the supposedly more religious lifestyle once common in the so-called Islamic City.

Frames of reference: New Urbanism and the Islamic City paradigm

Mohammed Eben Saleh has shown that there are structural parallels between a recent attempt by city planners in Saudi Arabia 'to reconcile the obvious desires to maintain traditions and security with equally strong desires for change to the built environment brought from the realities of 20th century life in a fairly affluent society' and a trajectory in urban planning known as New Urbanism (Eben Saleh 2002: 525; on New Urbanism see e.g. Grant 2006; Haas 2008; Katz 1994; Talen 2005).

Famous examples of developments where New Urbanism principles have been applied are Seaside, Florida, designed by Andrés Duany and Elizabeth Plater-Zyrberk in 1982, and Celebration, Florida, designed by Robert Stern and Jaquelin Robertson for the Walt Disney Company in 1994. Both Seaside and Celebration are self-contained, walkable new neighbourhoods with codified housing design inspired by historical American small towns (Duany and Plater-Zyberk 1991; Ross 1999). In the UK, Prince Charles commissioned the New Urbanist Léon Krier, the teacher of Duany and Plater-Zyrberk, to plan a community of 5,000 people in Poundbury, Dorset. Houses in a mix of vernacular and new classical styles were constructed from 1993 (Grant 2006: 82–9, 116–23). In post-Cold War Berlin, the 'critical reconstruction' of the fragmented inner city promoted by the Berlin Senate has much in common with the neotraditional principles of New Urbanism (see Bodenschatz 2005; *Die Welt* 2001; Hennecke 2010). Because of their attempt to revitalise the respective local architectural traditions, all these projects have often been lambasted as anachronistic kitsch (Ellis 2002).

In its charter, the Congress for the New Urbanism, founded in 1993 by Duany, Plater-Zyrberk, Peter Calthorpe and several other architects and planners, formulates its goals as follows:

> We advocate the restructuring of public policy and development practices to support the following principles: neighborhoods should be diverse in use and population; communities should be designed for the pedestrian and transit as well as the car; cities and towns should be shaped by physically defined and universally accessible public spaces and community institutions; urban places should be framed by architecture and landscape design that celebrate local history, climate, ecology, and building practice.
>
> (Congress for the New Urbanism 2001)

Eben Saleh identifies a larger trend in Saudi Arabia in line with these ideas. There, city planners intend 'to consider the traditions of Muslims, revive the social coherence and provide opportunities for pedestrianization between residences, mosques and schools' (Eben Saleh 2002: 527). In fact, Eyuce, Jomah, Shahrani and Sijeeni refer to architects and theorists generally associated with New Urbanism, such as Christopher Alexander, Rob Krier, Demetri Porphyrios and Robert Stern. Furthermore, Abu-Gazzeh, Fadan, Shahrani and Sijeeni draw on the works of authors who wrote in the spirit of, or paved the way for, New Urbanism before this trend had a name, notably Kevin Lynch and Jane Jacobs.[23]

The guidelines for the development of new neighbourhoods delineated by the Saudi Ministry of Municipal and Rural Affairs (MOMRA) in the mid-1990s are, according to Eben Saleh, inspired by New Urbanism (Eben Saleh 2002: 525–7). Alongside ecological and climatic considerations, support for pedestrian traffic, concern for religious and pastime activities as well as efficiency of service facilities, two of six objectives of the MOMRA development schemes pertain to questions of social interaction – more precisely, to the relation between public and private space. Objective number four, as summarised by Eben Saleh, is '[t]o strengthen the means for family privacy and recognize separate private/socialization spaces for women in the special organization of the community' (Eben Saleh 2002: 525). The sixth objective is paraphrased as follows: 'To enhance the security and safety of public, semi-private and private space through design principles' (Eben Saleh 2002: 525). The application of New Urbanist principles in Saudi Arabia which, in Eben Saleh's (2002: 527–8) opinion, requires giving special attention to the design of public, semi-public and private spaces, as well as to the segregated circulation of family and visitors, neighbourhood residents and strangers, would lead to a situation comparable to the so-called Islamic City.

The Islamic City paradigm has a long history in Orientalist research.[24] Key attributes of Islamic cities as defined by authors such as Albert H. Hourani (1970: 20–3), S.M. Stern (1970), Janet Abu-Lughod (1987: 160–73), Eugen Wirth (2000: 517–22) and Ludwig Ammann (2004: 93–5) include dense and irregular settlement patterns with tortuous streets, a division between commercial and residential quarters, a subdivision of the residential quarters into smaller neighbourhoods, blind alleys and dead-end courts shared by the residents of adjoining houses. The extension of rules governing behaviour in the private domain to certain alleys to which strangers had only limited access led, according to these authors, to the production of so-called semi-private spaces. Residential buildings in what they label as Islamic Cities are described as oriented towards the inside, positioned as the women's sphere, and as strictly private spaces. In addition, the Orientalists' association of the house with women on the one hand and of the public realm with men on the other caused them to assume that women do not have any public life at all. The distinction in Islamic law between members of the Muslim *umma* and outsiders, as well as other factors, are said to have caused the spatial segregation of ethnic and religious groups within so-called Islamic Cities. Furthermore, Islamic Cities are described as lacking municipal organisation.

Since the 1990s, the concept has been attacked repeatedly for being essentialist, Eurocentric and deficient in view of women's roles and regional particularities of legal and administrative structures (e.g. Hanssen et al. 2002: introduction; Neglia 2008; Raymond 2008; Stolleis 2004: 13–19; van Leeuwen 1995). Nevertheless, the concept features more or less prominently in books and articles on Jeddah or Saudi cities in general by Khaled Abdulgani (1993), Tawfiq Abu-Gazzeh (1994), Mohammed Eben Saleh (2002), Saleh al-Hathloul (1996), Hisham Mortada (1992, 2003), Fahad al-Mutawea (1987), Mohammad al-Shahrani (1992) and Tariq Sijeeni (1995).

In fact, hardly any characteristics of the Islamic City paradigm apply to the historic city of Jeddah. It is only possible to identify Jeddah with the paradigm of the Islamic City by way of omission and alteration. The fact that the highly diverse population of Jeddah did not have segregated neighbourhoods of different ethnic or religious groups (Freitag 2007), for example, is simply overlooked by the authors mentioned above. Jeddah's residential architecture and street pattern – tower houses instead of inward-oriented courtyard-houses, and thoroughfares instead of cul-de-sac streets – are not in accordance with the Islamic City paradigm. Neither is the existence of residential houses in the market area and the integration of commercial functions in residential buildings (Krause 1991: 53–4). The presence of strangers inside residential houses and the division between public and private spaces by means of social control and everyday practices rather than fixed architectural boundaries also challenge the paradigm of the Islamic City. Finally, since the specific forms of sociability framed and enabled by dead-end streets in other cities in the Islamic world did not exist in Jeddah (Krause 1991: 51), the *mirkāz*, or sitting platforms, in front of houses in the old town are declared semi-private spaces by some of the Saudi authors mentioned above. Considering that, as exclusively male spaces, they differed decisively from semi-private space in cities such as Cairo as well as from private space inside the home, this categorisation is a mismatch. While mentioning, to varying degrees, the particularities of Jeddah's urban structure, the authors referred to above do not call the validity of the Islamic City paradigm into question.

Knowledge production is always selective. What interests me in the framework of my analysis are the choices made in the selection process leading to the labelling of Jeddah as a typical Islamic City. Along with other Saudi architects and urban planners (e.g. Eyuce n.d.; Fadan 1983; Jomah 1992; al-Mutawea 1987), authors categorising Jeddah as an Islamic City share an overt nostalgia for the architecture, urban design and social life of the pre-oil era. They also have in common a desire to phrase this longing for the past in religious terms. What was lost, in their view, were not just antiquated architectural forms and old-fashioned social conventions, but rather a way of life conforming to Islam. They reject contemporary architecture because it purportedly hinders a life following the teachings of Islam. This argument is embedded, as numerous analogies indicate, in the wider discourse of Salafism and the Islamic Revival.

The Saudi architects and town planners did not propagate a reconstruction of historic structures, nor did they want to mimic the architecture of bygone days. Their intention was rather to revive what Hisham Mortada, for instance, has referred to as 'Traditional Islamic Principles of Built Environment' (Mortada 2003). They studied these principles in order to generate contemporary solutions appropriate to cultural traditions and social conventions. In this respect, their objectives showed striking parallels to New Urbanism. Some of them were even inspired by the architecture and writings of New Urbanists, but their criticism was, as I have shown, driven by concern about a perceived decline of Islamic moral values or, more generally, the loss of an identity defined to a significant degree as Islamic. This rootedness in local discourse on religious reform distinguishes them from New Urbanists elsewhere. Highlighting both frames of reference, New Urbanism and Islamic Revival, I propose to refer to this trend in architectural discourse in Saudi Arabia as 'New Islamic Urbanism'. It is not to be mistaken for a distinct architectural school or self-conscious movement, such as the Congress for the New Urbanism, for example. Rather, it should be seen as a loose network of architects and town planners sharing the same concerns, referencing each other's texts and promoting similar solutions. The many flaws, inherent biases and inconsistencies in their arguments suggest that different views and opinions on architecture, urban development and privacy must have coexisted. However, in the academic discourse on architecture and urban development, as manifested in the sources available to me, alternative opinions are not represented.

Conclusion

In the conservative climate of the 1980s and 1990s, architects and city planners strongly criticised the urban development and architecture of Jeddah beginning in the oil era. In line with Islamic reformers popular at that time, particularly the members of the *ṣaḥwa* movement, they argued that core Islamic values had been abandoned in favour of a Western lifestyle characterised by individualism and materialism. Their architecture criticism centred on the demise of an egalitarian society, weakening family bonds, the neglect of neighbourhood ties and the loss of privacy – all evident in the built environment, as they saw it.

As discussed in chapter 2, some scholars referred to the Quran and Hadith in order to demonstrate that, in the past, the architecture of Jeddah had helped maintain religious rulings on privacy. My discussion in this chapter reveals that their references to major sources of guidance for Muslims constituted part of a broader criticism of contemporary society. As these authors suggested, in the oil era people neglected not only their architectural and cultural traditions, but also the principles of social coexistence prescribed by Islamic law. Some scholars expressed their discontent with the status quo by arguing that, in recent decades, Jeddah and other Saudi cities had lost their identity as Islamic cities. In accordance with prominent religious reformers, the proponents of a 'New Islamic Urbanism' advocated a return to an idealised past. While the former demanded a religious renewal following the teachings of pious forefathers of the early Muslim period, the latter promoted a reorientation in urban planning and architectural design using the old city of Jeddah as a reference.

The thoughts and opinions of the architects quoted above were not merely expressed in journal articles and Ph.D. theses, which were made available at university libraries in Saudi Arabia and read and quoted by other Saudi students of architecture and urban planning. After earning a doctorate at a foreign university, in most cases a British or North American one, many architects and urban planners returned to Saudi Arabia to assume well-paid positions in the private or public sectors. Whether they taught architecture or environmental design at a Saudi university (e.g. Tawfiq Abu-Gazzeh, Yousef Fadan, Mohammed Eben Saleh, Hisham Mortada, Mohammad al-Shahrani and Tariq Sijeeni), worked as town planners for the municipality of a Saudi city or for a governmental institution (e.g. Abdulla Bokhari, Saleh al-Hathloul, Hisham Jomah, Tariq Sijeeni), or found a position in an architecture firm or established their own company (e.g. Fahad al-Mutawea), they had considerable influence on the development of Saudi cities and the public understanding of architecture.

The combination of architectural criticism and Islamic rhetoric manifest in the discourse of New Islamic Urbanism found fertile ground, given the widespread popularity of demands for Islamic reform. Indeed, the architectural vision of the experts had an impact on the architecture constructed in Jeddah. Fahad al-Mutawea, for example, noticed a 'revivalism and reassessment of … Islamic identity' in architecture and urban planning (1987: 38; cf. al-Hathloul 1998: 27). I will trace these developments – social practices pertaining to or challenging the discourse of piety and religious reform, as well as the question of how they relate to changing conceptions of privacy and new forms of public – in the next chapter.

Notes

1. Other authors complaining about the weakening of extended family networks are Fadan (1983: 310), Mortada (1992: 143, 260–5) and al-Mutawea (1987: 52–4).
2. Another example for a similar perspective on neighbourhood bonds is, again, Fadan, who writes: 'In a traditional neighborhood where several extended families live in a very intimate social environment ... each family assumes its obligation to support its neighbors during crises besides sharing happy occasions. In new neighborhoods, however, where villas are arranged in a gridiron layout, houses are built in the middle of lots and surrounded by ten foot walls. Cars can be parked in garages connected to the villas so that the family does not leave its home without the car. The small corner shop of the traditional neighborhood no longer exists in the new one, and the family must travel by car to do its daily shopping at a central supermarket located several blocks away. In short, structural features of the new neighborhoods discourage social integration among the families living there' (Fadan 1983: 309–10). Similar views are expressed by Jomah (1992: 339–49), Mortada (1992: 139–44, 226), and Sijeeni (1995: 147–63, 198–9).
3. Abu-Gazzeh is very drastic in his judgement: 'In comparison with the meticulous system of design and the authentic quality of architecture observed in Jeddah Al-Qademah [the Old Town], the modern built environment in Jeddah, as in other cities in Saudi Arabia, lacks the merits of traditional architecture. It is Western in form and style and maintains little continuity with local history. As a result, it stands apart from local culture. The rapid development of modern Jeddah city has demonstrated a restless search for the future and a constant denial of the past. A great architectural and design heritage has been lost as a result of the ruthless drive towards modernization and commercial gain' (Abu-Gazzeh 1994: 58).
4. Here is an excerpt: 'The visual intrusion by neighbouring balconies, windows and roofs also ... applie[s] to the front setback. Villa front setbacks are viewed from adjacent dwellings. Also, when the large front gate is open, the inside of the villa is visible to passers-by. This problem is maximised by the absence of a transitional space between the street and the space behind the gate. In the case of apartment housing, the privacy of the ground floor space is also intruded upon as the setback is completely open to the street. The rooms behind the front windows of that floor are visible to people passing in the street and to residents of the houses opposite' (Mortada 1992: 229–34).
5. Eyuce (n.d.: 38–9, 76, 140, 166) and al-Mutawea (1987: 64, 146–7, 164–5) present similar arguments.
6. 'There are several areas in both apartments and villas where the privacy of the resident family is within the visual range of visitors. For example, the entrance lobby of the villa cannot be used by female occupants when there are male guests entering the house or using the guests' section on the ground floor. In the apartment, the circulation between kitchen and dining room is also visible by a guest entering the bathroom or other spaces in the visitors' domain. This problem is more apparent in small apartments where the guests' toilet is not hidden and the main corridor between the family and guests' domains is relatively short. In this case, women are trapped either in the kitchen or in the living room' (Mortada 1992: 242).
7. '[M]odern houses ... depend more on physical privacy-regulators to compensate for the loss of social ones ... . The modern notion of privacy maintenance is mainly concerned with separating the individual from the outside world, and with self-image as opposed to traditional family privacy' (Jomah 1992: 336).
8. 'My observations led me to believe that this has allowed individuals more freedom to present themselves as independent beings. It has also allowed for more "choice" as to what to dress [sic] and eat, how to interact, behave and dwell. Naturally, the variability among individuals within one group has increased' (Jomah 1992: 339).

9. Muhtar Holland, born in 1935 in Durham, UK, is an Oxford graduate. As a scholar of, and convert to, Islam, he wrote on religious topics and translated classical Arabic and Turkish religious texts into English.
10. In the conclusion to his thesis, al-Mutawea maintains: 'Traditionally, islamic [sic] cultural values and beliefs strongly influenced the housing design.... It represented the family structure and growth, the role of men and women, the obligations towards family, relatives and neighbours and the attitude towards privacy. The traditional settlement and housing responded quite positively to the climatic and local conditions.... The King Abdulaziz university [sic] on-campus housing was almost opposite to this.... The effect of islamic [sic] culture was minimal, and the influence of the climatic and local conditions on the design was also absent' (al-Mutawea 1987: 193–4).
11. 'There is no question that if traditional principles are to be achieved in a built environment for Muslims, planning and regulating this environment should be carried out by Muslims or at least by those who are conversant with Islamic sharī'ah. In the case of Jeddah the opposite is true. The new dwelling environment is a result of master plans and building regulations set up by Western planners and rooted in non-traditional principles' (Mortada 1992: 199).
12. Jomah (1992: 372–87) formulates four criteria to achieve 'architectural authenticity': contemporary residential buildings must be developed within the cultural context in which they are supposed to exist; they have to serve the requirements of daily life, be connected with, not isolated from, the environment, and in conformity with religion.
13. 'What is happening in the Gulf is part of a larger Western design to dominate the whole Arab and Muslim world' (al-Ḥawālī quoted in Fandy 1999a: 61).
14. e.g. '[i]f we ignore God and choose the West we are the losers' (al-Ḥawālī quoted in Fandy 1999a: 66; on the same issue, see Teitelbaum 2000: 29).
15. Most of these women were educated in the United States, some of them holding doctoral degrees. A few of them had already entered the public arena before the drive-in with daring writings on the role of women in Saudi Arabia (see Doumato 1992; 1999).
16. The 'Memorandum of Advice' elaborated on the demands outlined in the 'Letter of Demands', by providing examples and detailing the suggested reforms. While principally following the same agenda as the previous document, it emphasised the role of individual preachers and *ʿulamāʾ* as well as of independent religious institutions in Saudi society, thus promoting the position of scholars of the Islamic Revival (see Champion 2003: 219–23; Dekmejian 1994: 630–4).
17. Salafis, or *al-salafiyyūn*, is a term used to describe the advocates of a return to the teachings of pious forefathers, *al-salaf al-ṣāliḥ*. The term is used by the followers of this trend themselves.
18. In a fatwa published in 1996, Ibn Bāz, for example, stated: 'Women driving leads to many evils and negative consequences. Included among these evil consequences is her mixing with men without her being on her guard.... Allah has ordered the wives of the Prophet ... and the women of the believers to remain in their houses, to wear hijab (Islamic dress) and not to display their adornments to non-mahram males (unrelated men who cannot serve as guardian) as that leads to promiscuity that overruns a society' (Ibn Bāz quoted in Doumato 1999: 578).
19. 'Removing a woman from her home, which is her kingdom, means removing her from what her natural state and her character require. Women entering the realm of men is a danger for Islamic society in that it leads to mixing of the sexes which is considered the main path to adultery, which splits society and wrecks morals' (Ibn Bāz quoted in Doumato 1999: 578).
20. In a speech delivered on 28 March 1992, King Fahd declared: 'We cannot import the methods used by people in other countries and apply them to our people. We have our Islamic beliefs that constitute a complete and fully-integrated system. Free elections are not within this Islamic system, which is based on consultation (*shura*) and the openness between the ruler and his subjects before whom he is fully responsible.... The system of free elections is not suitable to our country, the Kingdom of Saudi Arabia – a country that is unique in that it represents the Muslim world in supervising the holy shrines, and unique in other ways.... In my view, Western democracies may be suitable in their own countries but they do not suit other countries' (King Fahd quoted in Human Rights Watch 1992).
21. The group Edge of Arabia claims that the 2012 exhibition entitled 'We need to talk – *yajibu an nataḥāwar*' was 'the first major public exhibition of Saudi contemporary art in Saudi Arabia' (Edge of Arabia 2012: 10). Previously, Edge of Arabia had toured in London, Venice, Istanbul, Berlin and Dubai. Information on the project and selected artists belonging to the group is available on the website www.edgeofarabia.com and in a catalogue edited by Stephen Stapleton and Edward Booth-Clibborn (2012).

22. Drawing on Michael Warner (2002), Hirschkind (2006) refers to the preachers and audiences engaged in this piety movement, which challenged the secular Egyptian state, as Islamic counterpublics. The *ṣaḥwa* movement in Saudi Arabia, likewise in opposition to the state, can also be labelled as such, but less so the architects and urban planners who criticised certain social trends but did not challenge the Saudi state. I will discuss the concept of counterpublics in the Saudi context in more detail in chapter 6.
23. On the influence of Lynch and Jacobs on New Urbanism, see Grant (2006: 51–2, 81; 2011).
24. In a seminal article, Janet Abu-Lughod (1987) traces the origins of the quest for the essence of Islamic cities back to an article published in 1928, 'L'Islamisme et la vie urbaine' by William Marçais, as well as to Jean Sauvaget's work on Damascus (1934) and Aleppo (1941). Another important source often drawn on to identify differences between European cities and those in the Islamic world is Max Weber's text *The City* (1958), originally published in 1921. From 1970 on, the generalising concept of the Islamic City was subject to critical reassessment. In spite of profound criticism, authors such as Albert H. Hourani (1970), S.M. Stern (1970), Dale Eickelmann (1974) and Janet Abu-Lughod (1980; 1987) did not discard the concept entirely but rather attempted to modify and refine it. Until recently, urban historians, geographers, architects and town planners have used and reproduced it (e.g. Ammann 2004; Wirth 2000).

5
Residential architecture, from the 1970s to the early twenty-first century

In a modest apartment in al-Kandara, built in the 1960s, I was able to observe how New Islamic Urbanism's key idea of privacy protection was applied also to older residential buildings in Jeddah, and how it had an effect on the human body. I had just arrived in Jeddah in January 2012, and since I had not yet found a permanent place for myself, I spent a few nights at the home of the brother-in-law of my friend Mustafa. When Mustafa, who was also staying at his brother-in-law's, woke up after 10 a.m., he complained about the complete lack of daylight in the house, which was caused by numerous layers of different opaque materials covering windows (Figure 5.1). Mustafa, who was born and raised in Aden, Yemen, said that usually he would not have slept so long. The problem at his brother-in-law's place in Jeddah was that he could not tell the difference between day and night. When he tried to draw the curtains open and unbolt a window, his brother-in-law hurried to help him: 'Do you want to open a window? Sure you can! Just a second.' He pulled at the draperies of mixed materials which had not been moved for ages, causing the curtain to come off the rail. Obviously it was not meant to be drawn open.

The episode illustrates that the contemporary conception of domestic space in Jeddah follows particular local rules, even though residential architecture in Saudi Arabia and other Gulf states is sometimes perceived as faceless, lacking cultural identity and a distinctly local style. Mustafa's sister and brother-in-law, both native Yemenis who had moved to Saudi Arabia several decades ago, had long since adapted to the notions of home, domestic space and privacy prevalent in Jeddah. Keeping windows closed and covering them with plastic sheets and thick cloth as well as sealing off balconies and transforming them into storage rooms had

Figure 5.1 Living room/reception hall with windows covered by several layers of opaque materials, during the daytime. Photo: © Stefan Maneval 2012.

become normal for them. As a newcomer to Jeddah, Mustafa, in contrast, thought the insulation of the home peculiar and even felt affected by it in a disturbing way.

By emphasising the specificities of contemporary residential architecture in Jeddah, I do not intend to deny its diversity, especially as there are huge discrepancies in living quality between different social strata. The unequal distribution of oil revenues allowed some people to build splendid palaces adorned according to their owners' fancies, whereas large numbers of people still live in the concrete shacks hastily erected by the first wave of immigrants in the decades after the Second World War. To some extent, however, each larger city has a specific inner or intrinsic logic (*Eigenlogik*; Löw 2008: 73–82; Berking and Löw 2008). Cities are erected, organised and transformed according to the needs and desires of their inhabitants. People born and raised in a particular city perceive its specificities as normality and thus reproduce them in their everyday practices (Berking 2008). Newcomers to a city both consciously and unconsciously adapt to its specific structures – perhaps not assimilating entirely, but to a considerable extent. Local structures change, but the transformation itself follows the logic of each specific city. Social differences are not ignored in the concept of the intrinsic logic, but the focus is on the particularity of, and differences between, cities. One way of addressing social differences within the framework of this concept could be to ask how they are dealt with in Jeddah. I cover them by examining how the requirements of local notions of privacy are fulfilled in different social environments, and how different social groups construct public space and constitute publics.

This chapter treats changes in the residential architecture which occurred against the backdrop of the discourse of what I have defined as New Islamic Urbanism in the previous chapter. These changes were, as I will show, connected to new conceptions of private and public space. In order to identify common elements in the constitution of domestic space in Jeddah and, at the same time, take into account obvious differences between social milieus, I introduce, in the first part of the chapter, typical residential buildings of different social groups: single- and multi-family houses, remodelled old buildings and gated communities. I consider the dwellings of Saudis and immigrants, including members of the lower, middle and upper middle classes. My survey of different types of residential architecture leads to an analysis of common features of residential buildings inhabited by different social strata in Jeddah.

While the first part of the chapter deals with the question of how residential architecture serves to protect privacy as well as how it relates to a particular perception of the world outside the home, the second half inquires into the causes of these trajectories. What are the meanings attached to the home since the 1970s – not by experts, whose discourse I have analysed in the previous chapter, but by ordinary residents of Jeddah? I first discuss everyday practices as influenced by the discourse of Islamic Revival. Much of this discourse is known to revolve around what people, particularly women, are not supposed to do. I show that the residential architecture constructed since the emergence of New Islamic Urbanism and the Islamic Revival movement supports a pious lifestyle informed by this discourse. At the same time, as I highlight in the final section of this chapter, the same architecture creates new opportunities and enables diverse, sometimes conflicting social practices – and more than one notion of privacy.

New Islamic Urbanism in practice

From the 1970s on, the detached single-family house, or 'villa', became the most popular type of dwelling among the upper and middle classes in Jeddah as well as in other Saudi cities.[1] In the northern part of the city particularly, there are now large areas of villas built in a wide range of styles: a neo-classical temple-like home can be found next to an English hunting lodge of dressed stone, a Tuscan country house amidst futuristic, Scandinavian-style and neo-oriental buildings (Figure 5.2). All single-family units are surrounded by high walls (Figure 5.3). In some cases, family members live in separate buildings on the same plot of land or on neighbouring lots connected via gates within the enclosures. A comparison of descriptions of the walls shows that their height increased from 2 or 2.5 m in the 1970s to over 3 m in the 1990s (Bokhari 1978: 304, 347; Abu-Gazzeh 1996: 102). In addition, multi-storey houses are today separated from surrounding buildings by blends and extensions of iron sheet (Figure 5.4; al-Hathloul 1996: 213–16; Abu-Gazzeh 1996: 102–4; Mortada 1992: 229). The Riyadh-based architect Saleh al-Hathloul describes the widespread '[u]se of plastic corrugated sheets to ensure privacy' as follows: 'using a steel frame and plastic corrugated sheets, [a house owner] extends the height of the fence wall to the point where it breaks the line of vision coming from the windows of his neighbor's house' (1996: 215).

The only openings in the enclosures – entrances and garage doors – are usually made of non-transparent materials, such as metal and opaque glass, and are always kept closed (Figure 5.2). Families usually enter their villas only through the side door in the garage, whereas the main gate is used exclusively by guests. Different entrances lead to different sections of the house – the side door to the private area and the main entrance to the reception hall and the *ṣālūn*, a large sitting room for formal occasions and the entertainment of guests, and sometimes an extra dining room (Figure 5.5). The isolation of the *ṣālūn* from the private area of the house makes it possible to allow strangers in without any interference from family members of the opposite sex. The architectural setting indoors, as Mai Yamani has noted, is an extension of the clear-cut distinction between the inside and outside world which dominates the appearance of the villas as seen from the street (Yamani 2004: 125; see also Bokhari 1978: 347–8). The reception room, although located indoors, is associated with the outside world.

The increasing height of the walls and the blends of iron or plastic corrugated sheet as well as the interior division of the single-family home indicate that the discourse of New Islamic Urbanism was not limited to academic circles and a handful of architects. Its emphasis on privacy protection met a demand shared by large parts of the populace and hence became an essential feature of contemporary architecture in Jeddah and other Saudi cities. This can be observed not only in luxurious mansions. For practical reasons, middle-class apartment buildings

Figure 5.2 Villa in al-Sulaymāniyya district, combining neo-classical columns and a rustic crenellated tower. Photo: © Stefan Maneval 2011.

Figure 5.3 Wall surrounding a villa in al-Sulaymāniyya district. Photo: © Stefan Maneval 2011.

Figure 5.4 Blends of iron sheet between single-family houses. Photo: © Stefan Maneval 2010.

Figure 5.5 An upper middle-class family's reception hall. Photo: © Stefan Maneval 2010.

are not surrounded by walls. Nonetheless, in terms of appearance they share some characteristics with upper-class villas: the massive structures of both building types contain rather small windows, which often have panes made of tinted or polished sheet glass. In addition, windows are usually covered by grilles, shutters or curtains – night and day (Figure 5.6). Electric light and air conditioning, which is available even in the simplest flats, compensate for the loss of daylight and fresh air.

Bokhari mentions that balconies and terraces, which can be observed in many villas and apartment buildings constructed between the 1950s and 1970s, were hardly ever used (Bokhari 1978: 347). 'The customers don't want balconies. They are dust catchers, that's how they are seen here', an architect from Jeddah told me in an interview in January 2009, explaining why balconies are rarely constructed today. Many of the New Islamic Urbanists considered that balconies lacked privacy (e.g. Fadan 1983: 243–4; Mortada 1992: 234; al-Mutawea 1987: 185–6). In neighbourhoods dating from the 1950s and 1960s, such as Kandara and Baghdādiyya, one can see many balconies covered with canvas, wooden boards or moveable walls, sometimes forming small additional rooms or compartments (Figure 5.7; al-Mutawea 1987: 141–3). According to a high-ranking urban planner in the Municipality of Jeddah, this trend began in the 1980s (personal conversation, January 2009).

Figure 5.6 An apartment building in al-Ḥamrā᾽ district. Photo: © Stefan Maneval 2010.

Figure 5.7 Apartment building, built around the 1960s, in al-Kandara district. Photo: © Stefan Maneval 2009.

Newer apartment buildings often have small balconies, but their walls and blends are considerably higher than those constructed between the 1950s and 1970s.

Data collected by King Abdulaziz University building archaeologists from 14 contemporary houses in Jeddah in the early to mid-1980s reveals that openings made up an average of 11.6 per cent of a facade (Eyuce n.d.: Appendices VII–VIII). I have already summarised the study findings with regard to traditional architecture in chapter 2. Comparison of the average proportion of openings in the facades of houses built up to the mid-1940s with that of residential buildings of the early 1980s reveals that, within less than 40 years, the proportion of openings had decreased from two-thirds to little more than one-tenth. These figures are not distorted by an increase of building size: in relation to the floor area the proportion of openings decreased from 71.6 per cent to 7.8 per cent (Eyuce n.d.: Appendices III–IV, VII–VIII). Architects and citizens of Jeddah alike explain the reduced fenestration by a desire to protect rooms from the heat of the sun and the private sphere from the gaze of neighbours and passers-by (personal conversation, November 2009 and April 2011; Eben Saleh 2002: 523; al-Hathloul 1996: 201–24, 247, 256; Mortada 1992: 257, 267). Eyuce's study seems to be based on data collected in middle-class homes, but the pattern of few, small windows with opaque panes can also be observed in districts of lower-income groups like al-Hindāwiyya, al-Sabīl, al-Ṣuḥaifa, Ghulail and Nuzla, and in the poorest districts like al-Rawābī, where illegal immigrants live alongside Saudi migrant workers of rural or Bedouin family background.

Smaller houses and flats are not as strictly divided into a section for the family and one for guests as single-family buildings are, but as long as enough space is available one or two rooms may be reserved for entertaining guests. When male visitors occupy these rooms, the host makes sure that they do not meet female family members by mediating between the two spheres. Food prepared by women in the kitchen, for example, is brought to the door of the reception room, where the host takes it to serve male guests. Female guests are usually invited into the women's realm. In larger houses this can be a second floor, in smaller apartments another living room or the kitchen (personal communication and observation, February and April 2012). This means that the introduction of fixed functions for different rooms and sections of the house or apartment often brought about a gendered division of the home.

Houses in low-income areas of Jeddah often consist of only one or two small rooms shared by a whole family. If the front door leads directly into the living room of these simple dwellings, a screen is set up in front

Figure 5.8 Screen in front of the entrance to a small residential building in al-Hindāwiyya district. Men sitting in a *mirkāz* by the entrance. Photo: © Stefan Maneval 2011.

of the street entrance or immediately behind it inside the house, protecting the family from view when someone opens the door (Figure 5.8). In these areas, where houses and flats are often not big enough to include a reception room, one can still see many open-air meeting places consisting of sets of benches beside the wall of a house. The *mirkāz* described in chapter 2 has survived in these districts so that men can meet outside the home without disturbing female household members. One can regularly observe groups of men gathering there after sunset. Others hire a small room on the ground floor or in the courtyard of a building. Such indoor meeting places are usually furnished with cushions on the floor, a television and an air conditioner or fan. The practice of meeting at such a *nādī* (club) or a *mirkāz* ensures that family privacy is maintained at home (Figure 5.9). Since larger houses have a *ṣālūn*, the *mirkāz* has become obsolete in districts of the well-to-do.

The Old City is inhabited today almost entirely by migrant workers of poor social background. Only a small percentage of the old houses are still in existence, approximately 10–20 per cent (Maneval 2012a). The rest have been replaced by high-rise commercial buildings, hotels and modern apartments. Air conditioners set into the latticework of *rawāshīn* require the sealing of all windows as tightly as possible (Figure 5.10).

Figure 5.9 Men sitting in a *mirkāz* in front of their clubhouse in al-Hindāwiyya district. Photo: © Stefan Maneval 2011.

Figure 5.10 Wood panels, window panes and air conditioner: a *majlis* turned office in the old Nūr Walī building. Photo: © Stefan Maneval 2010.

To prevent the sunlight from heating up rooms, wooden panels are used to cover *rūshān* and window openings. Verbal communication and views through the bay windows have thus become impossible.

Gated housing developments are today a common type of dwelling for all social strata in Jeddah, from poor migrant workers to the royal family. The first gated communities in Saudi Arabia were constructed by ARAMCO, the Arabian American Oil Company, soon after the Second World War in the Eastern Province. Modelled after US suburbs, they, in turn, served as prototypes for other mass housing projects in the Kingdom (cf. Fadan 1983, 103–28; Citino 2006; Vitalis 2007).[2] The first gated developments in Jeddah were erected in the second half of the 1970s by the national Saudi airline, a private initiative under the auspices of Prince Fawwāz, and King Abdulaziz University respectively (Bokhari 1978: 327–34). Today, gated communities can be found all over the city. Migrant workers often live in overcrowded gated mass accommodation owned by the companies they work for. Students who do not have family in Jeddah lodge in dormitories provided by King Abdulaziz University. Located on the eastern fringes of Jeddah where the city ends and the desert begins, they are fenced in and guarded day and night.

Skilled foreign employees and upper middle-class Saudis alike live in luxurious gated communities owned and administered by private real estate companies. They do not live together in the same 'compounds', as these developments are called in Saudi Arabia. Saudis live in special Saudi-only compounds and foreign experts live in non-Saudi compounds, many of which are owned by a firm ironically named Arabian Homes. They offer residents a large range of facilities and services: janitorial, gardening and laundry services, retail shops, restaurants, travel agents and leisure facilities such as small libraries, gyms, children's playgrounds and swimming pools. Modelled after modern American or European residential neighbourhoods, the architectural style of these developments obscures which country you are in. Streets in al-Andalus Compound are named after Spanish towns with an Arab past such as, for example, Valencia, Toledo and Sevilla, promising a way of life far from the Saudi reality outside the gates. The housing units within gated communities are not as isolated as the villas outside. The number and proportion of windows is larger and the lots are divided by simple fences and hedges. However, each development as a whole is enclosed by high walls.

The resident of a gated expatriate community who had moved to Jeddah in 1984 told me that, after the first Gulf War in 1991, when the Islamic opposition grew stronger and demanded that infidels be expelled from the country, the walls of gated expatriate communities were strengthened with barbed wire and entry controls were tightened (personal communication, February 2012). Security measures were augmented even more in the first decade of the twenty-first century, when a series of bomb attacks targeted symbols of Western lifestyle. Since then, armoured military vehicles located in front of the main gates and soldiers with machine guns stationed at strategic points around the compounds have become standard. Speed bumps slow traffic on the access roads to the compounds, and steel gates, barbed wire, cameras and guards conducting pass checks 24 hours a day prevent unwanted visitors from entering the premises (Figure 5.11). Helen, my expatriate interlocutor, described the increasing fortification of her gated community as a 'progressive enclosure' (personal communication, February 2012). Nevertheless, the compound provides the only option for her family to live in Jeddah. The rent is paid by her husband's company, and a shuttle service provides transportation for schoolchildren. Apart from these pragmatic reasons, she stressed that, '[i]f you want to live something like a "normal" life here, you have to live in a compound'. The activities Helen mentioned as contributing to her sense of a normal life in what she perceives to be an anomalous environment include drinking beer, taking a swim in the pool and meeting friends. These activities also occur in beach resorts, health clubs, cafes, restaurants or at home, and not exclusively in

Figure 5.11 Entrance to a gated community in northern Jeddah. Photo: © Stefan Maneval 2009.

gated communities. But the gates and walls surrounding the gated communities certainly aim to protect a lifestyle Helen and other expats are used to, and that conservative Saudis and militant Salafis might despise. At the same time, the security measures reinforce the impression of 'cultural enclaves' (Glasze and Alkhayyal 2002) with their own rules – a living concept Helen disliked when she first moved to Jeddah.

Facets of enclosure (1): Fear and safety

The walls around single-family homes and gated housing compounds protect privacy in two different ways. Supported by metal sheet blinds, they block the view from streets and from the houses next door. Secondly, facilitating control over the entrance, they regulate access to the domestic sphere, allowing the inhabitants to feel safe.[3] The desire for safety is shared by Saudis and non-Saudis in Jeddah alike, and it is not limited to members of the upper and middle classes who can afford expensive fortification of their homes. Undertaking fieldwork for one month in early 2009, I was accommodated in the guest room – the unoccupied maid's quarters, to be precise – of a German expatriate family in a gated executive community. More than once, a taxi driver who dropped me off at the gate, normally a migrant worker from Bangladesh, Pakistan or the Philippines, expressed his admiration for the security offered by a gated development. Other examples from the middle-class expatriate community reveal that safety and a desire for protection are recurring themes in Jeddah that extend to many aspects of everyday life beyond the domestic sphere. A remarkably high proportion of Europeans in Jeddah can be observed driving around in SUVs and Jeeps. In view of the contentious reputation of these fuel-intensive vehicles in Europe, the owners explain their choice of car not simply in terms of the low fuel prices in Saudi Arabia. They tend to stress that traffic in the city is so dangerous that a strong and secure car is a necessity.

Both the security measures instituted in gated communities and the fondness for all-terrain four-wheel-drives (preferably bulletproof), demonstrate that the strong desire for safety is often connected with fear of the outside world. Asked about her childhood memories in an interview, the young artist Sarah S. Abu Abdallah from Jeddah vividly depicts the twofold feeling of safety at home and fear of the uncertainties loitering outside:

> Born in the nineties, I wouldn't claim to be born in the 'nicer times'. But my childhood was pretty peaceful and sheltered; my time was

> mostly spent indoors. Without much TV and barely any outdoors, I got an appetite for imaginary narratives. We read a lot, drew our stories and played them out, our activities ranged from designing a magazine to taping in-house movies. But normally growing up here, I was fed with so much female paranoia. It affected me deeply as a young girl and I keep drawing from it every time I make an artwork.
> (Interview in Edge of Arabia 2012: 102)

Women, especially young, unmarried ones, are often afraid of being harassed by men in the streets, getting into trouble with the morality police or, more generally, becoming subject to rumours that could harm their own or their families' reputation. This could make them undesirable for marriage (Le Renard 2011: 125–48; Le Renard 2014: 52–8, 99–101). Although Saudis are often described as more rigid when it comes to rules of gender segregation, public morality and the visibility of women (personal communication, March 2011, February 2012; see chapter 6), the 'female paranoia' Sarah Abu Abdallah speaks about is also common among non-Saudi subjects in Jeddah. During my fieldwork, a well-educated Franco-Lebanese woman who became a housewife after moving to Jeddah with her husband almost 30 years ago complained to me that she is forced to spend most of her time inside the house. Her husband, a Christian Lebanese like her, is not particularly conservative, but he works a lot and does not want her to leave the house alone. He is afraid that she might be kidnapped when she takes a taxi because local newspapers regularly report such cases of abduction (personal communication, February 2012). In her anthropological study of female public spaces in Riyadh, Amélie Le Renard (2014: 51, 56–7) quotes Saudi and Filipino women who share the fear of being abducted and raped by taxi drivers.

Everywhere in the world, human beings are afraid of something, and their anxieties are not always caused by serious threats. Although Saudi Arabia has the reputation of being a very secure country, when doing fieldwork I had the impression that a public 'discourse of urban fear' (Low 2001) exists in Jeddah – a discourse so ubiquitous that European expatriates used the perceived perils of Saudi streets as a pretext to fulfil their little boys' fantasies about big motor cars. Fear of terror attacks can explain the fortification of gated communities, and the perceived dangers of taxi drivers, youth in the streets and other people's gossip add another layer of discourse to the 'collective enunciations' (Deleuze and Guattari 1987) discussed in the previous chapter. Together, these discourses and debates help explain why, as Abu-Gazzeh maintained, in Saudi Arabia 'A man's home is his castle' (Abu-Gazzeh 1996: 283), and why the mobility of women in Jeddah and other Saudi cities is limited. In order to gain a more comprehensive picture, however, the contemporary architecture discussed above and the discourses related to it – the discourses of religious reform, New Islamic Urbanism and urban fear – need to be linked to social practices. The changing social practices related to the home are the topic of the following sections.

The changing architecture of social life

In her book *Changed Identities* the anthropologist Mai Yamani (2000) elucidates the point touched on by Sarah Abu Abdallah, that the social activities of women in the 1990s had, to a great degree, become confined to the boundaries of private dwellings. Due to the spatial division of commercial and domestic activities, stricter notions of gender segregation and the societal demand that men must care for female family members, young women in Jeddah were more tightly bound to the domestic sphere than their grandmothers 50 years before (Yamani 2000: 94–7; Le Renard 2014: 29–34). This phenomenon was not the result of a linear development. Several authors describe the 1960s and 1970s as a period in which women were more visible in public and gained more autonomy than in previous decades (Altorki 1986; Doumato 2000; al-Rasheed 2013; Yamani 1996). Although it was not yet accepted for women to engage in work that required leaving the home, a rising proportion of women went to school, and it was not uncommon for the daughters of privileged families to earn university degrees abroad (Doumato 2000: 2–4). It became normal for many Saudi women to go shopping in the *sūq* and, a little later, in the various shopping centres which were proliferating in the city. Some of these women were accompanied by their husbands or fathers while others went shopping without the company of men (al-Rasheed 2013: 104–5). Rising numbers of women ceased to cover their faces in public. Instead of seeking permission, they began to simply inform their husbands if they were going out, and they started to attend mixed gatherings at the homes of friends, often wearing casual clothing instead of an *ʿabāya*, the long black dress that Saudi women use to cover their bodies (Altorki 1986: 36–9, 56, 69).

This trend shifted in the conservative cultural climate of the 1980s and 1990s. Inspired by the teachings of the *ṣaḥwa* movement (Lacroix 2011), extensive religious instruction at school and religious TV broadcasts promoting the Wahhabi doctrine, men and women intermingled less during private festivities. Women who had not worn the veil in previous decades now started to veil their faces (al-Rasheed 2013: 109–10). In addition, young women in the 1980s started to wear black gloves and stockings as a conservative political statement and an expression of piety. Hiding hands, feet and especially the face became almost a social obligation in the 1990s. Women with uncovered faces risked harassment by the religious police, reprimand by other women or becoming the subject of slander (Doumato 1999: 577; 2000: 20–1). Unlike in previous decades, women were discouraged from studying abroad (Yamani 1996: 269–70). Fatwas such as the one issued by Ibn Bāz in 1996 (see chapter 4) censuring women's employment outside the home were not legally binding, and they did not necessarily cause those women working as teachers, nurses, etc. to leave their jobs (Doumato 1999: 579 n.43). However, considering Ibn Bāz's and other theologians' authority and the high esteem in which the Saudi populace held them, their words certainly discouraged many women from working outside the home.

In fact, the employment rate of Saudi women remained equally low between 1980 and the end of the 1990s although the number of women graduating from universities and colleges rose considerably (Doumato 1999: 570; 2000: 22; Prokop 2005: 63). In 1999, between 5.5 and 8 per cent of the indigenous workforce were women, and only 5 to 6 per cent of Saudi women of working age had employment (Doumato 1999: 571–2; Hamdan 2005: 47; Zaʿzūʿ 2004: 17).[4] Economic growth and distribution of wealth allowed more families to live solely on men's incomes. If economic circumstances no longer necessitated her work, a working woman's modesty appeared to be in doubt. In a quantitative study in social geography dedicated to the topic of 'Women's daily journey to work' (*riḥlat al-marʾa al-yawmiyya li-l-ʿamal fī Jiddah*), Laylā Zaʿzūʿ considers intermingling with men at work, the dependence on non-*maḥram* male drivers and – perceived as even worse than this – on public transportation as some of the major factors hindering women's employment (2004: 18–19, chapter 5). In addition, she sees long commutes to work and unpredictable congestion as obstacles for women who wish to combine children and work: being solely responsible for the rearing of her children, a mother ideally should not leave the home before her children and should be back from work when her children come home from school (Zaʿzūʿ 2004: 67–8, 185–6). Zaʿzūʿ does not call gender roles into question. Adopting, rather, a pragmatic approach in conformity with the prevailing moral values, she demands better opportunities for women to choose the location of their workplace, an improved network of streets and other enhancements of the infrastructure.

In the 1980s and 1990s, not only did veiling increase and work outside the home come to be considered immoral: a pious woman was also not supposed to leave the home except when absolutely necessary. Whereas in the past, avoidance of the public realm marked the social distinction of a woman and her family, it was now beginning to be perceived as an expression of piety. In fact, women of the relatively liberal, Western-educated elite came to be, and still are, more likely to leave the house in order to attend university, go shopping in the latest of Jeddah's opulent shopping malls or spend a day at a private beach resort than women of the lower and middle classes. According to Madawi al-Rasheed (2013: 120), fatwas that dealt with the female body, regulated women's behaviour and limited their movement offered women who could not afford the luxuries of Western-style modernity and consumption a way of asserting their own piety and morality. They provided an ideological framework which allowed them to condemn what was not affordable. In addition, better job opportunities for men created by the oil economy and the modernisation of the country enabled more Saudi families to live solely on men's income while the women remained at home. They were now able to leave the house less, thus adhering to the ideal of not being seen in public.[5]

As the domestic sphere became physically insulated from the outside world and women left it less often than before, the home, as both Mai Yamani (2000) and Tariq Sijeeni (1995) argue, became a place almost exclusively for the family. While Yamani's study is focused on women, Sijeeni has conducted interviews with Saudi men between 35 and 65 years of age. His interlocutors from relatively new districts like al-Bawādī recounted that, in spite of greater distances between members of an extended family, their social contacts in the 1990s were basically limited to relatives. They described social intercourse between neighbours even within the same apartment building as rare in comparison to the past (Sijeeni 1995: 149–63). The same impression was reported by one of my interlocutors in Jeddah in January 2009, an architect in his sixties: 'Today you don't know your neighbour any more, you're estranged by your neighbour'. A Saudi home today is normally inhabited by a married couple, their children and sometimes other family members. Visitors are predominantly kin – in contrast to the pre-oil era when an entire extended family had lived, worked and received customers as well as other guests in the same building. When guests visit, the division between the sexes today is, as indicated above, usually maintained with the help of physical barriers and fixed spatial arrangements: a *ṣālūn* or reception room ensures that the family section of the home is not intruded upon by visitors.

Tariq Sijeeni quotes an inhabitant of al-Bawādī district in Jeddah as saying:

> The sense of privacy in my house … is lost unless I keep my window shade down and I do not use my yard or swimming pool. This is because of several reasons: (a) My neighbors do not respect the issue of privacy because of their weakness of religious spirit and there are no social relations between us. (b) The building code today does not accommodate Muslim sociocultural values. (c) The building design enables the neighbors to look into each other's houses.
>
> (Sijeeni 1995: 159)

None of my own interlocutors linked the deliberate self-encasement of householders with building codes, the neglect of privacy protection in contemporary architecture or religious values being in decline. This line of argument seems to be strongly influenced by the discourse of the *ṣaḥwa islāmiyya*. However, several remarks gleaned during my fieldwork indicate that a connection between architectural seclusion, privacy and Islam is still being made. Having met several times, I dared to ask the owner of a house built in the 1950s, who was eager to help me with my research, whether he would let me see his house from the inside one day. This was the first and last time he gave me a categorically negative answer. '*Hunāk ḥurma*', there are women, he said to explain his refusal. Another interlocutor, Yasemin,[6] said in an interview (conducted in March 2011): 'We don't sit down where other people can watch us. We are conservative.' She was not talking about her own family then, but about society at large or 'all families', as she put it. An architect working for the Municipality of Jeddah also explained the concealment of balconies beginning in the 1980s in terms of religious conservatism (personal communication, January 2009). And when I talked to my friend Mustafa about my observations in Jeddah, he immediately thought he knew the reason for the secluded appearance of homes. 'This is due to the religion', he remarked (February 2012).

As I have indicated in chapter 2, in the first half of the twentieth century large latticed openings in walls as well as open balconies were not unusual in Jeddah. Furthermore, it was common to invite guests into the home. As the architecture and rules of behaviour ensured that unrelated men and women would not meet, this practice was not perceived as a breach of the precepts of Islam. Still, Mustafa's comment was not incorrect, since the interpretation of religious texts changed over the course of the twentieth century. Beginning in the 1980s, many residents of Jeddah enclosed domestic space with impermeable walls and visual screens and limited access to the home largely to family members because of their understanding of religion. It would be misleading to assume that the underlying conceptions of home and privacy were imposed on them by conservative scholars of Islam. In her inquiry into the women's mosque movement in Cairo in the 1990s, Saba Mahmood shows that non-liberal social practices, some of which appear to be merely outward markers of religiosity – such as veiling, punctuality in ritual prayers and particular ways of comporting oneself – constitute for the participants an essential part of the creation of a pious self. The 'pedagogical programme' of this particular branch of the Islamic Revival aims at cultivating a desire to follow these precepts, to the point that negligence comes to feel like disobedience to God's will (Mahmood 2005: 31, 123–31).

Saba Mahmood's observations help to explain why a large proportion of both men and women in Saudi Arabia in the 1980s and 1990s embraced a lifestyle which apparently limits people's, especially women's, mobility, access to work and healthy living conditions. One of my interlocutors, Muhannad, a Saudi from Jeddah in his late twenties whom I interviewed in 2011, mentioned that his wife, whom he described as much more conservative than himself, did not want to go shopping or on similar outings with him. 'Your realm is outside, mine is the home', she would tell him (personal communication, March 2011). For outsiders like myself, a statement such as this, or the one made by Sijeeni's interlocutor, quoted above, seem to contain excessive levels of self-imposed confinement and renunciation. The people who express these views, however, have made rules like remaining at home, limiting contact with unrelated members of the opposite sex, keeping the shutters drawn and refraining from using one's courtyard and swimming pool natural to their disposition. Disrespecting these or other rules derived from their particular reading of Islamic sources feels morally wrong to them.

Approximately two decades have passed since Tariq Sijeeni, Eleanor Doumato and Mai Yamani conducted their research. In the first decade of the twenty-first century the Saudi state, facing criticism from within the country and abroad, focused on women's issues as a means of enhancing its tattered image. Education and career opportunities for women were improved, more public debate on the position of women in Saudi society as well as criticism of conservative religious scholars and the religious police was permitted, and stronger participation of women in public life was promoted (see al-Rasheed 2013: 134–5,

146–52; Le Renard 2008, 2014: 36–46. Also see chapter 6, this volume). One of Sarah Abu Abdallah's works is a video installation which shows the artist painting a wrecked car pink (Edge of Arabia 2012: 76). She used video as a medium to appropriate the car symbolically, at a time when she was still not allowed to drive and move away from the protected home independently. Even the public display of such a video – or of Maha Malluh's 'Food for Thought' (see chapter 4) – must have been unthinkable in the 1990s.

Since then, more opportunities for women to work, study and engage in leisure activities outside the home have emerged – at least for some women – and in June 2018, women were finally allowed to drive. In February 2012, Effat University – a rather exclusive private school for women – kindly allowed me to interview six female students of both Saudi and non-Saudi origin.[7] None of these women in their early twenties felt forced to spend time at home if they did not want to, except at times when they could not find a driver. Besides their studies, one of them attended private art classes and was involved in publishing a magazine, the second student regularly met with friends in cafes and attended cultural events in one of these cafes or at a friend's home, the third often took a taxi to go shopping together with friends or her mother and sisters. These daughters of affluent Saudi and expatriate families on the one hand and the middle-class Lebanese woman who could not leave the house without her workaholic husband on the other represent extreme ends of a broad spectrum of women in Jeddah today; and yet they are also quite ordinary cases.

Facets of enclosure (2): Don't trust the concrete

Among the security measures introduced in the first decade of the twenty-first century to protect gated housing compounds, embassies, hotels etc. in Jeddah, as well as in other major cities in Saudi Arabia, from attacks by militant Islamists are massive concrete blocks in access ways to these buildings. An artwork by one of Saudi Arabia's most active and celebrated artists, Abdulnasser Gharem (see Stapleton and Booth-Clibborn 2012: 112–43), co-founder of the artists' project Edge of Arabia, comments on the phenomenon of these safety barriers. In early 2012 his 'Concrete Block' was displayed together with Maha Malluh's and Sarah Abu Abdallah's artworks in the exhibition 'We need to talk – *yajib an nataḥāwar*' in Jeddah (Figure 5.12). The block is covered with tiny letters, some of which, visible only at close sight, constitute the words *lā*

Figure 5.12 Abdulnasser Gharem's 'Concrete Block', at the 2012 Edge of Arabia exhibition in Jeddah. Photo: © Stefan Maneval 2012.

tathiq bi-l-ismant – don't trust the concrete! The block, which looks like concrete from a distance, is actually made of rubber stamps.

There are many reasons not to trust concrete. In the exhibition catalogue, Gharem comments on his own artwork, explaining that 'concrete and material things can not block the ideologies' (Edge of Arabia 2012: 50). In this sense, Gharem's calligraphic 'Concrete Block' reminds the viewer of the fact that, no matter how much concrete is used, safety can only be partially achieved if the fundamental problems which lead to acts of violence remain. No place inhabited by human beings who go in and out will ever be completely sealed off and secured. In a cultural climate in which militant ideologies thrive, acts of violence can therefore never be fully prevented. As Edward Blakely and Mary Gail Snyder (1997: 95–8, chapter 5) argue in their seminal book about gated communities in the United States, one can always find a way to pass through gates, a hole in the fence or a breach in the wall allowing outsiders to sneak into an enclosed estate.[8] Likewise, Setha Low (2003: 120–31) emphasises that, although people often move to gated communities because of a fear of crime, statistical evidence that gates actually deter criminal activity is very weak. The barriers that are supposed to protect potential targets of militant Islamists in Saudi Arabia actually make these targets much more identifiable.

Thus they become reminders of the fact that something needs to be hidden, shut in and defended.

Unlike gated communities in the US, Europe and other Middle Eastern countries, the walls, guards, snipers and tanks surrounding such developments in Saudi Arabia serve to protect a lifestyle deemed immoral or inappropriate – *ḥarām*, *ʿayb* or *bāṭil* – by a significant portion of the Saudi population. There is little doubt that many Saudis regard the relatively liberal lifestyle practised in gated communities in Jeddah and other Saudi cities critically. In other words, it is not just the radical minority articulating their disapproval by means of physical violence that views these communities in this way. It would nevertheless be wrong to believe that these places are the only ones in Jeddah where habits and conduct deviate from the religious ideal propagated by conservative Wahhabi preachers. The arrangement of daily life and social relations according to the ideals of gender segregation and visual privacy, achieved with walls, screens and barriers in Saudi homes, is indeed only one side of the coin. Just as airtight sealing of rooms enables air conditioners to generate an indoor climate that contrasts with outdoors weather, the architectural insulation of domestic space permits social practices that deviate completely from the rules governing behaviour in public. Headscarf, veil and *ʿabāya* have to be worn only outside the home. While adhering to the rules of gender segregation in public, unrelated liberal men and women intermingle inside residential houses. At dinner parties, women may leave their veils at the doorstep. While women can hardly ever be seen smoking in public, at home there is no one to tell them not to smoke – apart from their husbands, who may or may not care. Alcohol is strictly prohibited in Saudi Arabia and not even served at Western five-star hotels, as is common practice in other Arab countries where alcohol is banned. Yet at a rich Saudi businessman's party I witnessed a servant supplying some guests with alcoholic beverages, the glasses carefully wrapped in paper so as not to offend the puritans sitting at the next table (see also Altorki 1986: 130). In gated communities, Western expatriates engage in home brew contests in which they make wine out of grape juice bought in tetrapaks. Furthermore, social media and the internet enable people to get in touch, exchange messages and images, or view, talk to and flirt with one another via webcams. Young people seeking to connect with the opposite sex, for example, can thus satisfy their curiosity at least partially while sitting on a couch in their parents' living room.

Speaking about his dating habits, an unmarried migrant worker in his thirties told me about pre-arrangements he has to make in order to smuggle a woman into his flat (personal communication, January 2012).

After parking his car around the corner of his house so that none of his neighbours can recognise him together with a woman, he enters the buildings first to make sure that no one is on the stairs. His companion enters some moments later, which is unsuspicious because she might be visiting one of the families living in the same building. Once inside the flat, they are safe. He switches on the air conditioner so that his neighbours will not hear them. In most cases, the women he brings home are prostitutes. Prostitution has always been a part of life in Jeddah, just as in many other cities all over the world. But while, in the past, men visited prostitutes in separate settlements of huts, they now bring them home or, if they are married, to a friend's home or furnished apartment, as another informant told me (personal conversation, March 2011). Ethically speaking, prostitution practised in a separate district or in a customer's house or other residential building is more or less the same. In terms of the sociology of architecture, however, location is significant: illicit behaviour and prohibited actions are unlikely to occur in buildings – such as those representative of the traditional architecture of Jeddah – characterised by openness, permeability and social control. The screens and blinds common in Jeddah's contemporary architecture, in contrast, facilitate such practices. Described above as a response to the demands of a conservative Islamic way of life, the protection of the interior from prying eyes also allows residents to deviate from public moral codes or the law. In this context, the advice of Gharem's concrete block achieves yet another meaning if we apply it to residential buildings. Don't trust the concrete: you can never know what actually happens behind the walls shielding the domestic sphere in Jeddah today. They may be associated with a pious lifestyle in the spirit of the Islamic Revival, but they can also serve the opposite purpose.

In a society dominated by a rigid moral system, enclosures surrounding residential architecture thus provide space for heterogeneity. One of the happiest answers I have ever received to my question 'How do you like it here in Jeddah?' came from a gay man who had lived in several places considered more liberal than Saudi Arabia, including Canada and Lebanon (personal communication, March 2011).

'Good!' Omar said, 'you can really have a good life here'. Then he laughed and added: 'Well, a life in a bubble.' Unlike other places 'where people know everything about you and tell it to everyone', Jeddah represented a positive experience for him because people respected one another's privacy. 'Inside the houses, you can do anything you like, no one cares.'

His friend mentioned 'hundreds of different parties' at private homes.

‘Hundreds?’ I asked.

‘Well, at least five different kinds of parties. We have gay parties, straight parties, boring official parties and so on. Mostly you just invite a couple of friends.’

Yasemin, a divorced Saudi woman from Jeddah and mother of two adult sons and a teenage daughter, disagrees with the opinion that people in Jeddah do not care what other people do inside their homes. She struck me as an open-minded, straightforward woman with a sense of humour. She had met her former husband, a German, by saying hello to him in the street and striking up a conversation. Needless to say that this is something probably every girl growing up in Jeddah is told not to do. Interviewing her in March 2011, I asked how she perceived her relationship to her neighbours. She reported that ever since she got married and moved out of her parents’ home, she had had bad luck with her neighbours. One day in the late 1980s, her next-door neighbour pretended to have lost his keys in order to be allowed entry into the home she shared with her husband. Once inside, the neighbour climbed out of the window on the first floor, jumped to his own window and entered his bedroom. ‘Just to see the house, [and find out] if we are married or friends.’

Some days later, they found the police waiting for them in a car in front of their house. She believes that the ‘monkey neighbour’, as she called him, had reported to the police that she was not married to the man she was living with. The police left when they saw that she was carrying a little baby on her arm.

Affirmation of moral standards within the framework of the Wahhabi reading of Commanding Right and Forbidding Wrong (*al-amr bi-l-maʿrūf wa-l-nahī ʿan al-munkar*; see Cook 2000) was, in this case, given privilege over the principle of non-interference in a couple’s private sphere. At the same time, the anecdote illustrates the efficacy of the barriers erected to protect the private realm of an average Saudi home. Surmounting them is not an easy task. It requires at least a convincing pretext, if not the will to risk one’s life. As Yasemin said about her adventurous neighbour, ‘He could have dropped from the first floor!’

Sometimes social control aimed at the imposition of moral standards proves more powerful than the walls and curtains screening the comings and goings of household members. Yasemin used to sublet the upper floor of the single-family home where she was living when I interviewed her in March 2011 to foreigners. I wanted to know what neighbours thought about her sharing the house with unrelated men. She complained that the people next door were extremely curious and kept asking her intrusive questions. I wondered if this didn’t matter to her.

‘It does matter to me’, she replied. ‘And I interrupt them. Sometimes I don’t want to answer. When they ask too much, I say, “Sorry, I don’t want to reply.”’

The fact that she allowed foreigners to lodge in her house is rather exceptional in the Saudi context, and so is her way of coping with her prying neighbours’ remarks. However, 10 months later, when I asked one of her sons if I could rent their guest room, he said no, explaining that he was about to leave Jeddah for Riyadh because of a job assignment. With his elder brother having already moved out, only his mother and sister would remain in the house, and under these circumstances they could not take in male tenants. As far as he and his family were concerned, there was no problem, but they did not want to provoke a scandal. Even a fearless woman such as Yasemin could not completely ignore the opinion and gossip of neighbours, friends and distant relatives, or whoever else would fan the flames of scandal.

In spite of certain limitations such as those faced by Yasemin, homes in Jeddah provide shelter for a wide range of activities, many of them unconnected to domestic life. Without freedom of assembly, an institutional form of meeting has evolved in the private realm: affluent Saudi families often hold weekly gatherings, called *nadwa, dīwāniyya* or *majlis*,[9] with one or more invited speakers, whose talks are followed by lively discussion with the audience (Figure 5.13; see Diyāb 2003: 188–9; Matthiesen 2009; Yamani 2004: 37–8). Each session of a *nadwa* or *majlis* is dedicated to a specific social, religious, political or cultural issue. The Saudi Ministry of the Interior tolerates these gatherings because they take place within private homes, but monitors them closely and sends the police to shut them down if talks and discussions are suspected of promoting political opposition (Maneval 2010). In spring 2008, I was lucky to attend such a *majlis* featuring a joint concert of traditional Ḥijāzī musicians and a New York jazz band. The audience could even watch the host dancing – a performance unlikely to be seen in public at that time. By way of further example, Sufi rituals, which, since the beginning of Saudi–Wahhabi rule, have also been prohibited in public spaces in Saudi Arabia, survive today in Jeddah and other cities in the region only within the confines of residential buildings. Thus the walls and screens of residential homes offer a refuge for otherwise forbidden practices, heterogeneous identities and divergent worldviews, as well as platforms of exchange for dissident political opinions – in other words, these homes offer a refuge for publics and counterpublics (Warner 2002; see also the next chapter).

One of my interlocutors in the group interview with Effat students (February 2012) asserted that people in Jeddah are ‘just as reserved as

Figure 5.13 Discussion in a *majlis* held in the reception hall of a residential building. Photo: © Stefan Maneval 2012.

everywhere' in Saudi Arabia, 'but you got those little pockets'. She mentioned Saudia City – the gated housing development for Saudi Airlines staff – and the Bengali neighbourhood in Jeddah as examples. She came from a Bengali family herself. According to her, inside these limited and sometimes confined areas, life was 'completely different' from the rest of the city. 'So it's like a country with different countries inside', she concluded, and two other girls in the group who had formerly lived in gated communities confirmed her view. The form, materiality and technical equipment of the architecture, the range of building styles as well as the different lifestyles and multiple ways of making use of residential buildings, all contribute to creating this impression. New Islamic Urbanism with its emphasis on privacy protection through the help of physical boundaries between domestic space and the outside world enables these 'pockets', or cultural enclaves within the city. This helps to explain why, even though it used to be embedded in a discourse of piety and religious renewal, this architectural trend was also embraced by people who do not share the conservative view and lifestyle of its proponents – indeed, by the vast majority of Jeddah's diverse populace. The architecture of enclosure arguably became particularly attractive in the conservative cultural climate of the 1980s and 1990s because it facilitated the creation of 'bubbles' of alternative lifestyles.

Conclusion

Throughout the 1980s and 1990s, among architects and large segments of society, the opinion prevailed that the private sphere should be fortified with the aid of impermeable architectural elements. This approach to the creation and maintenance of private space differed profoundly from that of previous generations. Whereas in the pre-oil era, social conventions and control were used to secure private space within houses regularly frequented by all kinds of visitors, the New Islamic Urbanism proliferating since the 1980s aims at a high degree of enclosure and physical control. This is among the reasons why, in spite of repeated calls to find architectural solutions by seeking inspiration from the past, contemporary architecture looks completely different from its historical precedent.

Today, strict boundaries between inside and outside space exist, resulting in the insulation of interior spaces, which are disconnected from the environment. Air, light, views and unwanted people are prevented from entering a house by means of screens and barriers. As a consequence, it is both possible and necessary to create indoor conditions that constitute a stark contrast to the outside world. Although the sun shines outside, electric lights are required to light up dark interiors even during daytime; outside temperature and humidity are high, whereas air conditioners keep the atmosphere cool and dry indoors, turning houses into 'refrigerators', as two architects from Jeddah phrased it in separate conversations (personal communication, January and November 2009). The lush gardens and swimming pools of housing compounds and some villas contrast with the desert landscape of the surrounding Tihama region. Similarly, social rules imposed in public, for example gender segregation and the veiling of women, can be abandoned within the shelter of a residential building which, for the majority of residents, has become almost exclusively a family space. Residential units are predominantly inhabited by nuclear families, and visited mostly by members of the extended family.

What the inhabitants of these 'different countries within a country', or 'bubbles', as Omar put it, have in common is an extraordinary desire to protect their private sphere, albeit not necessarily for the same reasons as the New Islamic Urbanists. Their conception of private space is sometimes a very different one. It centres, as mentioned in the quotation by Hisham Jomah (1992: 336–9) cited in the previous chapter, around individualism, personal freedom and freedom of choice. I suggest that the architectural insulation of the interior should not be understood as an expression of an all-embracing religious conservatism. Rather, it has to be regarded as the material aspect of particular notions of privacy which find common ground in a strong preference for visual protection and the non-interference of outsiders. For a significant proportion of the population, enclosure of residential buildings constitutes part of their vision of a pious lifestyle. They believe that privacy, in the sense of a sphere protected from views of strangers, is dictated by Islamic law. For others it ensures that they do not have to adhere to the Wahhabi way of life. Inside the home, where no one can see them, they can abandon social rules that are imposed in public.

What has happened to the publics that gathered inside or in front of residential buildings in the past? According to the New Islamic Urbanists, some of whom misleadingly labelled these spaces as semi-public or semi-private, they have been erased without being replaced. Indeed, the gap between public and private space seems to have widened, as the residential home is more secluded than in the past, whereas public space has become an anonymous motorway, apparently devoid of human beings. This observation is, however, only partly correct. While the architectural framework has changed, the entangled relationship between public and private space has been reconfigured. As we have seen, the protected residential home can also serve as a shelter for activities usually associated with the public sphere, such as political debate, and for heterogeneous identities and counterpublics of, for example, gay people, banned religious minorities or political dissidents. On the other hand, there are enclaves of privacy in the public realm. The transformation of public space, the reinterpretation of privacy and the meaning of counterpublics in the early twenty-first century are the topic of the next chapter.

Notes

1. This trend is well documented, e.g. by Bokhari (1978: 304), Tuncalp and al-Ibrahim (1990: 112), al-Hathloul and Mughal (1991: 272) and Eben Saleh (2002: 523).
2. Among the first gated housing developments apart from ARAMCO was a new neighbourhood for state employees in Riyadh, ordered by the Saudi government in 1953 (Fadan 1983: 128–42).
3. As Tawfiq Abu-Gazzeh explains: 'The idea of territory is important in Saudi Arabia where "A man's home is his castle". The use of boundary walls around the house is just one example of the validity of the idea of personal territory. ... Invasion or unpermitted entry by outsiders is a serious matter, and control over access is highly valued' (Abu-Gazzeh 1996: 283).
4. In 2004, 72 per cent of employed women were working in girls' education, 22 per cent in the health sector, 5.3 per cent were social workers and 2 per cent were employed in a university (Za'zū' 2004: 17). In her study of female employment in Jeddah, Lailā bint Ṣāliḥ Muḥammad Za'zū' (2004) shows that, in the 1990s, women of all social strata were working in the education sector. While 59.4 per cent of women working in this sector had a university degree – 80.7 per cent of these being Saudi nationals – 22.4 per cent did not even have a high-school diploma

(Za'zū' 2004: 57–9, 73). Whereas 6 per cent of female employees in the education sector had an income higher than 9,000 SR (approx. 2,400 US $), 21 per cent – most of them non-Saudis – earned less than 3,000 SR per month, approximately 800 US $ at that time. The majority, around 60 per cent, earned between 5,000 and 9,000 SR, or 1,300 and 2,400 US $ (Za'zū' 2004: 77–9). Two-thirds of all female employees working in this field lived in middle-class neighbourhoods to the northeast of Jeddah such as al-Ṣafā, Mushrifa and 'Azīziyya. Yet one could find women working as teachers, kindergarten instructors, university professors or in the administration of a school distributed in all districts of the city (Za'zū' 2004: 90–4).

5. An indicator of the large amount of time these women spent and, even today, still spend at home is a high prevalence of vitamin D deficiency among women as well as children they care for in Jeddah and other Saudi cities – all places with abundant sunlight (see e.g. Abdullah et al. 2002; Siddiqui and Kamfar 2007). One study, for example, notes that, '[i]n Saudi Arabia, the exposure of people generally to the sun is limited, despite of abundant sunlight … Females tend to have less sun exposure due to sociocultural reasons, lack of awareness of the importance of sun exposure for bone health, and for cosmetic reasons thinking that it is harmful. It was noted that girls who had a severe vitamin D deficiency were rarely exposed to the sun and came from lower income families' (Siddiqui and Kamfar 2007: 443).
6. I have already quoted from the interview with Yasemin in chapter 2. The interview was conducted in Arabic.
7. The interviews, conducted in February 2012, were divided into one focus group of four students and two single interviews. The students were selected by an Assistant Professor at Effat University, Dr Gerald Naughton. I had asked him to choose students of both Saudi and non-Saudi origin in order to mirror the diversity of the city's population. After the interviews, Naughton told me that he had selected students he had got to know as unreserved and communicative in his classes.
8. In more general terms, in the conclusion to her discussion of current trends to regulate access to private homes and specialised workplaces, Doreen Massey highlights the fact that 'there will be adventures however the space is designed, whether it be the laboratory, home, or the urban park. The chance encounter intrinsic to spatiality cannot be totally obliterated' (Massey 2005: 180). The same point is made by Wendy Brown (2010) with regard to walls constructed to protect national states.
9. The same term (*majlis*) is used for 'living room', which is literally translated as 'the place/institution where people sit'.

6
Navigating urban space: Jeddah, early twenty-first century

'What is your research actually about?' Dr Hisham had asked me. As a professor of Islamic architecture at King Abdulaziz University (KAU), he had been assigned as my mentor in Jeddah. A few days after my arrival in March 2011, we met in his university studio to pay a visit to numerous deans, chairmen and heads of department at KAU who had provided Dr Hisham with their signature or other forms of support in his efforts to obtain a research visa for me and to arrange my accommodation in the on-campus students' hostel.

'I investigate public and private spaces in Jeddah, past and present', I explained. 'Therefore, I am looking for information about the old city and contemporary neighbourhoods alike.' While one of my benefactors, whom we visited that day, had serious doubts regarding my inquiries about the old city of Jeddah – made apparent in his question, 'Is there an old city?' – Dr Hisham was sceptical about a different part of my quest.

'Past and present, I see', he said, adding, 'but there aren't any public spaces in the contemporary city of Jeddah. Such a thing does not exist.'

For a moment I wondered if I was actually comparing something that had ceased to be with something that had never existed at all. Contemplating what Dr Hisham and the Dean of Graduate Studies and Research had meant and how their subjective experience may have influenced their views helped me regain confidence in my own work. In the case of the dean, the question was simple. As a scientist and a relatively privileged member of society, decrepit houses were perhaps not central to his interests. I soon encountered more people of a comparable social standing – both Saudi nationals and Western expatriates – who, after years of living in Jeddah, had never set foot in the old town. As for Dr Hisham, who had spent several years in the UK and the US and travelled all around the world, he was referring to the squares, plazas, marketplaces or public gardens he had encountered in the heart of many other cities where people meet, socialise, celebrate or assemble, make announcements, wear billboards and demonstrate. As a historian familiar with Jeddah's past he may also have had in mind the market streets and open spaces that had existed in this city in the past. Comparable places are indeed hard to find in the contemporary city. My impression when I visited Jeddah for the first and second times had in fact been similar to the view articulated by Dr Hisham. I was struck by the contrast between the seclusion and, in some cases, fortification of isolated private dwellings on the one hand, and the monotony of a gigantic gridiron motorway on the other (Figure 6.1). Yet, at the time of my conversation with Dr Hisham, I had also discovered forms and places of encounter which serve some of the social functions of a public space, albeit in different ways, and for a different cross-section of citizens. Moreover, I had learned about public expressions of political dissent and opinions that challenged the dominant moral code, which are barely known outside Saudi Arabia.

This chapter deals with the publics which produce these discourses and counter-discourses, as well as the architecture enabling their constitution. I first discuss different factors limiting the availability of public spaces of the type referred to by Dr Hisham. Assuming that opinions on gender segregation, mixing and privacy are essential to an understanding of public space in a Saudi city like Jeddah, I provide an overview of a debate on mixing in confined spaces of encounter, such as seminar rooms and workplaces. The overview of divergent opinions on gender segregation is followed by a presentation of social practices involving different strategies of dealing with the segregation regime. This leads to a discussion of how both Saudi citizens and migrant workers find ways to make their concerns public, although open space designed for public sociability is very limited, and opportunities for the constitution of publics are constrained by the Saudi state.

Routine human encasement in Jeddah

As explained in the previous chapter, people in Jeddah began fortifying their homes and avoiding the public realm because they felt the need to protect their privacy from intrusion and prying eyes. Is it possible that, as a consequence, the streets appear hostile and dangerous because they are largely devoid of human beings? Attempting to cross the dual carriageway to go shopping at a supermarket on the opposite side of Amir Sultan Street, or waiting for the next available cab on the dusty northern fringes

Figure 6.1 King Fahd Street, also known as Sittīn Street. Photo: © Stefan Maneval 2012.

of Medina Road, I had the feeling that I was the only person deliberately setting foot in what was undeniably public space. In Jeddah's contemporary neighbourhoods, only garbage collectors at work are seen walking distances longer than that between a parked vehicle and the next shop.

Everyone else in these districts, which were designed according to the American-style automotive city, seems to go everywhere by car. I learned this during my first period of fieldwork in early 2009, when I had an appointment at the Municipality of Jeddah. I asked the taxi driver to drop me in front of what was clearly the main entrance of the building – a giant flight of steps leading to an ornate entrance gate. Upon reaching the top of the steps, I found the gate closed. Wondering what I was looking for, a guard told me that the official entrance was only used on ceremonial occasions. Access to the building was in fact through the car park. Since my taxi had already left I had to walk around the huge office tower, past an outdoor parking lot in order to enter a multi-storey car park on foot. Sweating and exhausted from my involuntary promenade in the heat of the midday sun, I reached the car park lift, which carried me directly to the air-conditioned reception hall on the upper floor. The building was designed to minimise both visitors' exposure to the sun and the distance to be walked between the parked car and reception hall. This principle is very common in Jeddah. People living in neighbourhoods constructed in the 1970s or later normally enter their cars while still at home, that is to say in the integrated garage on the ground floor of an apartment building or in the car port within the enclosure of a detached house. They park and leave their car within the walled premises of their workplace, in the indoor car park of a shopping centre or office building, or immediately in front of a shop or restaurant. They may not even step out of the car at all before they return home again: not having much else to do, many young men spend the night drifting around aimlessly with friends, occasionally making use of the countless drive-ins at fast-food restaurants, juice bars and ATMs.

Avoidance of the elements certainly has climatic reasons: the weather in Jeddah is hot and humid throughout the year, reaching an average of 24–5°C (average max. 32°) in the winter and 31–2°C (average max. 41°) from May to September, with a relative humidity of approximately 60 to 70 per cent throughout the year.[1] The heat, especially during the summer, is experienced as unpleasant and enervating by expatriates from cooler places and Saudis alike – and much more so than in the past, it seems. Inhabitants of Jeddah constantly keep their cars and houses cool and dry due to the heat. Russell Hitchings and Shu Jun Lee (2008) have shown that the omnipresence of air conditioning in a hot and humid environment leads to decreased tolerance of the outside temperature among the local population. Individual thermal sensitivities are dynamic and can change over the course of months. The liberal use of air conditioning among long-term residents of Jeddah thus leads them to perceive the hot, humid weather of their own hometown as unbearable. As a consequence many people avoid exposure to the weather outside, particularly during the daytime.

But many in Jeddah cannot afford a car, or for that matter an apartment with an indoor car park, let alone a single-family home with a private car port. Male migrant workers from the lowest-income groups can occasionally be seen on bicycles, and a public bus service provides transportation on a small number of routes for those who do not have the money for a private car or taxi. Similarly, the *aswāq* (sing. *sūq*), or shopping areas, in low-income neighbourhoods such as al-Balad, al-Kandara, al-Hindāwiyya and al-Ṣabīl, as well as the narrow streets in densely populated *ʿashwāʾiyyāt* (informal settlements; sing. *ʿashwāʾiyya*) to the south of Jeddah, such as al-Ghulayl, Bitrūmin (Petromin) and al-Karantīna, are routinely frequented by pedestrians. That said, people in Jeddah avoid walking and those who can afford to prefer to bridge the passage from one place to another using a car, ideally one that is air-conditioned.

Urban design and state control

Many stay inside because they are intolerant of the weather. It may also be argued that streets in contemporary neighbourhoods in Jeddah have been designed for cars and not for pedestrians. The city's main streets consist of at least three lanes plus a service road in each direction, and still they are heavily congested since the number of cars keeps rising with the ever-growing populace. Except for a few streets in the old town and its adjacent neighbourhoods, there are no pavements, neither in shopping areas such as Taḥliyya Street nor along the subsidiary streets of residential districts. Public squares and gardens which are open to everyone simply do not exist. Whereas the coastline that reaches southwards from the historic city centre has become a vast industrial area, large strips of land to the north have been sold to private investors who have built exclusive hotels and restaurants or private beach resorts there, obstructing access to the sea for all but a small number of select customers. The remaining coastline has been turned into a sea promenade known as *al-kurnīsh* (corniche). It is the only place within the city area of Jeddah that is officially dedicated to outdoor leisure activities. Highly frequented after sunset by families of the middle and lower classes, it stands as a testament to the demand for more open spaces suitable for picnics, fishing and children's play, as well as walks in the evening breeze.

The construction of streets and facilities in Saudi Arabia is financed exclusively by oil revenues. The Saudi state, acting as the sponsor of infrastructure, does not depend on the taxpayer.[2] This provides the government with 'a strong tool to intervene in the planning and development of all settlements', explain Saleh al-Hathloul and Muhammad Aslam Mughal (2004: 611), both employees of the Saudi Ministry of Municipal and Rural Affairs. The Saudi government has an interest in providing utilities and services because these are key factors in rendering it legitimate. At the same time, the state and its administrative institutions, notably the Ministry of Municipal and Rural Affairs and the Municipality of Jeddah, can model the urban infrastructure in a way that best suits its own interests.

In his study of male youth subculture in contemporary Riyadh, Pascal Menoret (2014) discusses urban planning as a means of state control. His focus is mainly on the migrant rural communities who flooded the capital from the 1960s onwards, making up more than half the population of Riyadh already by 1968 (Menoret 2014: 82–3). The urban population and the authorities regarded the rural migrants who settled in slums constructed out of sheet metal, recycled wood panels and paperboard with anxiety and aversion.[3] The royal family, recalling the armed insurgency of the *ikhwān* movement of the late 1920s (Kostiner 1990; Steinberg 2002: 453–69; Vassiliev 2000: 268–81), feared an accumulation of under-privileged Bedouin in the cities for their potential to mobilise against the government and foment social unrest (Menoret 2014: 84–5).[4] From the mid-1970s onwards, rural migrants were moved to designated 'Low Income Neighbourhoods' well away from the city centre. More attractive pieces of land were, and presumably are still, frequently gifted to members of the royal family and their clients in return for loyalty (Menoret 2014: 62, 77–8, 91–2, 99).

Jeddah is not Riyadh and, to my knowledge, rural migration was regarded with less suspicion in the harbour city (see al-Turkī and Bāqādir 2006: 74–5). Yet the municipality of Jeddah struggled with urban sprawl and unplanned settlements as well, and the Āl Saʿūd's attitude to urban planning was roughly the same all over the country. Consequently, the urban development of Jeddah followed a similar course as in Riyadh, although different consulting firms were commissioned: both cities were designed for cars and not for pedestrians. The urban territory was segmented by a grid of streets. And residents who could not afford the down payment for a house, which was required in order to take out interest-free loans from the Real Estate Development Fund, were pushed to the margins of the city. There, the authorities were unable to put an end to the construction of shanties.

The grid pattern of Riyadh and Jeddah not only makes the provision of civic services easier, it also facilitates policing and the control of streets and citizens.[5] For the authorities, observing what is going on is much easier in the broad and straight streets of northern Jeddah than in the maze of irregular lanes and winding footpaths of the old town or adjacent low-income neighbourhoods of the 1950s. The design of the streets makes it unlikely that demonstrations and other activities that challenge the authority of the state will be carried out. 'The absence of separate pedestrian walkways in most local residential streets and the increase in street area exposed to the heat and dust ... discourage the residents from using the streets for social activities', writes the urban planner Waleed K. al-Hemaidi (2001: 187).[6] As an assistant professor at the urban planning department at King Saud University, Riyadh, al-Hemaidi is careful not to blame the authorities for the urban design he despises. Yet it is hardly surprising that the Saudi state, which does not grant citizens the freedom of assembly and the right to protest, does not provide public places suitable for such activities either. The urban design follows the logic that, if a public gathering place does not exist, it cannot be occupied by demonstrators.

Nevertheless, under flyovers and on empty lots, groups of youths can be observed playing football. Some of these young men are of African origin, and some are from Yemen, Saudi Arabia and other Arab countries (personal observation and conversation, January 2012). South Asian men sometimes gather at larger roundabouts, such as Maidān al-Baiʿa to the north of the historic city centre, to play cricket. When the temperature drops after sunset, Southeast Asians, chiefly Filipinos, unpack their camping equipment and have picnics on greened roundabouts in northern Jeddah. Fully veiled women can be seen jogging – or rather walking quickly, as jogging is considered inappropriate for women – along certain roads in Jeddah (Figure 6.2). As this habit is particularly popular among pregnant women advised to engage in some kind of physical exercise, it has earned King Abdullah Street, a street favoured by many joggers, the nickname *shāriʿ al-ḥāmil*, or Pregnancy Road. Men also jog, albeit to a lesser degree. In the historic city centre known as al-Balad today, people of all nationalities do grocery shopping, have a coffee at the Indonesian cafes in front of Corniche Plaza – an old-fashioned shopping centre opposite the ultra-modern National Bank tower – and buy cloth or *ḥajj*

Figure 6.2 A woman jogging on the roadside. Photo: © Stefan Maneval 2012.

souvenirs in the *sūq*, or spices and cosmetics at a Hadrami incense dealer. Low-income neighbourhoods, especially those to the east and south of the historic city centre, such as al-Sabīl, al-Hindāwiyya, al-Ṣuḥayfa and al-Kandara, are characterised by vibrant street life at night. In these districts, young men set up table tennis, table football and pool tables on roadsides (Figure 6.3). Youths spend their spare time there from around 9 p.m. until well past midnight. Other men gather in one of the numerous *marākīz* (sing. *mirkāz*), or sitting platforms, still in use in these districts. They may also have rented a small separate room, or *nādī* (club), for the purpose of meeting friends on a regular basis, watching football together, playing video games, exchanging news, joking and forging alliances and networks. Men's meeting places outside the home are particularly important in areas where houses are too small to provide an indoor division between female household members and male guests. Women are also a common sight in the streets of these neighbourhoods, much more so than in residential districts of the upper and middle classes. They fetch dinner at a restaurant around the corner in al-Hindāwiyya and they go shopping in the *sūq* of al-Kandara. Unlike men, however, they do not rest and socialise in the streets (personal observation, March 2011).

The only people unlikely to be seen in the poor southern districts of Jeddah are Western expatriates or middle- and upper-class Saudis, who

Figure 6.3 Youths playing table football along the roadside. Photo: © Stefan Maneval 2011.

avoid the so-called *ʿashwāʾiyyāt* or informal settlements of the lower social classes. Dr Hisham's urban planning perspective may explain why, in an earlier remark quoted at the beginning of this chapter, he denies the existence of public spaces in the contemporary city of Jeddah. Another explanation could be that he is unaware of these spaces. Even if Dr Hisham has observed migrant workers spending an evening with their families on a roundabout in Medina Road or youths playing football on the undeveloped area of the old airport when passing by in a car, partaking in them would be unthinkable for him.

The occupation of undeveloped land, car parks, roadsides and roundabouts by migrant workers, youths and the poor is regarded with suspicion by the authorities. As stated in the 2009 Jeddah Strategic Plan:

> Open space and leisure facilities include formal city and local parks and gardens and coastal recreation areas such as the Corniche as well as leisure centres, amusement parks, stadiums, public realm areas and streets. ... These facilities are currently limited in Jeddah, while those that exist are of variable quality and are often overcrowded. As a result, many people use vacant land, roundabouts and median strips along the sides of roads as open space.
>
> (Jeddah Strategic Plan 2009: 305)

Worried about 'significant', though unspecified, 'safety, health and management issues' resulting from the occupation of the margins of urban space, the Municipality of Jeddah has formulated the goal of providing more 'high quality open space and leisure facilities' (Jeddah Strategic Plan 2009: 326). The Jeddah Strategic Plan contains two images exemplifying how the planners in the Municipality envision 'high-quality open space'. The pictures show a vast car park in front of the shiny facades of high-rise buildings facing the sea at Jeddah's North Corniche. But who can afford to live in these buildings? Who owns the yacht lying near the shore? Who dines in the restaurant with the nice sea view? Certainly not the same people who picnic, socialise and play on median strips and undeveloped land. In other words, vacant land, roundabouts and median strips are not supposed to be used as public space. None of these places was designed for the purpose of outdoor sociability. Their unofficial function is not mentioned on the map. The appropriation of marginal open spaces is the undesired side effect of land speculation, social inequality and urban design which combines the logic of the authoritarian state with the American model automotive city.

Cars

A closer look at how people use their cars reveals that neither the climate nor the authoritarian state suffice to explain why so many people in Jeddah, particularly Saudi nationals, prefer to spend most of their time indoors and to reduce the passage between their home or another building and the car. Given that a car provides sufficient visual protection, passengers tend to behave according to the norms of domestic space. In the back seats of privately owned vehicles with tinted windows, for example, women do not feel the need to cover their faces. This also means that other people are expected to be mindful of female passengers and respect their privacy, as I have myself learned by way of a faux pas.

It is very common in Jeddah as well as elsewhere in Saudi Arabia to roll down the window and ask other drivers for directions. Everyone immediately responds by rolling down their own window and giving an answer, using roundabouts as landmarks or providing a count of intersections, crossings and traffic lights. Stopping at a traffic light with my rented car one night in January 2012, I rolled down the window to ask the driver of a large SUV for directions to a particular address in northern Jeddah. The driver responded only hesitatingly. Some days later, while driving with my friend Mustafa sitting next to me on the front seat, I found out why my request had been met with bewilderment. Mustafa, being a native speaker, was usually the one asking for directions.

'Why don't you ask this one?' I asked, desperate to end an odyssey during which we found ourselves back at the same intersection again and again.

'Impossible. There are women sitting in the car', he replied.

'But you'd only talk to the driver and not to his wife', I remarked in surprise.

'He might still feel offended', Mustafa explained. 'Here, if women are present, people are very careful not to disturb them.'

I suddenly remembered that there had been a veiled woman sitting next to the driver of the SUV the other day. The episode shows that people in Jeddah avoid walking not simply because they have little tolerance for the local climate and shun physical exercise. Amidst an unpredictable public space, a sphere characterised by chance encounters resulting in verbal and visual communication with strangers, many inhabitants of the city prefer to move from one place to another in the bubble of privacy provided by a car.

The secluded space of an individual car offers and assumes a level of privacy even without visual screens and tinted windows, as the following incident illustrates. One night I was sitting in a ramshackle Hyundai driven by my friend Mustafa's cousin, an elementary school teacher of religion who was born and raised in Mecca. In the car that stopped next to ours at a traffic light, we saw two women smoking. Conservative Saudis reject smoking – after the Saudi–Wahhabi conquest, it had even been prohibited for some years (Rathjens and von Wissmann 1947: 80). Even the less puritanical consider smoking to be unsuitable for women, which is why women are normally not seen smoking in public. The two women in the car were accompanied by two young men. They could have been their brothers, but more likely they were friends; at least, they did not appear to be on a family outing. They were playing loud music, smoking, partying and having fun right there in the car, and they did not bother to conceal it. Mustafa's cousin got upset.

'What is this?!' he yelled.

But he could not help it. As soon as the traffic light turned green, we heard tyres shrieking and watched the tail lights of the car speedily disappearing into the night (personal observation, January 2009). Even without tinted screens, the car grants its passengers privacy in the sense that no outsider can properly interfere. This can be a sort of privacy which has nothing to do with *ʿār* (honour) and *ʿayb* (shame; see chapter 2), but rather with *ḥurriyya*, or freedom. *Anā ḥurr* – 'I am free (to do what I want)' – is an expression used in the sense of 'This is none of your, or anyone else's, business'. The girls did not bother to speak to us, but their behaviour was an ostentatious display of this attitude made possible by the secluded mobility of the car.

Both cases described here indicate that a private vehicle, although moving in public, has much in common with the screened and isolated contemporary Saudi home (see chapter 5). In the first case, it serves as a physical barrier protecting the privacy of a family from undesired contact with strangers. In other cases it allows women to unveil and smoke, and men to pick up girlfriends, prostitutes and other men. If it does not provide enough visual protection, speed helps passengers to escape other people's control. The car is in this sense a private living room on wheels. Just like the fortified and visually protected home discussed in the previous chapter, it serves to enact different conceptions of privacy. One centres on non-interference with strangers of the opposite sex, as demanded by a particular version of piety. Another one emphasises personal freedom and permits, in some instances, the circumvention of a rigid moral code. Enabling these different, if not contrary notions of privacy – which all emphasise non-interference of strangers – a car, preferably one with tinted windows, provides a means of transportation that corresponds perfectly with the spirit, and ambiguity, of New Islamic Urbanism.

As is evident from the cases I have presented, people's notions of privacy determine how they access, or move and behave in, the public realm. In the following sections I will explore different attitudes to two Arabic concepts – *khalwa* and *ikhtilāṭ* – which inform divergent notions of privacy. In Arabic, these terms are used to distinguish between two forms of mixing. The former translates as intimacy or seclusion, and the latter refers to mixing in groups.

Encounters on the stairs: Strategies of avoiding *khalwa*

The transition between home and car, or interior and exterior space in general, presents a peril especially to women. I became aware of this when I visited my Lebanese friend Hamid, who had spent more than half his life in Jeddah. Climbing up the stairs to his apartment, we encountered a female neighbour. Much to my surprise, he turned around, pressed himself against the wall and demonstratively looked in another direction. I thought that there was enough space for her to pass by.

'She is Saudi', he explained. 'After a while you'll learn that they have to be treated differently.' Something can be gleaned about the precariousness of stairwells in Jeddah from this one instance. As a common space and interface between the home and the outside world, stairwells necessitate specific rules for simultaneous use by men and women. The prevalent rules of privacy forbid verbal, visual and physical contact between unrelated men and women. By pressing his body from top to toe against the wall, Hamid demonstrated that he would not take advantage of the opportunity to look at or touch his neighbour while passing her on a narrow flight of stairs.

Hamid's behaviour was not over-cautious, but expected of him, because shared spaces connecting the home with the street in apartment buildings are in fact seen as problematic by many Saudis, as the history of the Rush Housing Project (*mashrūʿ al-iskān al-sarīʿ*) on Jeddah's King Faḥd Street reveals. Due to a severe lack of housing, the Ministry of Public Works and Housing sponsored the construction of 32 pre-fabricated high-rise apartment blocks in an area between the old airport and the historic city centre (Figure 6.4).[7] After a construction period of less than two and a half years, the so-called Jeddah Towers, comprising a total of 1,936 generously sized middle-class apartments, were finished in 1979 – but

Figure 6.4 The Jeddah Rush Housing Project. In the foreground: facilities of the pilgrims' city at the old airport. Photo: © Stefan Maneval 2012.

no one moved in. The official explanation for the vacancies, which lasted for several years, was that, by the time of the completion of the development, a demand for housing did not exist any more and that there was now an over-abundance of residential units in Jeddah (al-Hathloul and Mughal 1991; Tuncalp and al-Ibrahim 1990: 115–17). Considering the accelerated growth of the city throughout the 1980s and given that other housing developments consisting of single-family units and small multi-family buildings did not stay tenantless, this explanation is hardly convincing. One of my interlocutors, an English-speaking Yemeni who moved to Jeddah in the 1960s, commented on the uninhabited apartment blocks as follows: 'It was a shame because there was a huge lack of houses among Saudis at that time, and from far away you could see those high towers standing there, all vacant.' According to him, the reason for the vacancy was reluctance among Saudis to move to a building with many shared spaces:

> Saudis were not used to living in a flat with all its consequences. They didn't like the idea that others could see when you come and leave and things like that. Sharing the same lift, for example: they didn't like the idea that their women would take the lift with

> another man. At least, that is what was said to explain why no one wanted to move in.
>
> (Personal communication, January 2009)

The towers had been built especially for Saudis, yet without taking their preferences and habits into consideration (Krause 1991: 30–1). Years later, the government decided to sell the apartments to Saudis who then rented them to foreigners with different conceptions of privacy, as my interlocutor explained.

While hinting at the lack of reliable information about the circumstances of the vacancies – 'that is what was said to explain why no one wanted to move in' – my informant corroborated the plausibility of the account by referring to his own Saudi neighbours' behaviour:

> Even where I live – there are four Saudi families living in the same house [an apartment block comprising six units] and it is something like an unwritten rule that, if you see one of them entering the lift with his wife, you try to avoid taking the same lift, even if you live on the same floor.
>
> (Personal communication, January 2009)

He added that neither would he share the lift with a Saudi woman in a public building.

The presence of a woman and an unrelated (non-*maḥram*) man in a closed room is termed *khalwa* and considered as *ḥarām*, or forbidden by Islamic law, by the vast majority of religious scholars in Saudi Arabia (al-Rasheed 2013: 159). Many Saudis thus regard shared spaces in apartment buildings as problematic, and a man entering a lift already occupied by a Saudi woman could cause her severe trouble. Unless she belongs to the liberal, Western-oriented elite, she would find herself in a situation which in her view conflicts with God's own rulings. The same can be said of pious men, who consider avoidance of *khalwa* as a religious demand. Even if someone does not have such strict beliefs, he or she would feel uncomfortable in a situation defined as *khalwa* due to other people's disapproval. My Yemeni interlocutor, for example, refrained from using the lift with Saudi women because he did not want to offend anyone, and many women in Saudi Arabia avoid being alone in a room together with a non-*maḥram* man because they do not want other people to speak or think ill of them. Hamid's reaction to meeting his neighbour on the stairs was an adequate answer to a situation when *khalwa* was unavoidable.

Debate on *ikhtilāṭ*

While Saudi religious scholars forbid *khalwa* more or less unanimously, there has been much debate about *ikhtilāṭ*, or mixing between the sexes in public and within groups of people, in recent years.[8] In 2004, at one of the 10 National Dialogue conferences held by the Saudi government between 2003 and 2015 (see Drewes 2010; Hamzawy 2008; Thompson 2014), conservative clerics dominated the debate, leading to recommendations which, according to critics, confirmed the status quo rather than initiating change that challenged it. Published in Saudi newspapers, the recommendations issued by the conference – which was especially dedicated to the topic of women in Saudi society – emphasised that women's 'natural role' and 'basic duty' was at home within the family. The document dealt with questions of education, employment and mobility only against the backdrop of this notion of 'the nature of women' (Dankowitz 2004). In contrast, four years later, at a National Dialogue conference on the topic of work and employment opportunities, prominent voices demanded greater acceptance not just of women working outside the home but even of mixed workplaces (Drewes 2010: 44–6; al-Rasheed 2013: 159–60). In the reign of King ʿAbdullāh (2005–15), the Saudi state was inclined to demonstrate commitment to gender equality and women's rights. In 2005, the election of two women to the administrative council of the Jeddah Chamber of Commerce was celebrated in the media. Mixed delegations started to accompany ministers and princes on travels abroad. Nūra al-Fāyiz was appointed the first female deputy minister in Saudi history in 2009. In the same year, the co-educational King Abdullah University of Science and Technology (KAUST) was inaugurated in the north of Jeddah (Le Renard 2014: 40–3; al-Rasheed 2013: 149–51). New women's universities were founded, and in the 2015 municipal elections, women were allowed to vote and stand as candidates for the first time.

Not all of these steps have gone unchallenged. Conservative *ʿulamā* condemned the increased mixing of the sexes at work and in education. In a TV interview on the occasion of the opening of KAUST broadcast by the private TV station al-Majd, Shaykh Saʿad al-Shithrī, member of the Council of Senior *ʿUlamā*, complained that 'in mixed-gender universities we see lots of evil/corruption'. He warned that, in those places, 'men can look at women and women can look at men, and their hearts might catch flame' (TV interview published in *al-Watan*, 30 September 2009, quoted in Meijer 2010: 86). His statement triggered an acrimonious debate between the relatively liberal press and the conservative *ʿulamā* supporting al-Shithrī. Although the shaykh had chosen his words with care, not failing to praise King ʿAbdullāh's initiative to establish the new, prestigious university, journalists writing for newspapers such as *Okaz* and *al-Watan* accused him of questioning the king's religious integrity. On 4 October 2009, one week after the TV interview, al-Shithrī was dismissed from his dual positions as a member of the Council of Senior *ʿUlamā* and the Permanent Council of Religious Studies and Fatwas (Meijer 2010: 85–7).

Two months later, in December 2009, Shaykh Aḥmad bin Qāsim al-Ghāmidī, head of the Committee for the Promotion of Virtue and Prevention of Vice in Mecca, published an article in the Jeddah-based newspaper *Okaz* in which he argued that *ikhtilāṭ* was a recent concept and its prohibition was not based on Islamic law.[9] In interviews and public talks al-Ghāmidī addressed other sensitive issues in a similarly radical tone. He cast doubts upon the authority of the *ʿulamā* on questions such as compulsory common prayers and the closing of shops during prayers, and he demanded a reform and reconstitution of the Committee for the Promotion of Virtue and Prevention of Vice. These opinions, voiced by a high-ranking member of the so-called *hay'a* (committee), scandalised conservative religious scholars. They tried to discredit al-Ghāmidī by questioning his expertise and competence. His publications were denounced on internet forums, and he was physically threatened. Yet, unlike Shaykh Saʿad al-Shithrī, he remained in office (Meijer 2010: 87–91).

The two cases indicate a shift in the political climate since the 1990s, when the state took the wind out of the Islamists' sails by introducing strict rules of gender segregation and giving greater power to the so-called religious police to execute those rules. Large parts of the Saudi population had embraced the conservative morality preached by the *shuyūkh al-ṣaḥwa*. In late 2009, in contrast, the Saudi government fired a hitherto loyal religious official for carefully repeating the *ʿulamā* establishment's mantra of gender segregation. At the same time it backed a leading member of the *hay'a* who doubted the validity of strict injunctions against *ikhtilāṭ* as it was currently practised in Saudi Arabia, called the authority of the *ʿulamā* into question and advocated a public debate on the mistakes of the Committee for the Promotion of Virtue and Prevention of Vice, which, above all, happened to be the organisation he worked for.

The disparate responses to both al-Shithrī's and al-Ghāmidī's public statements show that there is a variety of opinions about gender segregation among Saudis. A growing number of religious scholars maintain that *ikhtilāṭ* is permissible in certain situations. Outspoken opponents of *ikhtilāṭ*, on the other hand, can be found among the ranks of conservative ʿ*ulamā*, but also among female Islamists. For them, as for adherents of the Islamic Revival movement treated in chapters 4 and 5, avoidance of mixed spaces is a religious precept. Following this logic, the religious scholar Nūra al-Saʿad, for example, rejects mixing at workplaces and universities 'because it restricts us and limits our freedom at work and education' (al-Saʿad in an open letter published on the website www.harfnews.org, translated by al-Rasheed 2013: 162). She thus speaks for those whose reading of the sources of Islam leads them to reject *ikhtilāṭ* even while supporting women's work and engagement in spheres outside the home and family. Alongside other women Islamists she objects to *ikhtilāṭ* because, as many women and their families are against it, they would refrain from higher education and employment if those sectors involved mixing. Following al-Saʿad's line of argument, more gender-segregated spaces would be required to widen women's range of activities (al-Rasheed 2013: 159–63). As Amélie Le Renard (2014: 138) has observed in her study of female public spaces in Riyadh, even some progressive women prefer women-only workplaces because they enjoy greater freedom in the absence of men. Unlike in mixed spaces, where they have to wear an ʿ*abāya* all the time, they can wear different clothes, such as jeans, for example, use make-up and reveal their hair.

Masculine, feminine: The duplication of spaces

While the debate on *ikhtilāṭ* was going on, one could observe how the contrary positions manifested in two divergent trends in urban development and public space. The first, epitomised by the inauguration of the co-educational KAUST, embraces more mixed spaces. The second trend, favoured, among others, by conservative ʿ*ulamā* and female Islamists, is a duplication of spaces – the creation of male and female versions of the same public space, or of female institutions parallel to existing male ones. Since the 1980s, banks, large mosques, ministries and other government organisations have had female branches (Le Renard 2008, 2014: 36–40). During the reign of King ʿAbdullāh, this solution was more widely implemented: King Abdulaziz University, like many other Saudi universities, has both a male and a female campus; upscale cafes, larger restaurants, beach resorts and some shopping malls used to have a family section and an area reserved for men. Both trends have continued since King ʿAbdullāh's demise, with a noticeable tendency towards more mixed spaces.[10]

A small incident in 2012 illustrates the wavering course of action of the authorities vis-à-vis these two options and its implications for the social production of public spaces. Having discovered the art exhibition 'We need to talk' of the artists' group Edge of Arabia, I wanted to see it with my friend Mustafa. When we tried to enter the venue we were stopped at the entrance.

'You are not allowed to enter', the security guard told us, pointing to a sign at the entrance door, a sheet of paper affixed to the door with a piece of tape. *Li-l-ʿā'ilāt faqaṭ*, the sign read – families only. The previous times I had visited the exhibition no such sign had existed and the event had been open to men and women, families and bachelors alike. I had in fact been surprised at seeing elegant ladies next to unaccompanied young men and a mixed group of students, among them a young woman with short hair and no headscarf. On my first visit to the exhibition I had got to know Hamid from Lebanon, who later taught me how to behave on the stairs in the event that a Saudi woman passes by. He was at that time working as an exhibition guard inside the building. When the security guard refused to let Mustafa and me in, I called Hamid on the phone and asked if he could help us, which he immediately did. Once inside the exhibition space, Mustafa and I had plenty of time to see the artworks. Afterwards we went to one of the luxurious cafes in the same building, where I had previously enjoyed an espresso and a magnificent view of the Red Sea and the harbour of Jeddah. Soon, a waiter came. But instead of taking our order he told us that men were not allowed to sit where we had seated ourselves. We tried another cafe where screens were set up on the terrace to create a division between the male and the family sections. Small in size and with ample space between them, the screens were obviously only meant to serve as reminders of gender segregation rather than preventing male customers from catching sight of women. Still, I had seen women sitting on one side of the demarcation and men on the other side. Even here we were asked to leave.

'What's the matter?' I asked the waiter. 'I've sat here before.'

'*Amr malakī*', he replied – a royal order. It had been issued by Prince Nāyif (who died in June 2012), the Minister of the Interior known for his conservatism and rigour.

'Have there been any problems?' I wanted to know.

'Yes, there have been problems', was the answer. Hamid later told me that young men had haunted the cafes and restaurants to flirt with girls. The entire premises were therefore closed to single males now.

The brief period of mixing at a public event and of a merely symbolic gender division in the cafes on the same premises had come to an abrupt end. The closure of the venue for unaccompanied men reminds us that the duplication of spaces has its limits. Due to financial reasons, spatial constraints and logistical obstacles, not every space can be duplicated. In the case of the exhibition and cafe, this led to the closure of the place for single men. Other places, such as some cafes and restaurants, cannot offer a family section and are therefore not accessible for women. Nevertheless, I consider the episode to represent an experiment with *ikhtilāṭ*. It illustrates how the mixing of men and women in public places is negotiated not only in newspapers, TV interviews and fatwas, but also in situ, i.e. in the places concerned. By visiting certain places, such as the exhibition and cafes, and by pushing the boundaries of gender segregation in a specific direction, or even transgressing them, people contribute to these debates as well. The fact that such experiments were carried out in and around 2012, and that the sheet of paper at the door could be removed as easily as it had been affixed there, suggests that Prince Nāyif's 'royal order' was not the final word on the matter.

The duplication of spaces reflects an imaginary division of society into two distinct spheres – one for men and another for women – that produces powerful social structures. With the vast majority of political offices held by men, strong publics, to return to the terminology introduced in chapter 2, are still overwhelmingly masculine in Saudi Arabia today. Leadership positions in a university with both a male and a female campus, such as King Abdulaziz University, are occupied by men.[11] While more than half of the university students in Saudi Arabia are female, the list of subjects they are allowed to study is limited – mostly disciplines related to education, health, religion and design, but also IT and law. Many occupations are also restricted to men – women cannot become judges, for example. Under the reign of King ʿAbdullāh, companies were allowed to be run by women as long as they were women-only businesses (Le Renard 2014: 43), and in February 2018, women were granted the right to open their own businesses without the consent of a male 'guardian', normally the husband or father. Still, the employment rate of women is among the lowest in the world, and they made up approximately 16 per cent of the total workforce in 2018.[12] Women's choices and opportunities concerning their professional careers are thus far more limited than those of men (see Doumato 1999; Prokop 2005; Yamani 1996; Zaʿzūʿ 2004: 17). In addition, in cities designed for car traffic, the ban on driving for women severely constrained their movements for many decades. It was lifted in 2018, but the notion that women should not drive cars can be expected to persist, and prevent many women from driving, for many more years.

However, as critical studies on masculinity have shown for other patriarchal systems of society, access to the privileges that a state or a society grants men is often limited to certain types of men (see e.g. Carrigan, Connell and Lee 1985; Connell and Messerschmidt 2005; Ghoussoub and Sinclair-Webb 2000). In the Saudi case it depends heavily on factors such as social background, religious confession and nationality. Although certain professions and public offices are reserved for men, for example, they are beyond the reach of most male residents of Jeddah. Opportunities to make a career and gain access to decision-making positions differ tremendously. Family background is a decisive factor, and in Saudi Arabia a family name reveals much about a person's geographical origin as well as tribal affiliation or family background.[13] Political dissidents, religious minorities, especially the Shia in the Eastern Province,[14] and people labelled as Bedouin[15] are among those who, due to their social, religious or ethnic background, do not benefit from the patriarchal structure of the Saudi state and who face severe obstacles to constituting publics and obtaining public positions.[16] The most under-privileged members of Saudi society are the millions of migrant labourers who drive taxis, collect rubbish, clean toilets and floors of public buildings and shopping malls, sell garments and agricultural produce, construct buildings and roads, maintain the outdoor areas of gated housing estates, and serve tea, coffee and dinner in cafes and restaurants in every Saudi city.[17] Immigrants do not have the same rights and opportunities as Saudi nationals.[18] They are not allowed to keep their passport but have to give it to their respective employer or patron (*kafīl*), which makes them much more dependent on their employers than Saudi employees. Not all migrant workers are poor – white-collar workers and experts, doctors, pharmacists, architects, engineers and scientists from all around the world come to Saudi Arabia for higher salaries or better career opportunities than they can find in their home countries (Johnson 2010). However, the majority of the approximately 8 million immigrants, or 63 per cent of the working population (2004 statistics; cf. Dehne 2010), hold a position where they receive orders from Saudi employers or superiors, and not uncommonly from both male and female customers. Considered as unsuitable for marriage with a Saudi woman due to the difference in status, male migrant workers are allowed to work in places otherwise limited to women or families.[19]

Saudi women, on the other hand, are often far more powerful than these men. While not denying gender inequality in general, scholars such as Soraya Altorki (1986), Amélie Le Renard (2011, 2014), Madawi al-Rasheed (2013) and Mai Yamani (2000) have shown that gender segregation in Saudi Arabia does not preclude women from voicing their opinion, participating in public debate and having a social life beyond that of their own family. In sum, while women's opportunities in general are more restricted than men's, the social hierarchies within Saudi society and the structural racism separating Saudis from non-nationals can have a much deeper impact on a person's opportunities than the hierarchy of genders. This includes his or her access to the privilege of a private sphere or a public office, and to certain spaces in the city. The sign at the entrance to the Edge of Arabia exhibition indicates that women can access some places more easily than men. The episode also shows that being a white Westerner is an advantage when it comes to circumventing the rules of gender segregation, and that knowing the right person to call is another. One can only speculate whether I would have been stopped at the entrance had I come alone, but it is very unlikely that Mustafa would have been allowed to enter without a German at his side.

Whereas the impact of gender segregation on women's lives in Saudi Arabia has been discussed at length in books, journals and newspaper articles, male perspectives on gender segregation have been widely overlooked in both media coverage and scholarly writing on Saudi Arabia. My aim, in this and the following sections, is to consider various men's and women's views and experiences to provide a more balanced approach to gendered spaces and social practices.[20]

Negotiating gender segregation (1): A man's world

'That's how it goes in Jeddah', Hamid sighed, concluding our conversation on the closure of the exhibition venue to single males. 'As a single, life really sucks here.' For him as well as for other unmarried men I talked to it was beyond doubt that the segregation regime led to restriction of movement and opportunities for men as much as for women. Whereas women used to depend, and often still depend, on a male driver to reach any spot in the city, for unaccompanied men entry to many places is strictly forbidden. Gated public gardens, amusement parks or the food courts of some upmarket shopping malls, for example, used to be designated 'families only' – which meant that women had access with or without men, while men were only allowed to enter in the company of women (Figure 6.5).

In Saudi Arabia, men seem to enjoy greater freedom in public because the male dress code is less rigid than the female. The rule that women are allowed to see men, but men must not look at women,

Figure 6.5 Amusement park in northern Jeddah. Photo: © Stefan Maneval 2011.

however, sets narrow limits on men's freedom of movement. One night at the corniche in March 2011, I got to know Ahmad, a 25-year-old state employee working for airport security. I was sitting on the elevated walkway between the street and the beach, observing what was going on in front of me and taking notes. A Westerner sitting there alone, writing in a notebook, must have been a strange sight, so Ahmad sat down beside me and asked what I was doing. We spent an hour conversing. Ahmad's family was originally from Abha in the southwest of Saudi Arabia, but he was born and raised in Jeddah. Open-minded and outgoing, he called me on the phone the next day to meet up again. We agreed to meet in the same place on the corniche, which was one of Ahmad's favourite spots in the city, as he told me (Figure 6.6). After a walk, we sat down on a small concrete structure – a piece of modern art used as a playground by children. Two minutes later, a man picnicking with his family in front of us at a distance of several metres got up and asked Ahmad to look for another place to sit. Although all his female family members were fully veiled, sitting in our field of vision made him or them feel uncomfortable. As Ahmad could not find another place for us to sit without offending someone by looking in the direction of the women, we continued walking. Being male was not to our advantage that night.

Figure 6.6 Families picnicking at the Corniche. Photo: © Stefan Maneval 2011.

In mixed spaces accessible to all, men have to be very careful to avoid intruding into other people's privacy. Unmarried men like Ahmad or Hamid in particular are advised to keep a cautious distance from unrelated women in public. With hardly any public leisure facilities available, they can meet their friends either in the male section of cafes or at home. A woman, on the other hand, is officially not supposed to be accompanied by men other than her husband or closest kin (father, brother, son, uncle). Access to many male spaces is generally forbidden for women. According to one of my contacts, however, pretending to be siblings opens many doors. A Lebanese man in his mid-twenties, my interlocutor said he never had to prove that he actually was the woman's brother he claimed to be (personal communication, January 2009).

In order to pretend to be a woman's brother or cousin, a man has to get to know her first. This is not an easy task in a city which follows a strict segregation regime. But it is not completely impossible either. When I was out for a walk together with Ahmad at the corniche, he suddenly interrupted our conversation to call 'a friend who had run out of phone credit'. When his friend answered the phone, Ahmad's voice immediately turned softer. His use of the female forms of pronouns corroborated my assumption that his friend was a girl. He asked her to tell him her name, which she refused. So he called her *qalbī* – my heart. What followed was a mix of mutual exchange of biographic data – age, origin, profession – and flirtation. 'Qalbī' claimed to be 18 years old, she was from Egypt and worked in Jeddah as a hairdresser. When Ahmad finished the conversation after a few minutes of small talk, giggling and reciting verses from a passionate love song, I asked him how he had obtained the girl's phone number. He replied that he had given her his own number earlier that day in a shopping mall. She had responded with a text message while we were walking down the corniche.

Whereas some shopping centres for the lower- and medium-income groups have always been mixed, upmarket shopping malls in Jeddah used to be gender-divided before the reign of King Salmān. Situated near the coastline in the very north of Jeddah, an exclusive mall featuring several Western coffee bar franchises was particularly inventive in dealing with gender segregation. It had a rather common horizontal gender division: the ground floor was reserved for men, the upper floor for families and women. On the first floor, the entrance hall of the building is spanned by a bridge used as a 'families-only' sitting area for one of the coffee bars. Many female customers preferred the seats immediately next to the transparent balustrade facing the entrance of the building. From there, they could watch other customers entering the building and, exposed like actors on a stage, be seen by them. Since they were officially sitting in the family and female section, many of them did not feel obliged to wear the *niqāb*, the part of the veil covering the faces of most Saudi women in those years. Some did not even cover their hair. Women sitting on this stage obviously sought and found some public attention. Besides this coffee bar, the mall contained one of the few cafes in Jeddah where women could regularly be seen sitting at a table in front of the building, an area usually reserved for male customers. Although these women were mostly foreigners – my informant Helen claims to have started this trend – the place was exceptional. Even in upmarket shopping malls and cafes applying gender segregation in rather playful ways, and in mixed shopping centres for the medium- and lower-income groups in the city centre, it was not acceptable for men to strike up a conversation with women. Yet one could from time to time observe a man dropping a small piece of paper containing his telephone number while passing a young woman, as Ahmad had done.

Other men used to write their telephone numbers on the back of their own cars, hoping that some woman would call them (Figure 6.7). Still another means used to establish contact between men and women is the Bluetooth technology of mobile phones and laptop computers. This medium of communication allowed men to contact women, or women to contact men, without physically approaching one another. Since the range of the wireless interconnection is short, using it for this purpose requires a mixed environment, such as cafes and lounges in luxurious Western hotels, or access to the family section.

Figure 6.7 Telephone number written on the rear window of a car. Photo: © Stefan Maneval 2012.

Negotiating gender segregation (2): Encounters in cyberspace and the city

While public encounters between men and women are regarded with suspicion in Saudi Arabia, social media and the internet evidently provide opportunities for men and women to interact without being physically present in the same place. Among the questions I asked when I interviewed six students of Jeddah's exclusive private girls' college, Effat University, in February 2012, was how and where they spent their leisure time. Samira, whose family is from Bangladesh and who had lived in the US and Canada for four years and in Jeddah for 16 years, replied that she spent a lot of time at home, communicating with friends via social networking websites. Most of her online contacts were male. Another girl, Layla, whose family is from India and who had grown up 'in eight or nine different countries' also had male friends on the internet. Not only are men and women able to get to know each other online, but they can also, if both sides show interest, use the internet to arrange a meeting (see Le Renard 2014: 71–2). As for Samira and Layla, they both stressed that, in Saudi Arabia, they did not actually meet male friends. They only communicated with them online.

Considering the small size of my sample of Effat University students as well as the fact that all interviewees were in the same age group and had a similar socio-economic background, their interests, spare time activities, social networks and places where they spent their leisure time could hardly have been more disparate. Almost all of them frequently used the internet, but only Samira said that she spent large portions of her spare time at home on the computer. Two out of the group of six, Layla and a Saudi from Dhahran, Fatima, who had moved to Jeddah three and a half years ago, loved to go to shopping malls. Apart from these, Layla mentioned the Jarir bookshop and a whole host of other places she visited with her family or friends on weekends, including the corniche, the historic city centre, al-Balad, and the Shalal amusement park. Two others, Saba and Nur, said they disliked or even 'hated' shopping malls. Saba was a Saudi born and raised in Jeddah. Judging from her appearance and statements, she was probably the most conservative in the group. Still, she liked to visit cafes and restaurants in Tahliyya Street, a bustling shopping area for the well-off. The sixth girl, Faʾiza, was from a family from Mecca. Born in Riyadh, she grew up 'between the US and Bahrain' and had moved to Jeddah four years earlier. In the city she liked to attend cultural events and public discussions. One of the cafes she visited regularly, Bridges in Arafat Street, hosted open mic and movie nights. She added that the cafe was currently facing problems with the *hayʾa*, or religious police. Among Faʾiza's friends were also men. One of her male friends was Ahmad Angawi, a young artist whose artwork I had recently seen at the Edge of Arabia exhibition. Faʾiza often attended talks and cultural events in the house of Ahmad's father, the architect Sami Angawi. In contrast to Layla, Samira and Faʾiza, the other three students said they did not have any male friends, neither on a face-to-face basis nor on social networking websites.

Modes of travelling from one place to another in the city varied among the group of Effat students almost as much as the activities they engaged in. When I asked them how they travelled to all the places they had just mentioned, Saba jokingly replied: 'It's either you have a driver, or your dad, or your brother – or forget it.'

Fatima also had to ask a male family member or private driver to take her to any social activity she wanted to attend. When she or Saba went out with friends they would plan in advance whose driver took them to a place and who would later come to pick them up.

Layla, in contrast, said, 'For me it's either my father or taxis.' She reported that she was using taxis a lot, adding, 'I take them either with a friend or with my mother and sister.'

Samira surprised the other girls, and me as well, by laconically stating, 'I go by foot.' This led Layla to add that she also walked to the neighbourhood shopping area from time to time – something Saba and Fatima would not do. For the two Saudi girls in the group, neither walking nor taking a taxi was an option.

As Saba explained: 'Actually I'm afraid to get into a taxi here. So it's either the driver, or my friends can pick me up or something, or it's my dad.' She concluded with the remark 'We're *khāṣṣ*' – we are special – dropping an Arabic term into the English conversation.[21]

At times one can hear Saudis referring to an alleged Saudi *khuṣūṣiyya*, a noun derived from the same root as *khāṣṣ* denoting particularity or exceptionalism. Rather than explaining anything, this commonplace expression underscores the perception that Saudis are exceptional, thus broadening the gap between expatriates and Saudi nationals. Expatriates from diverse countries also stress the differences between their own and the Saudi way of life, or between Saudis and other people. I have already quoted Hamid as referring to Saudi exceptionalism when explaining why he pressed himself against the wall of the stairwell to make way for his Saudi neighbour. Ahmad had told me about different ways of approaching Saudi and foreign women. And my Yemeni informant who spoke about the Jeddah Rush Housing Project and the unwritten laws of Saudi lifts noticed differences in his Saudi neighbours' attitude to shared activities and spaces as well.

'The Saudis in the house where I live stay pretty much on their own. They do not socialise very much', he said.

I do not intend to question the validity of my interlocutors' perception in general. Yet my interviews with Effat University students show that the distinction between Saudis and non-Saudis is too simple. The young women's accounts mirror a large variety of attitudes to gender segregation and moral principles with respect to contact with the opposite sex. One can also say that they represent different conceptions of privacy which are informed by varying attitudes to *khalwa* and *ikhtilāṭ*. None of the students rejected *ikhtilāṭ* in all respects; otherwise they would not have been willing to meet me. Saba and Fatima, however, avoided *ikhtilāṭ* outside the university context. What appeared to be normal for Faʾiza – frequent contact with male friends, not just via social media, but also face-to-face encounters and joint activities, some of which might imply *khalwa* – was not the norm even for Samira and Layla. The two South Asian girls met with male friends in the US and in India, but not in Jeddah. Unlike Faʾiza, they as well as Nur had adapted to the rules of gender segregation that governed public space in Jeddah, but only for external reasons. Unconvinced of the religious necessity of rules which they did not have to follow outside Saudi Arabia, some of them used the internet to circumvent them.

The varying degrees of mobility, independence and contact with men among these young women suggest that attitudes to *khalwa* and *ikhtilāṭ* are not as strictly linked to ethnic origin or nationality as many people suggest by referring to Saudi exceptionalism; they are also dependent on personal experience, individual desires, religious beliefs and political opinions. Furthermore, the divergent notions of privacy and different attitudes to mixing are spatially manifested in the city, as I learned a couple of days after the interview when I visited Bridges, Faʾiza's favourite cafe, to see one of the few venues in Jeddah hosting public movie nights.

'Street Pulse': A public sphere utopia?

Bridges, or al-Jusūr, as the cafe is called in Arabic, was quite different from what I had expected. It consisted of only one oblong room at the rear of which a second floor had been built. Downstairs at the front were some bookshelves and tables offering a small and eclectic selection of new and second-hand English and Arabic books. Seven small tables and a tiny kitchenette in the corner hardly justified calling the place a cafe. The upper floor was used for the film screenings Faʾiza had mentioned: a moveable screen was set up in front of the wall at the rear of the room, and piles of chairs indicated the use of the space for public events.

On that day, a group of about half a dozen students, including both men and women, was seated on the floor, making a banner out of large pieces of paper on which they were writing slogans in Arabic. Among the students was the girl with short hair whom I had seen in the Edge of Arabia exhibition the other day. I asked her what they were doing.

'We are writing down our demands', she replied.

'What kind of demands?' I asked.

'Concerning the Syrian people', she said.

A young man came and asked suspiciously what I was up to. When I told him I was just wondering what was going on here, he explained that they were making these posters because they were not allowed to do anything else to voice their opinion, such as demonstrating in the streets.

'You know what is happening in Syria?' he asked me, alluding to the violent suppression of demonstrations against the regime of Bashar al-Assad taking place at the time. 'We want to do something, even if it's just a very small thing. We don't only want to watch.'

The short-haired woman asked me if I was a Syrian.

'No', I replied, slightly surprised, 'I'm German'.

'I'm Mariam', she introduced herself to me, and the young man and I followed her example.

Then I asked, 'And where are you going to set up these posters?'

'We don't know yet', the man said looking at Mariam, indicating to her not to talk too much.

'Some sort of flash mob', she added.

I was curious to learn more about what was probably going to be the first flash mob in Jeddah, but Mariam's friend hurried to say, 'Nice to meet you!' before I could ask any further questions.

Deeply impressed, I went downstairs. Bridges was obviously much more than a cafe housing film screenings. The rules of gender segregation were ignored here, or perhaps circumvented by declaring the place a bookshop. By creating its own rules and disregarding those dictated by the state, such as gender segregation, the cafe presents one method of calling the legitimacy of the state into question.[22] This may explain why, as Faʾiza had mentioned in the interview, Bridges faced problems with the morality police. Furthermore, as a space where exceptional things – such as the preparation of a flash mob, for example – were allowed to happen, Bridges served as a meeting place for liberal-minded young people like Faʾiza and Mariam (Zacharia 2011). Faʾiza had told me that she had met some of her friends at Bridges. Bringing together like-minded people, this cafe constituted a microcosm with its own rules, or its own bubble, to quote Omar once more. Yet, unlike the insulated bubbles in the private realm that Omar was talking about, Bridges was a bubble with public access.

The contribution to the Edge of Arabia exhibition by Faʾiza's friend Ahmad Angawi was an installation entitled 'Street Pulse' – a huge ball covered with microphones (Figure 6.8). Next to it was a map of Jeddah on which the artist had marked different places in the city: spots where he would like to install voice recorders into which residents of Jeddah could speak their mind. He had already sent a proposal to the authorities asking for permission to make his vision real. The exhibition guide doubted that the artist would get permission, 'but it's the idea that is most important' (personal communication, February 2012). In Saudi Arabia, where freedom of opinion is not granted, Ahmad Angawi's artwork is a political statement. I had hardly expected that a group of young people

Figure 6.8 Ahmad Angawi's 'Street Pulse' installation at the 2012 Edge of Arabia exhibition in Jeddah. Photo: © Stefan Maneval 2012.

in Jeddah were already doing what Ahmad Angawi had envisioned. On Angawi's 'Street Pulse' map, Cafe Bridges could have been marked as a spot in the city that had already been claimed and started to be used as a space where people sought out ways to express their opinion and make it public.[23]

My experience at Bridges thus led me to think of Ahmad Angawi's artwork in a new way. Perhaps the spots he had marked on the map should not be seen as representing Utopia. Perhaps more places already existed where the inhabitants of Jeddah challenged state authority and made their concerns public. I knew about the publics that convened in residential buildings – the Sufi conventions and *majālis* (sing. *majlis*) or *nawādī* (sing. *nādī*) of affluent families mentioned in the previous chapter, for example. Now I started to look for publics which assembled outside the home. I soon discovered that various groups of people had found modes of publicly articulating their opinions and expressing discontent. I found that each public is associated with particular architecture and social practices, similar to the way in which Cafe Bridges provided space for a small but subversive public to convene and prepare a concerted action.

Claiming public spaces: protest and resistance

Anyone who is perceived to present a peril to the stability of the regime must fear to lose his job, as the aforementioned case of Shaykh Saʿad al-Shithrī shows. Critics of the state voicing their opinions in demonstrations, newspapers, reform petitions or blogs are regularly banned from travelling, physically punished or detained for years – often without trial – and thus rendered silent.[24] Yet the silence is never complete, and discontent is not only voiced by a handful of prominent critics. Protest flares up frequently in different regions of Saudi Arabia; it is expressed in various forms and sometimes supported by significant numbers of people.[25]

In Jeddah, a flood caused by heavy rainfall on 25 November 2009 sparked heated public debate on mismanagement and corruption (Hagmann 2011). One hundred and twenty-three people died in the flood, according to official figures considered far too low by both Saudi activists and foreign media. Shocked by the catastrophic events and the Municipality's inability to cope with them, residents of Jeddah organised help at the grassroots level. Blogs, newspaper articles, petitions to the king and social networking websites discussed the shortcomings of the authorities prior to and during the disaster. A Facebook group called 'People's campaign for support of the rescue of Jeddah' (*al-ḥamla ash-shaʿbiyya li-l-musāhama fī inqādh madīnat Jiddah*) attracted more than 40,000 followers in just a few days. The group abandoned its initial goal of suing the Municipality of Jeddah when King ʿAbdullāh promised that persons and organisations responsible for malpractice in the management of the response to the flood would be prosecuted. The king also announced that families of victims of the flood would receive 1 million Saudi riyals (approximately €190,000) in compensation. These steps, as well as the blocking of websites used to circulate petitions initiated as a response to the disaster, show that the government took notice of the furore and viewed some of the agitation involved as a serious threat to the regime.

The debate on malpractice in the city administration of Jeddah in the context of the 2009 flood is an example of how the internet can be used to voice criticism and forge alliances. As the 2011–12 protests in Tunisia, Egypt, Libya and Syria have shown, even mass protests can be organised online. But no dictator has so far been forced to resign via Facebook. The fact that loosely organised networks of people like Faʾiza, Ahmad Angawi, Mariam and her fellow activists exist also beyond the internet, that is to say, that some people not only join a Facebook group because they are temporarily upset but also take further political action, is of importance. Constituting what virtually all theorists of the public sphere would call a public, the group of young men and women I had met at Bridges, students probably, organised an act of civil disobedience. This is remarkable especially in view of the fact that any demands made public are regarded with suspicion by the Saudi authorities and can be interpreted as criticism of government policy. The activists who met at Bridges that night were very few, and they did not plan a revolution. The flash mob they were preparing, however, is a way of occupying a place in the city and contesting the state's monopoly over public space (cf. Butler 2011).

Pascal Menoret (2014: 162–73, 205) interprets the widespread phenomenon of car drifting (*tafḥīṭ*) by young men in Saudi cities in terms of a similar frame of reference. Saudi youths, according to Menoret, engage in joyriding with stolen or rented cars out of frustration over lack of freedom and opportunities. They are rebels without a cause: dissatisfied with the rigid moral standards prevalent in Saudi society, humiliated by autocratic teachers and despotic parents, and bored because there is nothing much to do for unmarried men in Saudi cities, they do not follow a specific political goal, but appropriate public space in a destructive way. Taking cars, driving like crazy, dodging the police, risking their own and other people's lives, and openly challenging heteronormativity is their way of expressing discontent. Through actions and behaviour, clothes and haircuts, as well as through songs and YouTube videos of drifting sessions, they deconstruct the image of a clean and secure country ruled and inhabited by deeply religious people. They thus challenge the official narrative according to which law and order have been established on the Peninsula by the Āl Saʿūd.[26]

Migrant workers employ similar 'weapons of the weak' (Scott 1985) to mount resistance and make their concerns public, in spite of the fact that the Saudi state neither grants them sufficient legal protection nor permits the constitution of formal publics that can speak on their behalf. Many Saudi households have a private driver for female family members at their disposal, the vast majority of whom are non-Saudi nationals. Their employers' dependence on their services puts drivers in a position that they can take advantage of to negotiate better working conditions and higher salaries (Le Renard 2014: 51). Migrant workers who are not capable of exerting pressure on their employers by refusing to work – due to the over-supply of workers in certain professions, for example – sometimes benefit from informal expatriate networks that offer support. In an article dealing with Filipino migrant workers in Saudi Arabia, Mark Johnson (2010) presents several cases of Filipino middle-class families helping compatriots to escape from abusive employers or providing escapees with accommodation and new employment. NGOs promoting legal protection of migrant workers, though not permitted in Saudi Arabia itself, operate within countries which export labour forces to Saudi Arabia and other Gulf countries. Activists in Indonesia, for example, have drawn public attention to the miserable situation of many Indonesian migrant workers in Saudi Arabia, thus urging the Indonesian government to launch monitoring and support initiatives for domestic workers abroad (Silvey 2004; 2006). Some support organisations have informal branches in Saudi Arabia. As the abuse of Overseas Foreign Workers, as they are often referred to, has received much attention in the media of countries such as Indonesia and the Philippines in recent years, support groups can effectively exert pressure on their respective consulates even though they are not officially registered (Dehne 2011: 84–6).

Paradoxically, the very fact that migrant workers and runaways lack institutional support has led to their increased public visibility. Finding no other refuge, Southeast Asian escapees began setting up shacks under flyovers in the city centre of Jeddah or in front of their home countries' consulates (Dehne 2011: 89–90). At times, more than 1,000 people lived in these makeshift tent cities, sometimes waiting for their deportation for months (see e.g. *Arab News*, 21 June 2011). This caused the local press to report about them. The Jeddah-based English daily *Arab News*, for example, wrote on 27 October 2010:

> Residents and business owners in the area near the Kandara flyover along King Fahd (Sitteen) Road are complaining about the havoc created by hundreds of illegal immigrants who live in a Hooverville beneath the overpass. Most of these people, a mix of runaway workers and pilgrim-visa overstayers, living here beneath tarps and other flimsy temporary housing are of Asian origin. The phenomenon of illegal immigrants camping out under the bridge has been going on for quite some time, but the situation has turned nasty recently when disturbances broke out and police were called in to make arrests. The overstayers were reportedly creating troubles on purpose so they would be picked up by immigration police and deported from the country free of charge. Some of the squatters vandalized parked cars and caused damage to nearby properties.

Although primarily concerned about the maintenance of public order, media reports occasionally mention reasons why individual migrant workers abscond from their employers:

> Housemaids who flee their sponsors due to bad working conditions to seek work in the black labor market often end up in a situation of jumping out of the frying pan and into the fire.... 'They seize our IDs, lock us up in secluded rooms and make us live in very difficult conditions, which is no less than indentured servitude,' a maid told *Arab News* on condition she not be named. Nuriyyah, an Indonesian maid who has been working for two years in Saudi Arabia, describes the situation she found herself in as 'slavery' after being legally recruited and brought to the Kingdom. The wage she ended up receiving was not enough to feed her family back home.
>
> (*Arab News*, 13 January 2011)

In another article, telling readers why it is not a good idea to abscond and camp in the streets, *Arab News* mentions 'A maid from the southern Philippine region of Davao [who] said she ran away from her employer in Riyadh to avoid getting raped' (*Arab News* 2008). For people like her, the private home is a place of violence, whereas the street, perceived as hostile and dangerous by others, becomes a refuge. By occupying certain spots in the city, talking to the press and sporadically turning to more aggressive forms of protest, runaway migrant workers thus manage to draw attention to their issues.

The cases presented in this section illustrate that large groups within Saudi society that are denied access to so-called 'strong' publics – such as critics of the Saudi government, dissatisfied Saudi youths and migrant workers – have different informal options of publicly expressing frustration, formulating political demands and mounting resistance. The informal or 'weak' publics constituted by members of these groups are not powerless; on the contrary, by exerting pressure on their respective embassies, their employers or the Saudi authorities, they sometimes manage to improve their own situation. Some criticism is voiced on the internet or through other media of mass communication. Often, publicity is generated via the occupation of a portion of urban public space, either sporadically, as in the case of car drifters or a flash mob, or for longer intervals, as illustrated by the camp of escaped migrant workers. What renders these activities effective is their public visibility: they introduce some degree of chaos into the image of orderly public space which the state wishes to impose. Since the Āl Saʿūd portray themselves as granters of social, political and moral order as well as of security, justice and stability (al-Rasheed 1996; 2004), the disorder produced by squatters, drifters and protesters against basically anything calls the ruling family's legitimacy into question.

By focusing in the remaining section of this chapter on a particular form of dissent, which is inextricably linked with certain types of architecture – shopping malls, gated communities and beach resorts – I draw together different strands of my argument as developed thus far. The aim is to show how the public articulation of nonconformist opinions on *ikhtilāṭ*, gender and sexuality, enabled by a specific architecture, lead to the entanglement of public and private space in a way that challenges conceptions of privacy prevailing in the context of Saudi Arabia.

Gated publics, counterpublics[27]

I asked a 29-year-old Saudi architect what I had also asked the six Effat University students: where do young people in Jeddah spend their spare time? At that time, in the year 2009, my informant was living in Germany, where he was working on a Ph.D. Here is the reply I received in an e-mail:

> Young men and women meet their friends in cafes, restaurants or shopping centres. When the weather is nice they spend their time with friends and relatives in vacation spots at the seaside in Obhur. Some families have their own holiday cottage on their private piece of land. Others rent chalets for several years or for a limited period of time in one of the 'holiday villages' run by hotel firms. In those neighbourhoods in Obhur one spends time with other people in some kind of closed circle of acquainted families. Like this it is possible to use public spaces and green areas together with others. Normally there is no opportunity to do so in the city.... Boys go to the gym and diving, girls have a lot of parties at home.
>
> (e-mail received on 4 July 2009, originally in German, my translation)

During my stays in Jeddah I got to know some of the holiday villages and beach resorts in Obhur mentioned in the e-mail (Figure 6.9). Except for a small parcel of a few hundred metres, the entire coastline in Obhur to the north of Jeddah is private property. Some areas are owned by individuals,

Figure 6.9 A beach resort in Obhur. Photo: © Stefan Maneval 2012.

others by luxurious hotels in the city centre. The hotels offer visitors door-to-door shuttle services to the remote beach resorts. The remaining properties belong to companies which have built gated holiday developments either exclusively for their high-ranking employees or for holidaymakers in general. Tenants of chalets in one of these developments can invite guests. This is the most comfortable way of gaining access to these resorts as a mere visitor. Another option is leaving one's passport at the entrance gate of one of the beaches belonging to luxury hotels and paying a fee of approximately 100 Saudi riyals per person, about €20 in 2012.

When I visited a beach resort in March 2011, I learned that Saudi nationals are not permitted to enter. I was surprised that Saudis were kept out of beaches in their own country whereas I, a German visitor, and the two men who gave me a ride back to the city at the end of the day, both migrant workers from other Arab countries, had access to them.

'The place would quickly change if ordinary Saudis were allowed to enter', the driver of the car explained. 'There used to be a beach where Saudis could go. Young Saudis went there with their girlfriends. When the police found out about this, the place was shut down for a while. Now, Saudis are not allowed to enter any more.' The *hayʾa* had the normal police shut down the place, he explained (personal communication, March 2011).

The places mentioned by the young architect in the e-mail quoted above are not considered to be genuinely public spaces by many researchers critical of current trends that privilege privatisation and securitisation of urban space.[28] According to their logic, beach resorts, shopping malls, amusement parks and gated communities are not fully public because they are owned by individuals or companies who have the right to police who enters the premises and prohibit unwanted activities, among them the assertion of civil rights. Access to these places depends on people's financial resources, personal contacts, racial identities at times or, as in the case of non-Saudi beach resorts in Obhur, on nationality. These are therefore often perceived as intensifying social, economic and racial segregation (Low 2003: 11, 224–8). Following this line of thought, one may argue that the exclusion of Saudi nationals from beach resorts in Jeddah reinforces the stereotype of a Saudi exceptionalism.

However, access to publics and counterpublics often depends on different factors such as language skills, education, social status, money, nationality, race, sex, gender identity and acceptance of certain ethical values. A state-owned 'public' museum in many cities of the world also costs around €10–15, a price not affordable to everyone. Access to public libraries is only granted to registered users, with registration requiring valid personal papers, residency in the same country or a valid visa, and perhaps a fee. Habermas's (1989) bourgeois publics of the Enlightenment era, which were convened in private homes, were not accessible to everyone, and neither were public spaces in Jeddah in the past, such as the *sūq*, the *mirkāz* or women's gatherings in the residential buildings. Furthermore, counterpublics of gays and lesbians, people of colour and religious or other minorities often meet in secluded private spaces because behaviour practised by the participants contradicts the norms of their cultural environment (Fraser 1992: 121–4; Warner 2002: 109–24).

It is not my intention to deny the discriminatory practices facilitated by the privatisation and securitisation of urban space. My point is, rather, that although indisputably exclusive in some way, shopping centres, restaurants and gated holiday developments can be considered as public spaces in the sense that they enable or encourage encounters and conversations between strangers or acquaintances (Abaza 2001; Nissen 2008).[29] In beach resorts in Jeddah, unrelated men and women talk to each other. Men wear shorts that do not cover their knees, women wear swimsuits and bikinis. Some smoke cigarettes and shisha, some play loud music and some go swimming. The e-mail quoted above indicates that similar developments exist for Saudis, too. Although not permitted entrance into many resorts in Obhur, they rent holiday cottages in the Mövenpick resort in northern Jeddah or north of Obhur in a famous resort called Durrat al-ʿArūs. In YouTube videos one can see young men dancing in the streets within the precincts of that resort, or in a car park, or on a stage-like elevation of ground, in front of a camera in order to be seen by strangers. These young men want to have an audience, they want to be public.

Partying outside the home is possible in Durrat al-ʿArūs because the walls surrounding the premises keep out views, unwanted visitors and, most of the time, the morality police. These young people make public what others regard as immoral, and they can only do so in a secluded space, in the company of people who largely share their attitudes to gender, sexuality and the body. Conflict with the norms of a cultural context of domination and restriction is, following Michael Warner (2002), what distinguishes counterpublics from other publics. Not every tenant of a chalet in Obhur or Durrat al-ʿArūs is participating in a counterpublic. Some are mere holidaymakers, divers, shisha smokers or bored youths. But with regard to those who have a desire to make their own deviation from the norms public, the concept is a useful analytical tool.

A photo essay by the British photographer Olivia Arthur (2012) titled *Jeddah Diary* shows Saudi girls riding bicycles and walking down the streets of Durrat al-ʿArūs at night, unveiled, wearing tight-fitting

Figure 6.10 Girls riding bicycles in the Durrat al-ʿArūs holiday resort. Photograph from Olivia Arthur's *Jeddah Diary* (2012), reproduced with the permission of the artist. © Olivia Arthur.

Figure 6.11 A group of veiled women posing for Olivia Arthur's camera. Photograph from Arthur's *Jeddah Diary* (2012), reproduced with the permission of the artist. © Olivia Arthur.

Western clothes and no *ʿabāya* (Figure 6.10). In other images by the same photographer women wearing fashionable – and extremely short – dresses and hot pants are partying with men in a gated community. Apart from these pictures, the book contains many scenes from the daily life of women in Jeddah, mostly taken at their private homes in kitchens, living rooms and bedrooms. The women in the pictures did not object to the publication of their pictures. They only demanded that their faces were not visible in them (Figure 6.11).

Nevertheless, when Olivia Arthur showed them the pictures she had taken, one of the women remarked, 'That's great ... but can't you show a bit more of her eyes so that people can see how beautiful she is?' (Arthur 2012: 30). This statement is surprising, given that not even the omission of their faces makes the circulation of their images legitimate in the eyes of many Saudis. Women are not supposed to be seen by outsiders, and so they are not supposed to be photographed, at least not by anyone who might circulate their pictures to outsiders. Occasionally, people who saw me walking around with a camera in Jeddah were very anxious that I was taking pictures of women. One old lady in Hindāwiyya started yelling at me while she continued walking down the street. A man passed by and asked what the fuss was about.

'*Hadha yuṣawwir an-nās!*' she exclaimed – 'He's photographing people!'

I explained to the man that I was only taking pictures of houses and showed him some of my images on the display of the digital camera. He did not seem completely convinced but let me go. I heard the same phrase, *yuṣawwir an-nās*, on another occasion at the corniche in al-Ḥamrā. That time, a woman said it to another woman, again not to me directly because she would not talk to unrelated men. She said it loudly enough for me to hear, though, and I stopped taking pictures. Men in the streets of districts such as al-Hindāwiyya, al-Kandara or al-Balad, in contrast, often asked me to take their pictures – only when no woman was present. All the women who were worried that I might photograph them were completely veiled, enveloped in black from head to foot, exposing only face and hands and sometimes not even that.

Many of the young women in Olivia Arthur's photographs do not veil their bodies, but their faces are disguised. Some wear casual Western clothes, which leave much skin uncovered, but they make sure that their long hair screens their faces. Or an object is placed between the camera and their faces. Or they hide their faces with their hands. Or Arthur photographed her own prints under bright light, so that the reflection of the light blurs the faces, but not the entire image. Thus, rather than legitimising the circulation of the portraits, the techniques employed by Arthur to erase or omit the women's faces serve the purpose of making the women unrecognisable in the first place. The women want to be photographed, they want to be seen. But as this can damage their reputation, they prefer to hide their identity. The request to show more of the depicted woman's eyes attests to the play with revelation and concealment. They do not want to refrain from showing that they are beautiful women, but they need to conceal who they are.

Olivia Arthur's images were not produced to be shared with family and friends, and the women were completely aware of this fact. Some women wearing an *ʿabāya* and a veil covering their faces are unmistakably posing for Arthur's camera – and for an unknown viewer, an imaginary public. Having one's picture taken by a professional photographer from Europe and agreeing to the circulation of these pictures, as well as posting videos on YouTube, are ways of seeking publicity. Some videos of Saudi men dancing have been watched more than 200,000 times. One extremely popular video, for example, depicts three youths dressed like religious scholars imitating Michael Jackson. Arthur is a member of the renowned cooperative Magnum Photos. Her pictures from Saudi Arabia were shown in exhibitions in New York and London, her *Jeddah Diary* was written about in the German weekly *Die Zeit*. It can also be purchased and viewed from anywhere in the world via the internet. The dancers of Durrat al-ʿArūs as well as the women hiding their faces but not their bodies in Arthur's photographs are obviously addressing a global public.

Yet the practices documented in Olivia Arthur's photographs and in YouTube videos can take place only within an architecture which keeps certain parts of the Saudi public out, thus creating a more or less private setting. Moreover, wearing, before the eyes of strangers, tight-fitting jeans, swimsuits and hot pants instead of an *ʿabāya*, or shorts instead of a *thawb* (the white dress worn by many Saudi men), dancing in the streets or in the clubhouse of a gated community, and posing for the camera are not only public forms of display of deviant behaviour. What is made public is, according to the prevailing social norms, part of the private realm: naked skin, the female body, certain types of movements and gestures, as well as communication between unrelated men and women.

Once more: the private setting of secluded and privately owned facilities enables encounters between strangers, and thereby the constitution of publics. The people who meet at these places make practices normally restricted to the private sphere public. Things get complicated at this point. Yet this phenomenon is not entirely unique. In many ways it resembles the drag queens written about by Michael Warner (2002) in the introduction to *Publics and Counterpublics*. Around 1960, they regularly met in a New Jersey house and documented their parties with several cameras. They met in a private setting to avoid social stigma, but they were taking photographs so that, in principle, an infinite number of outsiders could see what they were doing. The imagined publicity created a feel of glamour, as Warner puts it, which allowed them 'to experience their bodies in a way that would not have been possible without this mutual witnessing and display' (2002: 13).

If we are speaking about tens of thousands of viewers of a video, tens of thousands of readers of a German weekly and hundreds of visitors to an exhibition, as in the examples from Jeddah referred to here, we are also dealing with real publicity. Communication with the world beyond the gates is important. It aims at making public what otherwise cannot be openly articulated in this particular cultural environment. Just like the 'counterpublics of sex and gender' elsewhere (Warner 2002: 62–3), the counterpublics in Jeddah presented here challenge prevailing notions of what public and private mean within a wider social context. They are offering the Saudi public alternative opinions on gender segregation, definitions of shameful nudity, female modesty and desire. Above all, men and women claim their right to have what for them is a sexually attractive body – a body that can dance, has long legs, breasts, curly hair or beautiful eyes. They show off this body to anyone they want to outside the private realm: friends, strangers, men and women. And they enjoy being admired for it. They enjoy being public. They are engaged in renegotiating the border between public and private space.

These people certainly do not epitomise Saudi youth. Perhaps they represent only a minority. Although their voices are just some among many other voices which may be more powerful, they are able to say that they do not care about the rules. It would be a terrible mistake to believe that this message is addressed only to a Saudi audience, especially in view of the media involved in these cases – the internet, a Magnum photographer's exhibition in New York City and the German press. The artists and their protagonists promote new perspectives on what it means to be young and male, or young and female in Saudi Arabia. They demonstrate that, within their own bubble, they are free to do what they want. They are told not to play music in the streets. But they do. They are not supposed to dance. But they do. Women should stay away from men. But they don't. They can have fun if they want to – and they want to. Like the girls smoking in a car mentioned earlier, having a space where they do not need to care what other people tell them to do or not to do is their version of privacy.

Conclusion

Public space doesn't simply exist. A desert is not what we call a public space, and neither is a motorway, so long as it is only used to move from one place to another by means of a car. It takes people, strangers who interact with each other, to turn a place into public space. In other words, public space is socially produced. This is not a new insight; geographers and sociologists have elaborated on this point for some decades (e.g. Lefebvre 1991; Löw 2001; Massey 2005). The question that has captured my interest and imagination in this chapter is whether or not, in a place like Jeddah, where the political environment is plainly hostile to the emergence of critical publics, the social production of public spaces is in fact possible. And if so, in what ways does this social production manifest itself?

In the first part of the chapter I discussed key factors that hinder the emergence of lively public spaces facilitating face-to-face communication between strangers as they are known elsewhere. However, the local climate, or rather the perception of it as unpleasant, the automotive city, an autocratic regime suspicious of open spaces with their potential for assembly and collective expressions of dissent, and local conceptions of privacy and its accompanying politics of gender, do not prevent people from constituting publics. Rather, these factors lead to the appropriation of urban places that were not designed for the purpose of public sociability for alternative, ad hoc and at times guerrilla-style public articulations of discontent. They also lead to the use of privately owned facilities for public encounters.

The architecture of public space and men and women's social practices connected to it are, I have argued, indivisible from local conceptions of privacy. In Jeddah, these are informed by varying positions on two main categories of mixing, *khalwa* and *ikhtilāṭ*. People's attitudes to these concepts determine their respective modes of travelling in the city, the places they visit and activities they engage in. The fact that dominant forces in society prevent people from doing what they want to do in public, or compel them to hide what they may want to display, leads to increased entanglement between public and private spaces. Practices associated with publics take place within the protected sphere of the private home or other built spaces that keep viewers and visitors out, such as beach resorts or gated holiday developments. The duplication of spaces for the segregation of sexes, the use of private cars often with tinted windows, the ubiquity of gates and guards, and a culturally prescribed avoidance of contact between unrelated men and women, also create islands of privacy within the public realm.

Within these islands, practices that are considered to be part of, and otherwise limited to, the private sphere can take place undisturbed. Such practices are sometimes deliberately made public as a challenge to the border between public and private. This is the case with the young women in Jeddah portrayed by Olivia Arthur, youths dancing in Durrat al-ʿArūs and young men and women exposing their half-naked bodies at beach resorts in Obhur. Following Michael Warner (2002), I have referred to these practices, which challenge prevailing norms and moral principles, as counterpublics.

In the 1980s and 1990s, as could be seen in chapters 4 and 5, the Islamic Revival movement was engaged in a process of challenging the

Saudi state as well as common notions of public and private. The transformation of the Saudi society initiated by these 'Islamic counterpublics' (Hirschkind 2006) demonstrates how powerful such dissident movements, unauthorised expressions of discontent and deviant social practices can be. The latter parts of this chapter have focused on contemporary forms of protest, resistance, counterpublics and the revision of existing rules and norms. Although some of the voices presented here may seem feeble, their contribution to an ongoing transformation of Saudi society can hardly be overestimated. At the same time, it is important to bear in mind that there are other publics with different agendas, informed, for example, by a conservative imagination of social coexistence.

I have summarised in this chapter a recent debate on gender segregation and *ikhtilāṭ*, and I wish to emphasise once more that many men and women support a strict spatial division between the sexes. Many Saudis strongly reject the mixing that occurs at workplaces and parties in gated enclaves. Some consider women unqualified 'by nature' to perform a public role whereas others support the creation of more segregated workplaces as a way to enhance opportunities for women. Even though, as I have shown, gender segregation constrains the movement of both men and women, many people also use it to their advantage. Men of different social strata benefit in terms of job opportunities and powerful positions, while women gain access to secure and harassment-free spaces. For others, such as the female Islamist Nūra al-Saʿad, it is an important factor in the cultivation of a particular type of piety (see Mahmood 2005; also see chapter 5 of this volume).

It may be said that the royal family is attentive to these divergent opinions and different visions of society. To maintain stability, it carefully adjusts its policy, dismisses leaders of state institutions and inaugurates new ones, according to the way the wind blows. While the negotiation of what is public and private continues, different and also divergent versions of these concepts circulate and are enacted in everyday life, enabled by particular forms of architecture.

Notes

1. Source: National Oceanic and Atmospheric Administration, ftp://ftp.atdd.noaa.gov/pub/GCOS/WMO-Normals/RA-II/SD/41024.TXT (accessed 16 June 2015).
2. VAT was first introduced in 2018, at a standard rate of 5 per cent.
3. The 1971 master plan for the development of Riyadh produced by Doxiadis Associates (DA) states that the Bedouin dwellings, 'of which a large number are unauthorized … are the cause of unhealthy conditions and unrest. They definitely bring serious problems to the development, servicing and management of the city' (quoted in Menoret 2014: 76–7). The migrant

population was seen as a source of 'trouble [to] the security and health departments' and of 'moral … problems' (DA 1963 work report, quoted in Menoret 2014: 86).

4. In 1968, Prince Salmān bin ʿAbd al-ʿAzīz, then governor of Riyadh, ordered the removal of approximately 60,000 Bedouin from the centre of Riyadh, then a city of around 300,000 inhabitants. The DA experts objected to the relocation site proposed by Prince Salmān, an area next to National Guard barracks and a cement factory miles away from the built-up city area, but not to the idea of displacing residents and rehousing them in remote areas (Menoret 2014: 74–7).
5. As James C. Scott writes in his book *Seeing Like a State*: 'Delivering mail, collecting taxes, conducting a census, moving supplies and people in and out of the city, putting down a riot or insurrection, digging for pipes and sewer lines, finding a felon or conscript (providing he is at the address given), and planning public transportation, water supply, and trash removal are all made vastly simpler by the logic of the grid' (Scott 1998: 57).
6. Hemaidi's complaint that 'foreign experts' commissioned with the planning of Saudi cities failed to understand 'the local traditional urban fabric of the city and the Arabic-Islamic cultural background of its people' may sound familiar from the discourse of New Islamic Urbanism presented in chapter 4. These experts introduced 'foreign planning principles' which, in Hemaidi's view, proved 'inadequate to the people's needs and local conditions' (Hemaidi 2001: 188–9).
7. The story of the Rush Housing Project is documented by Bokhari (1978: 304), Farahat and Cebeci (1982) and Fadan (1983: 225–30).
8. See al-Rasheed (2013: 159–72), Meijer (2010), van Geel (2016). Van Geel (2018: 113–14) highlights that, in the Saudi context, in which gender segregation is the norm and the mixing of unrelated men and women an exception, the language does not provide an adequate term for segregation, but there is much debate about *ikhtilāṭ*. She presents a detailed discussion of the different meanings of the term to Saudi women, thus emphasising also its vagueness. Whereas the meaning of *khalwa* – the presence of a woman and a non-*maḥram* man in a confined space – is relatively clear and undisputed, there are many different understandings and definitions of the term *ikhtilāṭ* (van Geel 2018: chapter 3).
9. According to al-Ghāmidī, *ikhtilāṭ* 'is natural in the life of the *umma* [community of believers], and forbidding it does not rest on clear religious evidence' (al-Ghāmidī in *Okaz*, 9 December 2009, quoted in Meijer 2010: 88).
10. While *ikhtilāṭ* was introduced in certain places, such as shopping malls, cafes and some restaurants, under King Salmān and crown prince Muḥammad bin Salmān, others remain gender segregated.
11. Since the reign of King ʿAbdullāh, a few women's universities, such as Effat University in Jeddah, have been headed by women.
12. Estimates based on data collected by the International Labour Organization, the ILOSTAT database and World Bank population estimates (https://data.worldbank.org/indicator/SL.TLF.TOTL.FE.ZS?locations=S; accessed 14 April 2019).
13. At the top of the social hierarchy stands the royal family, above all the senior princes occupying key ministerial offices. Counting more than 5,000 members, the Āl Saʿūd form a powerful network of patrons and clients, interlinked with the economic elite and most of the important tribes and families through intermarriage (Glosemeyer 2002). Members of the royal family engage in business themselves and own the largest media companies in the country (Hagmann 2010). Closeness to the royal family is a crucial asset in a man's path to success and political or economic power. The king appoints ministers, members of the Shura council and heads of other government organisations, and ministers appoint bureaucrats as well as chief editors of newspapers. In addition, the Āl Saʿūd reward loyal clients with pieces of land, employment in the state apparatus, state contracts and monopolised import licences, all sources of enormous wealth (see Hertog 2005; 2011: 86–94; Menoret 2014: 121–8). The relationship between tribes and the state is discussed in Maisel (2014).
14. Saudi Arabia's Shiite population, approximately 8–15 per cent of the entire populace, are gravely under-represented in the political and educational system. This is true even for the Eastern Province, where the Shia account for half the population. In the Universities of al-Qatif and al-Ahsa, two major cities in the Eastern Province, only 5 per cent of faculty members are Shiites (Dinkelaker 2010; Meijer and Wagemakers 2013).
15. 'Bedouin' is a term used for nomads, their sedentary descendants and poor rural migrants in general, another group discriminated against within the Saudi state and society (Menoret 2014: 82–7, 140–7).

16. The emphasis here is on the patriarchal structure of the *state*, not of society in general, or of tribes and families. Men from these social groups and strata can still have more power within their own families than their wives, daughters and sisters.
17. Although the 2005 Saudi Labour Law grants migrant workers basic rights such as regular payment, breaks and a maximum workload of eight hours per day and 48 hours per week, as well as respect for religion and human dignity, many immigrants complain about appalling living and working conditions (see Dehne 2010). Many of them face non-payment of wages, excessive workloads and racism (personal communication, March 2011 and January 2012; see also Human Rights Watch 2004). They have hardly any rights in respect of their employers and are not organised in workers' unions, as these do not exist in Saudi Arabia, either for non-nationals or for Saudis. For many, the only way to escape in cases of maltreatment and abuse is to turn to their embassy and wait for deportation (oral communication with runaway migrant workers from Indonesia, March 2011). Female migrant workers – nurses, nannies or domestic servants, for example – are even less mobile and sometimes confined to their employers' homes.
18. The children of migrant workers are not permitted to study at a Saudi university even if they are born and raised in Saudi Arabia, for example.
19. The rules of gender segregation do not apply to these migrant workers of low social status in the same way, as though they are not males to the same degree as Saudi men (Le Renard 2014: 33). Similar observations on the connection between gender hierarchies and ethnic stratification in Kuwait have been made by Longva (1993).
20. A few years after I finished my fieldwork in 2012, gender segregation was abolished in some of the places described here. Yet it continues to be an important social principle that structures men's and women's movements, behaviour and interaction in public. Even though the cases presented in the following pages are already history, the points I want to make with regard to the constitution of public and private spaces remain valid.
21. The Arabic term *khāṣṣ* can denote private property, such as in *sayyāra khāṣṣa*, private car. Just like the related noun *khuṣūṣiyya*, it is also used in the sense of special or different.
22. In this respect I follow de Certeau (1984), who emphasises the capability of seemingly trivial practices of everyday life to challenge powerful structures.
23. A few years later, Cafe Bridges was closed. It was purportedly shut down by the authorities as a response to its hosting of public political debates. I owe this information to Ulrike Freitag.
24. Such cases are reported e.g. by the BBC (2015), Doumato (1992), *Elaph* (2007), Giglio (2012), *Gulf News* (2013), Maneval (2010) and al-Rasheed (2012).
25. For political commitment in Saudi Arabia in the 1950s and 1960s, see Ghrawi (2015). Violent and non-violent forms of protest have frequently been adopted by Shiites in the Eastern Province. Their publications, although banned inside Saudi Arabia, can nevertheless be bought by Saudis in bookshops in many neighbouring Arab countries (al-Rasheed 1998). Since 2011, encouraged by the protest movements in Tunisia, Egypt and Libya, Shiites demanding an end to religious discrimination and economic inequality have regularly demonstrated in the streets of towns and villages in the coastal region of Qatif, particularly in Awamiya. Many of these protests resulted in violent clashes with the security forces, during which approximately 20 young Shia activists as well as several policemen were killed (Aljazeera 2012; Alahmad 2014; Matthiesen 2012).
26. For examples of the official historiography see e.g. al-Ḥārithī (2003/4) and al-Simari (2011). For a critical analysis of this narrative, see Maneval (2014) and al-Rasheed (1996; 2004).
27. The argument and some of the material presented in this section have previously been published as an article (Maneval 2019).
28. See e.g. Klein (2000: 182–6), Madanipour (2003), Scharoun (2012: 88–96) and Sorkin (1992). For a critical overview of the academic debate on the privatisation of urban space, see Nissen (2008).
29. Based on this criterion, Amélie Le Renard (2011; 2014; 2015), for example, treats the gated and highly securitised women's campus of King Saud University, as well as shopping malls in Riyadh, as public spaces. She reports that on 25 September 2008, the national day commemorating the foundation of the Saudi Kingdom, customers of a shopping mall in Riyadh spontaneously put up a fight against the Committee for the Promotion of Virtue and Prevention of Vice (Le Renard 2014: 115–16). They turned the mall into a stage for civil disobedience and posted videos of their action on the internet, thus making their dissatisfaction with the morality police public.

7
Conclusion

My intention in this book has been to gain a better understanding of what, in the city of Jeddah and to some extent in Saudi society at large, can be considered as public and private and, by doing so, to contribute to Western debates on the meaning of these terms in gender-segregated Muslim contexts in general. With regard to Saudi Arabia, media coverage and, to some extent, scholarly literature deals with these questions almost exclusively from the perspective of women, reinforcing opinions and common knowledge about Saudi Arabia in the West: that women there are marginalised, excluded from the public sphere and, on the whole, subjugated by Saudi men. This general picture is lucidly expressed in a series of photo collages by the Saudi artist Manal al-Dowayan: the black-and-white images of her series 'Landscapes of the Mind' show veiled women in desert landscapes, amidst the petrochemical industry and ornamental palm trees, or walking alongside fences that separate and exclude them from who-knows-what. In other collages of the same series, one can see women's eyes floating in the sky or women's hands decorated with henna growing out of petroleum tanks and desert mountains. In Saudi Arabia, eyes and hands are usually the only body parts of a woman exposed to the public. The collages thus illustrate the way Saudi Arabia is perceived in the West: through the lens of the oil business and women's rights.

In terms of Islamic conservatism and gender inequality, Saudi Arabia is considered to be an extreme case. At the same time, due to notoriously strict public morals and the strong position of religious scholars and institutions in the Saudi state, Saudi society is regarded as a prime example of Islamic patriarchy. As such, it fuels Western unease about Islamic politics of gender, if not with Islam as a whole. Western criticism of Islamic politics of gender as enacted by Saudi–Wahhabi Islam is animated by two core values, liberty and gender equality. Although these are ideals rather than a social reality even in the West, these principles appear to be indisputable and of universal validity from a liberal-secular point of view. From such a standpoint, the fact that Islam is the predominant religion in Saudi Arabia and many other Middle Eastern countries is not in itself regarded as a problem, because religion is considered as a matter of personal choice that everyone should be able to make for him- or herself. Within a secular logic, however, religion is only acceptable as long as it stays within the private realm and does not muddy the waters of a purportedly 'neutral' public sphere. The veil and its contemporary Saudi variant, the *ʿabāya*, which help to make women invisible to men, render Islam publicly recognisable to Western eyes. Moreover, the fact that women's veiling is considered to be compulsory by certain Muslims, among them prominent male Saudi clerics, runs counter to liberal premises that prioritise the freedom of the individual. In addition, women in Saudi Arabia were long known not to be allowed to drive cars, to be forced to shroud their bodies in black cloth when they leave the house, to depend heavily on male guardians and so on. All of this apparently contradicts liberal-secular assumptions.

Criticising the liberal-secular premises of Habermas's discourse ethics and conception of the public sphere, Schirin Amir-Moazami (2010) contends that it is impossible to bracket off one's ideological disposition – secular or religious – when entering the political arena or any other public. Such inalienable persuasions and world views provide orientation in all aspects of life, not just in private affairs, and necessarily express themselves publicly. Religion therefore remains visible and socially productive in the public sphere – through ethics, moral principles and the tremendous power of religious beliefs to channel desires. By virtue of the same qualities, religion also plays a role in demarcating the private sphere from the realm of the public. The boundary between these spheres affects gender relations and the human body, because sexuality, as an intimate act and source of erotic pleasure, is simultaneously the primary source of social reproduction and kinship relations and, as such, of concern to a wider community – in every society. As a result, binary gender roles, gendered bodily practices and unwritten rules of conduct exist in so-called secular and Muslim societies alike and determine the way men and women behave in public and private spaces. Gender-specific modes of maintaining one's privacy, traversing public urban spaces, comporting oneself and interacting with strangers survive today in most, if not all, parts of the world, even in places where the principle of gender equality is widely recognised.

The boundaries between the public and the private thus vary from context to context, producing different gendered bodily practices, different inequalities and exclusions. In secular societies, indicators of one's religious belief, especially if it is the belief of a religious minority, are regarded with more suspicion and less likely to be publicly shown than in societies that acknowledge or demand that religion remains an essential element of public life. On the other hand, in liberal-secular contexts people have more, but by no means unlimited, freedom to wear what they want and publicly display their bodies than in a Muslim context such as the one I have studied in this book. These distinct norms and conventions, boundaries and exclusions are informed by different imaginations of the common good. The need to distinguish between right and wrong is answered by different inalienable beliefs in key principles that provide guidance in all aspects of life (Delitz and Maneval 2017). If we wish to understand how public and private spaces are conceived of and socially produced in a Muslim context like Saudi Arabia, we need to accept that the key principles governing these conceptions and motivations are considered as just as sacrosanct and unquestionable as liberal-secular assumptions in the West. Aiming to comprehend the motivation behind certain forms of inequality and exclusion, then, neither implies justifying them, nor entails using them to corroborate one's own moral superiority.

Without denying or defending gender inequality and gender-based exclusion in Saudi Arabia, my purpose in this book has been to challenge a reductive normative discourse in the West that equates gender segregation and veiling with the subjugation of Muslim women. In this discourse, gender equality in the West tends to be taken for granted and the violation of women's rights in Muslim contexts such as Saudi Arabia is seen as proof of the misogynist character of Islam or the inferiority of Muslim culture. In order to offer a more balanced view of public and private spaces in Jeddah, which are inseparable from questions of gender, this book has taken both men's and women's perspectives into account. It has looked at the spheres of the public and the private not as spatially divided, in a physical sense, but as entangled, mutually determining and situational. What I mean by this is that in Saudi Arabia, much as anywhere else, culturally dependent notions of privacy govern the way men and women of different social groups partake in public activities, as well as how they move and communicate. People protect their privacy while being public. Moreover, maintaining one's privacy – by avoiding display of what is considered to be nudity, for example – is a precondition for entering public space. The perception of public spaces, on the other hand, shapes the very boundaries that are drawn to demarcate one's private sphere as well as the social practices that serve to maintain it. In addition, based on the assumption that access to all publics is in one way or another limited, this study has focused on various forms of exclusion as well as on counterpublics.

The material collected and presented in this book, with these considerations in mind, suggests that gender segregation and other social norms and rules limit public activities and the freedom of movement not just of women, but also of men; and this corresponds to the religious views held by a significant portion of the male and female population. Those who do not share these views seek and find ways to express their discontent, or to circumvent, and call into question, prevailing moral standards. In doing so, they renegotiate the border between the public and the private. We are hence facing a range of positions and ongoing conflict around these concepts. The public sphere is a battleground, also in Saudi Arabia.

Architecture is an important means of defining boundaries between the public and the private, and key to an understanding of the different ways of doing so. My focus on the architecture of public and private spaces in Jeddah has revealed that a particular architectural style, for which I have chosen the term New Islamic Urbanism, has evolved and gained popularity, because it serves entirely different conceptions of public and private space. Although New Islamic Urbanism emerged from a discourse centred, among other aspects, on privacy protection, it enables the formation of publics in an extraordinarily restrictive political environment. In the remainder of the conclusion I want to revisit my findings in more detail.

In Jeddah, throughout the period covered in this book, the twentieth and early twenty-first century, the social construction of these boundaries has created divisions between the public activities of men and women and various social groups. Although they are informed by binary categories of gender, these divisions have never been equivalent to a female private and a male public sphere. Neither have they ever been congruent with the architectural division between inside and outside, or home and street. They have always been relational. Gender, social status and age, as well as a person's individual attitude to socially constructed norms of publicness and privacy, all play a role in defining the boundaries between these spheres, within the context of a particular situation. Due to the local ideal of women's privacy in early twentieth-century Jeddah, which I explored in chapter 2, women of some wealth and standing avoided being visible to unrelated men. As much as was possible, they retreated from outdoor public spaces, such as streets, the bazaar, cafes and sitting areas in front of residential buildings, as these were customarily occupied by men. Nevertheless, they participated in formal and informal networks and held social gatherings in the upstairs living rooms of residential buildings. A combination of architectural structures and social practices ensured that men did not disturb these female publics: stairwells, walls and doors served as barriers which screened them from view, and men were obliged to keep out of rooms occupied by women other than their wives and closest relatives. Buildings were designed in such a way that the privacy of the families residing in them was maintained, but they were not conceived of as strictly private spaces. They fulfilled various public functions, too. Unwritten rules existed regulating who met where, who was allowed to join and who was not supposed to disturb certain spaces. Similarly, unwanted guests were prevented from entering houses primarily by means of social control.

Not only women had to avoid places of encounter with men: men were also required to respect women's privacy, which included not looking at them and not disturbing their gatherings. This caution was a precondition for women's public activities. However, there were many women who, out of economic necessity or due to their disadvantageous position in society, were not able to meet the ideal of female privacy. Women of poor families could be seen vending food and groceries in the streets, and the privacy of slaves and prostitutes was severely limited. Whereas these women's public visibility marked their low social status, women of higher social standing achieved social distinction by avoiding being seen, and by staying away from male publics. While acknowledging the political scope of women's publics, it is important to note that they were not formally granted the power of decision-making. Only men could hold positions and partake in institutions which had such power; yet not all men had equal access to the same publics. A man's involvement in a particular public, decision-making or not, depended on his wealth, family reputation and profession.

New building materials, construction techniques and types of houses which were increasingly introduced to the country in the oil era profoundly changed the material framework of public and private spaces. They created clearer distinctions between inside and outside, as compared to the older buildings, and often did not offer flexible solutions for the division of male and female activities. Most of the new residential buildings constructed from the 1950s onwards were designed to serve domestic purposes only. Simultaneously, the large number of external workplaces created by new facilities, services and employment possibilities led to a division of work and domestic life. As a consequence, the home lost many of its public functions and became a place almost exclusively dedicated to family life. While a residential building in Jeddah was previously inhabited by an entire extended family, the majority of new homes were built to accommodate nuclear families. Also, larger family compounds now divided the segments of an extended family more effectively than Jeddah's old tower houses. Privacy was increasingly understood as an enclosed space of non-interference for the conjugal couple and its children. As the distance to parents, parents-in-law and grandparents increased and domestic space became more insulated from the environment, sociability within the home decreased. At the same time, possibilities for social control were reduced. This also provided new opportunities for the younger generation.

In the 1980s and 1990s, architects and urban planners from Jeddah asserted that homes built in Jeddah from the beginning of the oil era contradicted traditional principles of social coexistence, especially traditional Islamic notions of privacy, family bonds and connectedness to the wider neighbourhood. In their opinion, the contemporary architecture of Jeddah prevented people from leading their lives according to the teachings of Islam. Claiming that large-scale imports of architectural solutions from abroad led to housing design that was detached from local sociocultural and religious traditions, they called for a return to principles of environmental design in the historic city of Jeddah. I have argued that this criticism was embedded in a broader discourse of Salafism and Islamic Revival (*al-ṣaḥwa al-islāmīya*). Islamic reformers from the 1970s to the 1990s warned against Westernisation, the decline of Islamic values and moral decay, especially with respect to the politics of gender. Instead of the teachings of pious forefathers, architects and urban planners used the idealised architectural tradition of Jeddah and the Ḥijāz as a reference point. These authors, whose discourse I have termed New Islamic Urbanism, pursued careers at Saudi universities, in the Municipality of Jeddah or in private architecture companies. They thus had an influence on later generations of students of architecture, on planning processes and on home builders' and buyers' choices. Due to the widespread popularity of the Islamic Revival movement, their opinions fell on fruitful ground.

As many Saudis consider privacy protection, with the help of impermeable architectural elements, to be an essential part of a pious lifestyle, New Islamic Urbanism became overwhelmingly popular in Jeddah and other Saudi cities. Characterised by screens, metal blinds, walled enclosures, tinted windows, shutters etc., it disconnects interior spaces and residents from the outside world. However, high walls and screens also enable a wide range of activities which are prohibited in public. At home, away from the public eye, people do not have to follow the rules of conduct derived from Wahhabi theological exegesis that govern public urban spaces. The architecture of seclusion thus enables different conceptions of privacy: one centres on concealing the body and avoiding contact between unrelated men and women; another emphasises the non-interference of outsiders in personal affairs and the freedom of the individual. My assumption is that New Islamic Urbanism was so successful because it served different needs and even contrary desires.

I do not mean to divide the population of Jeddah into two groups with distinct conceptions of privacy. People can enact different conceptions of privacy at different times, as they may identify with these conceptions to varying degrees. A member of a Sufi order, for instance, may consider it important to protect family members from view. At the same time, the screens and blinds of his home allow him to conduct Sufi rituals, which neighbours and the Saudi state regard with suspicion. By way of further example, the women in Olivia Arthur's photographs discussed in chapter 6 agreed to have their pictures taken and published – an act regarded as shameful by more conservative Saudis. Some of the women in Arthur's photos, however, preferred to wear clothes which cover most of their bodies. In both cases, visual protection and personal autonomy are equally valued.

As I argued in chapter 6, notions of privacy in Jeddah today are informed by the concepts of *khalwa*, which denotes the presence of a man and an unrelated woman in a confined space, and *ikhtilāṭ*, the mingling of unrelated men and women in groups and open spaces. Divergent attitudes to these concepts lead to the formation of different types of publics within particular architectural assemblages: gender-segregated workplaces, universities and shopping malls on the one hand, and mixed art exhibitions, cafes and parties within privately owned facilities on the other. Varying conceptions of privacy, and their corresponding politics of gender, thus determine the way men and women access and contribute to the constitution of public space: the modes of transport they use to travel from place to place and the way they interact with strangers, as well as how, where and with whom they spend their time.

The Saudi state does not remain neutral in this regard. In the conservative cultural climate of the 1980s and 1990s, the Saudi regime drew legitimacy from limiting the public visibility of women. Under the reign of King ʿAbdullāh (2005–15), the state promoted a more active role for women and began to experiment with mixing in certain places. Yet strong forces in Saudi society object to the mixing of the sexes. Therefore, two parallel trends of gender policy emerged in the early twenty-first century: on the one hand, more gender-segregated spaces have been created, especially during the reign of King ʿAbdullāh. Simultaneously, the mixing of men and women in public spaces, known as *ikhtilāṭ,* has become more common – a trend that has increased under King Salmān. Based on my fieldwork observations, I have argued that gender segregation restricts both men's and women's movements. However, the costly duplication of spaces also creates opportunities. In the context of Saudi Arabia, women-only universities, for example, offer chances for women not only to study, but also to have a public life outside the home. Those women who reject *ikhtilāṭ*, but wish to study, work and participate in public events, do not necessarily regard gender segregation and veiling as confining. For them, maintenance of their privacy through spatial separation and concealment of their bodies from men who are not closely related are preconditions for any and all engagement in public activities.

At the same time, other women and men seek to circumvent a segregation regime which does not reflect their personal attitude to gender and religion. Alternative ideas of what it means to be public and what should be private, and hence inaccessible to outsiders, are negotiated and enacted within privately owned, secluded spaces, such as homes, cars, beach resorts, gated communities and a few cafes. Privacy for them means doing what they want to do because it is no one else's business. This includes activities and behaviour that conflict with the dominant norms and moral standards. It may also include transgression of the rules of moral conduct in public. Some participants in these counter-discourses perform and publicly display their own conceptions of privacy and publicness by means of mass communication. By doing so, they constitute counterpublics which challenge the prevailing norms and rules of public and private life in Saudi Arabia and contribute to their transformation.

As the Saudi state does not grant its citizens the freedoms of assembly, association, speech and opinion, it is within the reception halls of private homes, gated developments and privately owned facilities that Saudis gather, articulate dissent and constitute publics and counterpublics. While critics warn that the proliferation of shopping malls, gated communities and similar forms of privatisation and securitisation of urban spaces result in curtailed civil liberties, cases from Saudi Arabia suggest a slightly different reading. The selling, fencing in and gating of territories formerly owned by the community and administered by the state to private investors does indeed cement social differences and result in further marginalisation of the under-privileged, including in Jeddah. However, critics of these trends sometimes overlook the fact that privatised and securitised public spaces produce not only consumers, but also new forms of sociability, out of which new publics can emerge. These publics can articulate criticism and stage concerted action. In the context of an authoritarian state that supports a restrictive moral regime, a gated housing or holiday development can provide protection for social activities otherwise banned in the streets of the city, and opportunities for counterpublics to convene. Paradoxically, the walls and gates of such developments in Jeddah are therefore experienced as granters of social freedom, albeit only by those who have access to these spaces.

'[B]eing public is a privilege', writes Michael Warner (2002: 23), commenting on nineteenth-century debates on women's access to the public sphere of politics. This holds true for Saudi Arabia as much as for many other contexts, including contemporary Western societies. But having privacy is a privilege too, I would add. In Jeddah in the pre-oil era, the capacities of slaves, prostitutes and the poor to maintain a private sphere that corresponded to the cultural ideal were severely limited. Conforming to the ideal of privacy was a privilege of the wealthy who could afford large houses with many rooms on several floors and who did not depend on women's commercial activities to make ends meet. In contemporary Saudi society, various forms of privacy are likewise not available to everyone. Migrant workers, for example, who often have extraordinarily long work days and share rooms with several co-workers, barely have space of their own where others do not interfere. Maids working and living in Saudi households are denied the visual privacy which forbids pious Saudi women to be seen by and communicate with unrelated men. Furthermore, not everyone can afford access to one of the islands of privacy within the Saudi public realm. Not everyone can pay the rent for a chalet in Durrat al-ʿArūs or the entrance fee for a beach resort in Obhur. And many families in Jeddah cannot afford private cars with tinted windows that enable them to avoid unwanted contact with strangers and to feel safe when travelling across the city. One needs to have money or to know the right people to gain access to a privately owned facility which can be used as a weekend retreat, to enjoy an atmosphere of individual freedom beyond the control of the authorities or as a stage for enactments of alternative conceptions of nudity and publicness. Besides cultural differences, religious beliefs and political opinions, the question of what kind of public someone in Jeddah attends and how much privacy one can have in the city has therefore always depended on wealth and social status.

In Saudi Arabia, opportunities to constitute and participate in publics are limited – for men and women alike. Nevertheless, certain forms of publicness can be achieved even if the privilege of being public is not formally granted in the form of civil liberties. This holds true, for example, for meetings of dissidents, religious minorities and sexual counterpublics within residential buildings. In recent years, the internet has widened opportunities for public debate and criticism of the state. The authorities' scope to control and intervene in cyberspace is fairly limited. Incapable of effectively censoring public expressions of dissent in blogs and on social networking websites, the regime silences internet activists by detaining, physically punishing or murdering them. As the Saudi state draws legitimacy from its image as a provider of security and order, an effective means to make one's concerns public is to challenge state authority by occupying public urban territory. This strategy is employed by drifters: frustrated young men who drive rented or stolen cars at high speed across Saudi cities, sliding around on highways, drifting sideways, left and right, damaging vehicles and dodging the police. It is also deployed by migrant workers who, having absconded from their employers due to maltreatment, non-payment of wages or other forms of abuse, set up tents and makeshift homes in the streets of Jeddah. Their public visibility captures media attention and prompts embassies and Saudi authorities to respond to their concerns.

Many publics discussed in this book are largely unknown outside Saudi Arabia. Apart from a few spectacular cases, which temporarily garner global media attention, the existence of critical publics and opposition movements, as well as sexual, religious, migrant workers' and other counterpublics is largely ignored, as are their respective concerns. Some of these publics and counterpublics address first and foremost a Saudi audience. Others make use of global channels of communication: foreign newspapers and magazines, international art exhibitions, YouTube and English-language websites. Seeking publicity within Saudi Arabia and abroad, they aim to transform Saudi society as much as they intend to cast it in a different light. Renegotiating the boundary between public and private, they challenge assumptions of what life in Saudi Arabia is like. With this book, I hope to draw attention also to the diversity of the discourse in which they and representatives of other societal groups and forces are engaged as well as to the various strategies they use to constitute publics and articulate their opinion.

References

Abaza, Mona. 2001. 'Shopping Malls, Consumer Culture and the Reshaping of Public Space in Egypt.' *Theory, Culture & Society* 18 (5): 97–122.

____. 2006. *Changing Consumer Cultures of Modern Egypt: Cairo's Urban Reshaping*. Leiden: Brill.

Abdulaal, Waleed Abdullah. 2011. 'Large Urban Developments as the New Driver for Land Development in Jeddah.' *Habitat International* 36 (1): 36–46.

Abdulgani, Khaled. 1993. 'Jeddah: A Study of Metropolitan Change.' *Cities* 10 (1): 50–9.

Abdullah, Mohamed A., Hamad S. Salhi, Lina A. Bakry, Emi Okamoto, Abdullah M. Abomelha, Brian Stevens and Fawzi M. Mousa. 2002. 'Adolescent Rickets in Saudi Arabia: A Rich and Sunny Country.' *Journal of Pediatric Endocrinology & Metabolism* 15 (7): 1017–25.

Abu-Gazzeh, Tawfiq M. 1994. 'Built Form and Religion: Underlying Structures of Jeddah Al-Qademah.' *Traditional Dwellings and Settlements Review* 5 (2): 49–55.

____. 1996. 'Privacy as the Basis of Architectural Planning in the Islamic Culture of Saudi Arabia.' *Architecture & Comportement* 11 (3/4): 93–111.

Abu-Lughod, Janet. 1980. 'Contemporary Relevance of Islamic Urban Principles.' *Ekistics* 47 (280): 6–10.

____. 1987. 'The Islamic City: Historic Myth, Islamic Essence, and Contemporary Relevance.' *International Journal of Middle East Studies* 19 (2): 155–76.

Abu-Lughod, Lila. 1986. *Veiled Sentiments: Honor and Poetry in a Bedouin Society*. Berkeley, CA: University of California Press.

____. 1990. 'The Romance of Resistance: Tracing Transformations of Power through Bedouin Women.' *American Ethnologist* 17 (1): 41–55.

____. 2002. 'Do Muslim Women Really Need Saving? Anthropological Reflections on Cultural Relativism and Its Others.' *American Anthropologist* 104 (3): 783–90.

Ahmed, Leila. 1992. *Women and Gender in Islam: Historical Roots of a Modern Debate*. New Haven, CT: Yale University Press.

Alahmad, Safa. 2014. 'Reporting Saudi Arabia's Hidden Uprising.' BBC. 30 May. www.bbc.com/news/world-middle-east-27619309 (accessed 22 April 2015).

Alireza, Marianne. 2002 [1971]. *At the Drop of a Veil*. Costa Mesa, CA: Blind Owl Press.

Aljazeera. 2012. 'Saudi Forces Clash with Protesters in Qatif.' 13 January. www.aljazeera.com/news/middleeast/2012/01/201211314391756712 4.html (accessed 8 July 2015).

Alshech, Eli. 2004. '"Do Not Enter Houses Other Than Your Own": The Evolution of the Notion of a Private Domestic Sphere in Early Sunnī Islamic Thought.' *Islamic Law and Society* 11 (3): 291–332.

Altorki, Soraya. 1986. *Women in Saudi Arabia: Ideology and Behaviour Among the Elite*. New York: Columbia University Press.

Amar, Paul. 2011. 'Middle East Masculinity Studies: Discourses of "Men in Crisis", Industries of Gender in Revolution.' *Journal of Middle East Women's Studies* 7 (3): 36–70.

Amir-Moazami, Schirin. 2007. *Politisierte Religion: Der Kopftuchstreit in Deutschland und Frankreich*. Bielefeld: transcript.

____. 2010. 'Fallstricke des konsensorientierten Dialogs unter liberal-säkularen Bedingungen: Entwicklungen in der Deutschen Islam Konferenz.' In *Migrationsreport 2010: Fakten, Analysen, Perspektiven*, edited by Marianne Krüger-Potratz and Werner Schiffauer, 109–38. Frankfurt am Main: Campus Verlag.

Ammann, Ludwig. 2004. 'Privatsphäre und Öffentlichkeit in der muslimischen Zivilisation.' In *Islam in Sicht: Der Auftritt von Muslimen im öffentlichen Raum*, edited by Nilüfer Göle and Ludwig Ammann, 69–117. Bielefeld: transcript.

Anṣārī, 'Abd al-Quddūs. 1972. *History of Aziziah Water Supply, Juddah and Glimpses on Water Sources in the Kingdom of Saudi Arabia*. Beirut: Mu'assasa 'Abd al-Ḥafīẓ al-Basāṭ.

____. 1982. *Mausū'a tārīkh madīna Juddah*. Cairo: Dār Miṣr li-ṭ-ṭibā'a.

Arab News. 2008. 'Consulate Warns Against "Fixers" as More Filipinos Seek "Backdoor Exit".' 26 January. www.arabnews.com/node/308171?quicktabs_stat2=1 (accessed 25 July 2015).

____. 2010. 'Residents near Kandara Bridge Decry Migrants' Shantytown.' 27 October. www.arabnews.com/node/358838 (accessed 20 July 2015).

____. 13 January 2011. 'From Frying Pan to Fire: Runaway Maids End Up in Harsher Conditions.' www.arabnews.com/node/365279?quicktabs_stat2=0 (accessed 20 July 2015).

____. 21 June 2011. 'Last of Stranded Sri Lankans Leave Kandara Bridge.' www.arabnews.com/node/381413 (accessed 20 July 2015).

Ardener, Shirley. 1993. *Women and Space: Ground Rules and Social Maps*. Oxford: Berg.

Arthur, Olivia. 2012. *Jeddah Diary*. London: Fishbar.

Ballantyne, Andrew. 2007. *Deleuze and Guattari for Architects*. London: Routledge.

BBC. 2015. 'Saudi Blogger Badawi "Flogged for Islam Insult".' 9 January. www.bbc.com/news/world-middle-east-30744693 (accessed 16 February 2015).

Benhabib, Seyla. 1992a. 'Models of Public Space: Hannah Arendt, the Liberal Tradition, and Jürgen Habermas'. In *Habermas and the Public Sphere*, edited by Craig Calhoun, 73–98. Cambridge, MA/London: MIT Press.

____. 1992b. *Situating the Self: Gender, Community, and Postmodernism in Contemporary Ethics*. New York: Routledge.

Berking, Helmuth. 2008. '"Städte lassen sich an ihrem Gang erkennen wie Menschen": Skizzen zur Erforschung der Stadt und der Städte.' In *Die Eigenlogik der Städte: Neue Wege für die Stadtforschung*, edited by Helmuth Berking and Martina Löw, 15–31. Frankfurt am Main: Campus.

Berking, Helmuth, and Martina Löw, eds. 2008. *Die Eigenlogik der Städte: Neue Wege für die Stadtforschung*. Frankfurt am Main: Campus.

Bille, Mikkel, and Tim Flohr Sørensen. 2007. 'An Anthropology of Luminosity: The Agency of Light.' *Journal of Material Culture* 12 (3): 263–84.

Blakely, Edward J., and Mary Gail Snyder. 1997. *Fortress America: Gated Communities in the United States*. Washington, DC: Brookings Institution Press.

Bodenschatz, Harald. 2005. 'Council for European Urbanism (CEU) – ein Netzwerk für Städtebaureform in Europa.' *Die neue Stadt* 1. www.die-neue-stadt.de/archiv/ausgabe_i_v/goerlitz.html (accessed 13 April 2015).

Böhme, Gernot. 2006. *Architektur und Atmosphäre*. Munich: Wilhelm Fink Verlag.

Bokhari, Abdulla Y. 1978. 'Jeddah: A Study in Urban Formation.' Ph.D. diss., University of Pennsylvania.

Bourdieu, Pierre. 1967. Postface to *Architecture gothique et pensée scolastique*, by Erwin Panofsky, 133–67. Translated by Pierre Bourdieu. Paris: Minuit.

____. 1979. *Algeria 1960*. Cambridge: Cambridge University Press.

____. 1984. *Distinction: A Social Critique of the Judgement of Taste*. Cambridge, MA: Harvard University Press.

Brown, Wendy. 2010. *Walled States, Waning Sovereignty*. New York: Zone.

vom Bruck, G. 1997. 'A House Turned Inside Out: Inhabiting Space in a Yemeni City.' *Journal of Material Culture* 2 (2): 139–72.

Burckhardt, John Lewis. 1829. *Travels in Arabia*. London: Henry Colburn.

Butler, Judith. 2011. 'Bodies in Alliance and the Politics of the Street.' *transversal texts*. September. eipcp.net/transversal/1011/butler/en (accessed 23 April 2015).

Cache, Bernard. 1995. *Earth Moves: The Furnishing of Territories*. Cambridge, MA: MIT Press.

Carrigan, Tim, Bob Connell and John Lee. 1985. 'Toward a New Sociology of Masculinity.' *Theory and Society* 14: 551–604.

Champion, Daryl. 2003. *The Paradoxical Kingdom: Saudi Arabia and the Momentum of Reform*. New York: Columbia University Press.

Chatty, Dawn, and Annika Rabo, eds. 1997. *Organizing Women: Formal and Informal Women's Groups in the Middle East*. Oxford: Berg.

Citino, Nathan. 2006. 'Suburbia and Modernization: Community Building and America's Post-World War II Encounter with the Arab Middle East.' *The Arab Studies Journal* 13/14 (2/1): 39–64.

Commins, David. 2006. *The Wahhabi Mission and Saudi Arabia*. London: I.B. Tauris.

Congress for the New Urbanism. 2001. 'Charter of the New Urbanism.' www.cnu.org/charter (accessed 25 July 2015).
Connell, R.W., and James W. Messerschmidt. 2005. 'Hegemonic Masculinity: Rethinking the Concept.' *Gender & Society* 19 (6): 829–59.
Cook, Michael. 2000. *Commanding Right and Forbidding Wrong in Islamic Thought*. Cambridge: Cambridge University Press.
Dankowitz, Aluma. 2004. 'A Saudi National Dialogue on Women's Rights and Obligations.' *MEMRI Inquiry & Analysis Series Report* 183. www.memri.org/report/en/0/0/0/0/0/0/1158.htm (accessed 22 January 2015).
Davis, Mike. 1992. 'Fortress Los Angeles: The Militarization of Urban Space.' In *Variations on a Theme Park: The New American City and the End of Public Space*, edited by Michael Sorkin, 154–80. New York: The Noonday Press.
de Certeau, Michel. 1984. *The Practice of Everyday Life*. Translated by Steven Rendall. Berkeley, CA: University of California Press.
Dehne, Philipp. 2010. 'Eine Beziehung mit Zukunft? Arbeitsmigranten in Saudi-Arabien.' In *Saudi-Arabien: Ein Königreich im Wandel*, edited by Ulrike Freitag, 135–64. Paderborn: Schöningh.
____. 2011. 'MigrantInnen im saudi-arabischen Kontext.' MA thesis, Freie Universität Berlin.
Dekmejian, Hrair. 1980. 'The Anatomy of Islamic Revival: Legitimacy Crisis, Ethnic Conflict and the Search for Islamic Alternatives.' *Middle East Journal* 34 (1): 1–12.
____. 1994. 'The Rise of Political Islamism in Saudi Arabia.' *Middle East Journal* 48 (4): 627–43.
Dekmejian, Richard. 2003. 'The Liberal Impulse in Saudi Arabia.' *Middle East Journal* 57 (3): 400–13.
Deleuze, Gilles. 1995. *Negotiations*. Translated by Martin Joughin. New York: Columbia University Press.
Deleuze, Gilles, and Félix Guattari. 1987. *A Thousand Plateaus: Capitalism and Schizophrenia*. Translated by Brian Massumi. Minneapolis, MN: University of Minnesota Press.
Delitz, Heike. 2009. *Architektursoziologie*. Bielefeld: transcript.
____. 2010. *Gebaute Gesellschaft: Architektur als Medium des Sozialen*. Frankfurt am Main: Campus.
____. 2017. 'Architectural Modes of Collective Existence: Architectural Sociology as a Comparative Social Theory.' *Cultural Sociology* 12 (1): 37–57.
Delitz, Heike, and Stefan Maneval. 2017. 'The "Hidden Kings", or Hegemonic Imaginaries: Analytical Perspectives of Post-foundational Sociological Thought.' *Im@go: Journal of the Social Imaginary* 10: 33–49.
DeLong-Bas, Natana J. 2004. *Wahhabi Islam: From Revival and Reform to Global Jihad*. Oxford: Oxford University Press.
Demetriou, Demetrakis Z. 2001. 'Connell's Concept of Hegemonic Masculinity: A Critique.' *Theory and Society* 30: 337–61.
Didier, Charles. 1857. *Séjour chez le grand-chérif de la Mekke* Paris: Hachette.
Dinkelaker, Christoph. 2010. 'Im Osten nichts Neues? Zur Situation der Schia in Saudi-Arabien.' In *Saudi-Arabien: Ein Königreich im Wandel*, edited by Ulrike Freitag, 189–220. Paderborn: Schöningh.
Diyāb, Muḥammad Ṣādiq. 2003. *Jiddah: al-Tārīkh wa-l-ḥayāt al-ijtimā'iyya*. Jeddah: Maṭābi' mu'assasat al-madīna li-l-ṣaḥāfa.
Dornhof, Sarah. 2011. 'Regimes of Visibility: Representing Violence against Women in the French "Banlieue".' *Feminist Review* 98: 110–27.
Doumato, Eleanor. 1992. 'Gender, Monarchy, and National Identity in Saudi Arabia.' *British Journal of Middle Eastern Studies* 19 (1): 31–47.
____. 1999. 'Women and Work in Saudi Arabia: How Flexible Are Islamic Margins?' *Middle East Journal* 53 (4): 568–83.
____. 2000. *Getting God's Ear: Women, Islam, and Healing in Saudi Arabia and the Gulf*. New York: Columbia University Press.
Drewes, Frauke. 2010. 'Das Nationale Dialogforum in Saudi-Arabien: Ausdruck politischer Reformen oder Stagnation?' In *Saudi-Arabien: Ein Königreich im Wandel*, edited by Ulrike Freitag, 29–60. Paderborn: Schöningh.
Duany, Andrés, and Elizabeth Plater-Zyberk. 1991. *Towns and Town-making Principles*. New York: Rizzoli.
Duncan, George Orr. 1987. 'The Planning and Development of Jeddah 1970–1984.' Ph.D. diss., University of Durham.

Eben Saleh, Mohammed A. 2002. 'The Transformation of Residential Neighborhood: The Emergence of New Urbanism in Saudi Arabian Culture.' *Building and Environment* 37: 515–29.

Eco, Umberto. 1986. 'Functionalism and Sign: The Semiotics of Architecture.' In *The City and the Sign*, edited by M. Gottdiener and A. Lagopoulos, 56–85. New York: Columbia University Press.

Eickelman, Dale. 1974. 'Is there an Islamic City?' *International Journal of Middle East Studies* 5: 274–94.

Eickelman, Dale, and Jon W. Anderson, eds. 2003. *New Media in the Muslim World: The Emerging Public Sphere*. Bloomington, IN: Indiana University Press.

Edge of Arabia, ed. 2012. *We need to talk = yajibu an nataḥāwar* (exhibition catalogue). Jeddah: self-published.

Elaph. 2007. 'al-Ghamidi li-Ilaf: ghadartu mujbiran.' 19 September. www.elaph.com/ElaphWeb/AkhbarKhasa/2007/9/264283.htm?sectionarchive=AkhbarKhasa (accessed 16 February 2015).

Elias, Norbert. 1983. *Die höfische Gesellschaft: Untersuchungen zur Soziologie des Königtums und der höfischen Aristokratie*. Frankfurt am Main: Suhrkamp.

Ellis, Cliff. 2002. 'The New Urbanism: Critiques and Rebuttals.' *Journal of Urban Design* 7 (3): 261–91.

Eyuce, Ahmet. n.d. [1985?]. 'A Comparative Analysis of Solid–Void Relationships of Traditional and Contemporary Houses in the Western Region of Saudi Arabia.' Working paper, Faculty of Environmental Design, King Abdulaziz University Jeddah.

Fadan, Yousef. 1983. 'The Development of Contemporary Housing in Saudi Arabia (1950–1983): A Study in Cross-Cultural Influence under Conditions of Rapid Change.' Ph.D. diss., Massachusetts Institute of Technology.

al-Faḍlī, 'Abbās bin Muḥammad Sa'īd. 2010. *al-Nuzla al-Yamāniyya: Ḥayy fī dhākira Jiddah*. Jeddah: Maktaba Dār Zahrān.

al-Fahad, Abdulaziz H. 2005. 'Ornamental Constitutionalism: The Saudi Basic Law of Governance.' *Yale Journal of International Law* 302: 375–96.

Fandy, Mamoun. 1999a. *Saudi Arabia and the Politics of Dissent*. New York: St Martin's Press.

____. 1999b. 'CyberResistance: Saudi Opposition Between Globalization and Localization.' *Comparative Studies in Society and History* 41 (1): 124–47.

Farahat, Abdelmohsen M., and M. Numan Cebeci. 1982. 'A Housing Project: Intentions, Realities and Alternatives.' *Housing Science* 6 (3): 209–27.

Fernando, Mayanthi L. 2009. 'Exceptional Citizens: Secular Muslim Women and the Politics of Difference in France.' *Social Anthropology/Anthropologie Sociale* 17 (4): 379–92.

Fischer, Joachim. 2004. 'Exzentrische Positionalität: Der Potsdamer Platz aus der Perspektive der Philosophischen Anthropologie.' *Potsdamer Platz: Soziologische Theorien zu einem Ort der Moderne*, edited by Joachim Fischer and Michael Makropoulos, 11–32. Munich: Wilhelm Fink Verlag.

Fischer, Joachim, and Heike Delitz, eds. 2009. *Die Architektur der Gesellschaft: Theorien für die Architektursoziologie*, Bielefeld: transcript.

Fischer, Joachim, and Michael Makropoulos, eds. 2004. *Potsdamer Platz: Soziologische Theorien zu einem Ort der Moderne*. Munich: Wilhelm Fink Verlag.

Foucault, Michel. 1972. *The Archaeology of Knowledge, and The Discourse on Language*. Translated by Alan M. Sheridan Smith. New York: Pantheon.

____. 1977. *Discipline and Punish: The Birth of the Prison*. Translated by Alan Sheridan. New York: Pantheon.

Fraser, Nancy. 1992. 'Rethinking the Public Sphere: A Contribution to the Critique of Actually Existing Democracy.' In *Habermas and the Public Sphere*, edited by Craig Calhoun, 109–42. Cambridge, MA/London: MIT Press.

Freitag, Ulrike. 2007. 'Handelsmetropole und Pilgerstation: Djidda in spätosmanischer Zeit.' *Comparativ: Zeitschrift für Globalgeschichte und vergleichende Gesellschaftsforschung* 17 (2): 64–79.

____. 2015a. 'The Falah School in Jeddah: Civic Engagement for Future Generations?' www.jadaliyya.com/pages/index/21430/the-falah-school-in-jeddah_civic-engagement-for-fu (accessed 5 August 2015).

____2015b. 'Symbolic Politics and Urban Violence in Late Ottoman Jeddah.' In *Urban Violence in the Middle East: Changing Cityscapes in the Transition from Empire to Nation State*, edited by Ulrike Freitag, Claudia Ghrawi, Nelida Fuccaro and Nora Lafi, 111–38. New York/Oxford: Berghahn.

____. 2016a. 'Urban Space and Prestige: When Festivals Turned Violent in Jeddah, 1880s–1960s.' In *Violence and the City in the Modern Middle East*, edited by Nelida Fuccaro, 61–74. Stanford, CA: Stanford University Press.

____. 2016b. 'Urban Life in Late Ottoman, Hashemite and Early Saudi Jeddah, as Documented in the Photographs in the Snouck Hurgronje Collection in Leiden.' *ZMO Working Papers* 16.
____. 2017. 'Heinrich Freiherr von Maltzan's 'My Pilgrimage to Mecca': A Critical Investigation.' In *The Hajj and Europe in the Age of Empire*, edited by Umar Ryad, 142–54. Leiden: Brill.
Frers, Lars. 2007. *Einhüllende Materialitäten: Eine Phänomenologie des Wahrnehmens und Handelns an Bahnhöfen und Fährterminals*. Bielefeld: transcript.
Friedman, Thomas L. 2017. 'Saudi Arabia's Arab Spring, at Last.' *New York Times*. 23 November. https://www.nytimes.com/2017/11/23/opinion/saudi-prince-mbs-arab-spring.html (accessed 28 March 2019).
Fürtig, Henner. 2007. 'Reformkampagne in Saudi-Arabien: Brise oder Sturm?' *GIGA-Fokus* 11. www.giga-hamburg.de/dl/download.php?d=/content/publikationen/pdf/gf_nahost_0711.pdf (accessed 8 June 2008).
Gazzaz, Abdulrahman, and Turki Gazzaz. 2019. *Public/Private*. Jeddah: Bricklab/Saudi Arts Council.
van Geel, Annemarie. 2016. 'Separate or Together? Women-only Public Spaces and Participation of Saudi Women in the Public Domain in Saudi Arabia.' *Contemporary Islam* 10: 357–78.
____. 2018. *'For Women Only': Gender Segregation, Islam, and Modernity in Saudi Arabia and Kuwait*. Self-published.
Gell, Alfred. 1998. *Art and Agency*. Oxford: Clarendon Press.
General Authority for Statistics. 2016. 'Statistical Yearbook of 2016.' https://www.stats.gov.sa/en/5305# (accessed 28 March 2019).
Ghoussoub, Mai, and Emma Sinclair-Webb, eds. 2000. *Imagined Masculinities: Male Identity and Culture in the Modern Middle East*. London: Saqi.
Ghrawi, Claudia. 2015. 'In the Service of the Whole Community? Civic Engagement in Saudi Arabia (1950s–1960s).' www.jadaliyya.com/pages/index/21479/in-the-service-of-the-whole-community-civic-engage (accessed 5 August 2015).
Gieryn, Thomas F. 2002. 'What Buildings Do.' *Theory and Society* 31 (1): 35–74.
Giglio, Mike. 2012. 'Saudi Writer Hamza Kashgari Detained in Malaysia Over Muhammad Tweets.' *The Daily Beast*. 10 February. www.thedailybeast.com/articles/2012/02/08/twitter-aflame-with-fatwa-against-saudi-writer-hamza-kashgari.html (accessed 5 August 2015).
Gilsenan, Michael. 2008. *Recognizing Islam: Religion and Society in the Modern Middle East*. London/New York: I.B. Tauris.
Glasze, Georg, and Abdallah Alkhayyal. 2002. 'Gated Housing Estates in the Arab World: Case Studies in Lebanon and Riyadh, Saudi Arabia.' *Environment and Planning B: Planning and Design* 29: 321–36.
Glosemeyer, Iris. 2002. 'Saudi-Arabien: Wandel ohne Wechsel?' In *Elitenwandel in der arabischen Welt und Iran*. SWP-Studie, edited by Volker Perthes, 172–88. Berlin: Stiftung Wissenschaft und Politik.
Glover, William. 2008. *Making Lahore Modern: Constructing and Imagining a Colonial City*. Minneapolis, MN: University of Minnesota Press.
Göle, Nilüfer. 1997. 'The Gendered Nature of the Public Sphere.' *Public Culture* 10 (1): 61–81.
____. 2000. 'Snapshots of Islamic Modernities.' *Daedalus* 129 (1): 91–117.
Göle, Nilüfer, and Ludwig Ammann, eds. 2004. *Islam in Sicht: Der Auftritt von Muslimen im öffentlichen Raum*. Bielefeld: transcript.
Grant, Jill. 2006. *Planning the Good Community: New Urbanism in Theory and Practice*. London/New York: Routledge.
____. 2011. 'Time, Scale, and Control: How New Urbanism (Mis)Uses Jane Jacobs.' In *Reconsidering Jane Jacobs*, edited by Max Page and Timothy Mennel, 91–103. Chicago/Washington, DC: Planners Press.
Greenlaw, Jean-Pierre. 1995. *The Coral Buildings of Suakin: Islamic Architecture, Planning, Design and Domestic Arrangements in a Red Sea Port*. London: Kegan Paul.
Grubbauer, Monika. 2011. *Die vorgestellte Stadt*. Bielefeld: transcript.
Guardian. 2013. 'Dozens of Saudi Arabian Women Drive Cars on Day of Protest against Ban.' 26 October. www.theguardian.com/world/2013/oct/26/saudi-arabia-woman-driving-car-ban (accessed 23 April 2015).
Guha, Ranajit. 1996. 'The Small Voice of History.' In *Subaltern Studies IX: Writings on South Asian History and Society*, edited by Shahid Amin and Dipesh Chakrabarty, 1–12. Delhi: Oxford University Press.

____. 1999. *Elementary Aspects of Peasant Insurgency in Colonial India*. Durham, NC/London: Duke University Press.
Gulf News. 2013. 'Saudi "Blasphemy" Prisoner Hamza Kashgari Tweets for First Time after Release.' 29 October. gulfnews.com/news/gulf/saudi-arabia/saudi-blasphemy-prisoner-hamza-kashgari-tweets-for-first-time-after-release-1.1248548 (accessed 5 August 2015).
Haas, Tigran. 2008. *New Urbanism and Beyond: Designing Cities for the Future*. New York: Rizzoli.
Habermas, Jürgen. 1989. *The Structural Transformation of the Public Sphere*. Translated by Thomas Burger with Frederick Lawrence. Cambridge, MA: MIT Press.
Hagmann, Jannis. 2010. 'Medienkontrolle durch Medienbesitz? Presse, Rundfunk und Internet in Saudi-Arabien.' In *Saudi-Arabien: Ein Königreich im Wandel*, edited by Ulrike Freitag, 107–34. Paderborn: Schöningh.
____. 2011. 'Regen von oben, Protest von unten: Eine Analyse gesellschaftlicher Mobilisierung infolge der Flutkatastrophe in Jidda, Saudi-Arabien, anhand von Presse, Petitionen und Facebook.' Working Paper No. 4, Center for North African and Middle Eastern Politics, Freie Universität Berlin.
Halbwachs, Maurice. 1980. *The Collective Memory*. Translated by Francis J. Ditter, Jr, and Vida Yazdi Ditter. New York: Harper & Row.
Hale, Sondra. 1986. 'Sudanese Women and Revolutionary Parties: The Wing of the Patriarch.' *Middle East Report* 138: 25–30.
Hamdan, Amani. 2005. 'Women and Education in Saudi Arabia: Challenges and Achievements.' *International Education Journal* 6 (1): 42–64.
Hamzawy, Amr. 2008. 'The Saudi Labyrinth: Is there a Political Opening?' In *Beyond the Façade: Political Reform in the Arab World*, edited by Marina Ottaway and Julia Choucair-Vizoso, 187–210. Washington, DC: Carnegie Endowment for International Peace.
Hanssen, Jens, Thomas Philipp and Stefan Weber, eds. 2002. *The Empire in the City: Arab Provincial Capitals in the Late Ottoman Empire*. Würzburg: Ergon.
al-Ḥārithī, Nāṣir bin ʿAlī. 2003/4 [1425 AH]. *Aʿmāl al-malik ʿAbd al-ʿAzīz al-miʿmāriyya fī munṭaqat Makka al-Mukarrama 1343–1373 AH/1924–1953*. Riyadh: Dārat al-Malik ʿAbd al-ʿAzīz.
Hassan, Fayza. 2001. 'Abdel-Rahman Makhlouf: A Passion for Order.' *Al-Ahram Weekly Online* 565. 20–26 December. http://weekly.ahram.org.eg/2001/565/profile.htm (accessed 7 November 2009).
al-Hathloul, Saleh. 1996. *The Arab-Muslim City: Tradition, Continuity and Change in the Physical Environment*. Riyadh: Dar al-Sahan.
____. 1998. 'Continuity in a Changing Tradition.' In *Legacies for the Future: Contemporary Architecture in Islamic Societies*, edited by Cynthia C. Davidson, 18–31. London: Thames and Hudson.
al-Hathloul, Saleh, and Muhammad A. Mughal. 1991. 'Jeddah.' *Cities* 8 (4): 267–73.
____. 2004. 'Urban Growth Management: The Saudi Experience.' *Habitat International* 28: 609–23.
Hawting, G. R. 1984. 'The Origin of Jedda and the Problem of al-Shuʿayba.' *Arabica* 31 (3): 318–26.
Hegland, Mary Elaine. 1986. 'Political Roles of Iranian Village Women.' *Middle East Report* 138: 14–19, 46.
al-Hemaidi, Waleed K. 2001. 'The Metamorphosis of the Urban Fabric in an Arab-Muslim City: Riyadh, Saudi Arabia.' *Journal of Housing and the Built Environment* 16: 179–201.
Hennecke, Stefanie. 2010. *Die kritische Rekonstruktion als Leitbild: Stadtentwicklungspolitik in Berlin zwischen 1991 und 1999*. Hamburg: Verlag Dr Kovač.
Hertog, Steffen. 2005. 'Segmented Clientelism: The Political Economy of Saudi Economic Reform Efforts.' In *Saudi Arabia in the Balance*, edited by Paul Aarts and Gerd Nonneman, 111–43. London: Hurst.
____. 2011. *Princes, Brokers, and Bureaucrats: Oil and the State in Saudi Arabia*. Ithaca, NY: Cornell University Press.
Hirschkind, Charles. 2006. *The Ethical Soundscape*. New York: Columbia University Press.
Hitchings, Russell, and Shu Jun Lee. 2008. 'Air Conditioning and the Material Culture of Routine Human Encasement: The Case of Young People in Contemporary Singapore.' *Journal of Material Culture* 13 (3): 251–65.
Hoexter, Miriam, Nehemia Levtzion and Shmuel N. Eisenstadt, eds. 2002. *The Public Sphere in Muslim Societies*. Albany, NY: State University of New York Press.
Holland, Muhtar. 1988. *The Duties of Brotherhood in Islam*. Leicester: Islamic Foundation.
Hollier, Denis. 1992. *Against Architecture: The Writings of George Bataille*. Cambridge, MA/London: MIT Press.

Hourani, Albert. 1970. 'Introduction: The Islamic City in the Light of Recent Research.' In *The Islamic City*, edited by Albert H. Hourani and S.M. Stern, 9–24. Oxford: Bruno Cassirer.

Hourani, Albert H., and S.M. Stern, eds. 1970. *The Islamic City*. Oxford: Bruno Cassirer.

Human Rights Watch. 1992. 'Empty Reforms: Saudi Arabia's New Basic Laws.' www.hrw.org/legacy/reports/1992/saudi/INTROTHR.htm (accessed 25 July 2015).

____. 2004. 'Bad Dreams: Exploitation and Abuse of Migrant Workers in Saudi Arabia.' www.hrw.org/en/reports/2004/07/13/bad-dreams-0 (accessed 23 April 2015).

Idārat al-ʿAyn al-ʿAzīziyya. n.d. [2000?]. *Lamaḥāt ʿan al-ʿayn al-ʿzīziyya bi-Jiddah: wafq jalālat al-malik ʿAbd al-ʿAzīz Āl Saʿūd ṭayyaba Allāh tharāhū*. Jeddah: self-published.

Jeddah Strategic Plan. 2009. 'Building our Future, Preserving our Heritage and Values.' Jeddah: Amāna Muḥāfaẓa Jiddah.

Johnson, Mark. 2010. 'Diasporic Dreams, Middle-Class Moralities and Migrant Domestic Workers Among Muslim Filipinos in Saudi Arabia.' *The Asia Pacific Journal of Anthropology* 11 (3): 428–48.

Jomah, Hisham Abdul Salam M. 1992. 'The Traditional Process of Producing a House in Arabia during the 18th and 19th Centuries: A Case-study of Ḥedjāz.' Ph.D. diss., University of Edinburgh.

Jones, Paul. 2011. *The Sociology of Architecture*. Liverpool: Liverpool University Press.

Jones, Toby. 2003. 'Seeking a "Social Contract" for Saudi Arabia.' *Middle East Report* 228: 42–8.

Joseph, Suad. 1983. 'Working-Class Women's Networks in a Sectarian State: A Political Paradox.' *American Ethnologist* 10 (1): 1–22.

____. 1997. 'The Public/Private: The Imagined Boundary in the Imagined Nation/State/Community: The Lebanese Case.' *Feminist Review* 57: 73–92.

____. 2000. 'Gendering Citizenship in the Middle East.' In *Gender and Citizenship in the Middle East*, edited by Suad Joseph, 3–30. New York: Syracuse University Press.

Kamali, Mohammad Hashim. 2008. *The Right to Life, Security, Privacy and Ownership in Islam*. Cambridge: Islamic Texts Society.

Kandiyoti, Deniz. 1996. 'Contemporary Feminist Scholarship and Middle East Studies.' In *Gendering the Middle East: Emerging Perspectives*, edited by Deniz Kandiyoti, 1–27. London: I.B. Tauris.

Katz, Peter. 1994. *The New Urbanism: Toward an Architecture of Community*. New York: McGraw-Hill.

Kechichian, Joseph A. 2001. *Succession in Saudi Arabia*. New York: Palgrave.

Khashan, Hilal. 2017. 'Saudi Arabia's Flawed "Vision 2030".' *Middle East Quarterly* 24 (1). https://www.meforum.org/6397/saudi-arabia-flawed-vision-2030#_ftnref30 (accessed 28 March 2019).

King, Geoffrey. 1998. *The Traditional Architecture of Saudi Arabia*. London: I.B. Tauris.

Klein, Naomi. 2000. *No Logo*. New York: Picador.

Korsholm Nielsen, Hans Christian, and Jakob Skovgaard-Petersen. 2001. *Middle Eastern Cities 1900–1950: Public Places and Public Spheres in Transformation*. Aarhus: Aarhus University Press.

Kostiner, Joseph. 1990. 'Transforming Dualities: Tribe and State Formation in Saudi Arabia.' In *Tribes and State Formation in the Middle East*, edited by Philip S. Khoury and Joseph Kostiner, 226–51. Berkeley, CA: University of California Press.

Krause, Rolf Friedrich. 1991. *Stadtgeographische Untersuchungen in der Altstadt von Djidda/Saudi-Arabien: Eine Dokumentation*. Bonner Geographische Abhandlungen 81. Bonn: F. Dümmler.

Krawietz, Birgit. 1991. *Die Ḥurma: Schariatrechtlicher Schutz vor Eingriffen in die körperliche Unversehrtheit nach arabischen Fatwas des 20. Jahrhunderts*. Berlin: Duncker & Humblot.

____. 2016. 'From Prescriptive Modernity to Shame at Large: Muslim Sportive Bodies and (Fe)Male Nudity.' In *Muslim Bodies: Body, Sexuality and Medicine in Muslim Societies*, edited by Susanne Kurz, Claudia Preckel and Stefan Reichmuth, 61–96. Berlin: LIT.

Lacroix, Stéphane. 2004. 'Between Islamists and Liberals: Saudi Arabia's New "Islamo-Liberal" Reformists.' *Middle East Journal* 58 (3): 345–65.

____. 2011. *Awakening Islam: Religious Dissent in Contemporary Saudi Arabia*. Cambridge, MA: Harvard University Press.

Lagrange, Frédéric. 2000. 'Male Homosexuality in Modern Arabic Literature.' In *Imagined Masculinities: Male Identity and Culture in the Modern Middle East*, edited by Mai Ghoussoub and Emma Sinclair-Webb, 169–98. London: Saqi.

Lange, Christian. 2012. 'Privacy.' In *Princeton Encyclopedia of Islamic Political Thought*, edited by Gerhard Bowering, 430–1. Princeton, NJ: Princeton University Press.

____. 2013. 'Vom Recht, sich zu verhüllen: Dimensionen der Privatsphäre im muslimischen *fiqh*.' In *Jahrbuch für Verfassung, Recht und Staat im islamischen Kontext 2012/2013*, edited by Peter Scholz, Christine Langenfeld, Jens Scheiner and Naseef Naeem, 35–50. Baden-Baden: Nomos.

Lecocq, Baz. 2015. 'Awad El Djouh and the Dynamics of Post-Slavery.' *International Journal of African Historical Studies* 48 (2): 193–208.

van Leeuwen, Richard. 1995. 'The Quest for the "Islamic City".' In *Changing Stories: Postmodernism and the Arab-Islamic World*, edited by I. Boer, A. Moors and T. van Teeffelen, 147–62. Amsterdam: Rodopi.

Lefebvre, Henri. 1991. *The Production of Space*. Translated by Donald Nicholson-Smith. Oxford: Blackwell.

Le Renard, Amélie. 2008. '"Only for Women": Women, the State, and Reform in Saudi Arabia.' *Middle East Journal* 62 (4): 610–29.

____. 2011. *Femmes et espaces publics en Arabie Saoudite*. Paris: Dalloz.

____. 2014. *A Society of Young Women: Opportunities of Place, Power, and Reform in Saudi Arabia*. Stanford, CA: Stanford University Press.

____. 2015. 'Engendering Consumerism in the Saudi Capital.' In *Saudi Arabia in Transition*, edited by Bernard Haykel, Thomas Hegghammer and Stéphane Lacroix, 314–31. New York: Cambridge University Press.

Lewis, Bernard. 2012. 'Ḥadjdj.' In *Encyclopaedia of Islam*, 2nd edition, edited by P. Bearman, Th. Bianquis, C.E. Bosworth, E. van Donzel and W.P. Heinrichs. referenceworks.brillonline.com/entries/encyclopaedia-of-islam-2/hadjdj-COM_0249 (accessed 29 May 2012).

Leys, Ruth. 2011. 'The Turn to Affect: A Critique.' *Critical Inquiry* 37 (3): 434–72.

Long, David E. 1979. *The Hajj Today: A Survey of the Contemporary Makkah Pilgrimage*. Albany, NY: State University of New York Press.

Longva, Anh Nga. 1993. 'Kuwaiti Women at a Crossroads: Privileged Development and the Constraints of Ethnic Stratification.' *International Journal of Middle East Studies* 25: 443–56.

Löw, Martina. 2001. *Raumsoziologie*. Frankfurt am Main: Suhrkamp.

____. 2008. *Soziologie der Städte*. Frankfurt am Main: Suhrkamp.

____. 2009. 'Materialität und Bild: Die "Architektur der Gesellschaft" aus strukturierungstheoretischer Perspektive.' In *Die Architektur der Gesellschaft: Theorien für die Architektursoziologie*, edited by Joachim Fischer and Heike Delitz, 343–64. Bielefeld: transcript.

Low, Setha. 2001. 'The Edge and the Center: Gated Communities and the Discourse of Urban Fear.' In *The Anthropology of Space and Place*, edited by Setha M. Low and Denise Lawrence-Zúñiga. 387–407. Malden, MA: Blackwell.

____. 2003. *Behind the Gates: Life, Security, and the Pursuit of Happiness in Fortress America*. New York/London: Routledge.

Madanipour, Ali. 2003. *Public and Private Spaces of the City*. London/New York: Routledge.

Mahmood, Saba. 2001. 'Feminist Theory, Embodiment and the Docile Agent: Some Reflections on the Egyptian Islamic Revival.' *Cultural Anthropology* 16 (2): 202–36.

____. 2005. *Politics of Piety: The Islamic Revival and the Feminist Subject*. Princeton, NJ: Princeton University Press.

Maisel, Sebastian. 2014. 'The New Rise of Tribalism in Saudi Arabia.' *Nomadic Peoples* 18 (2): 100–22.

Maltzan, Heinrich von. 1865. *Meine Wallfahrt nach Mekka: Reise in der Küstengegend und im Inneren von Hedschas*. Reprint of the 1st edition, Hildesheim: Olms Verlag, 2004.

____. 1873. *Reise nach Südarabien und Geographische Forschungen im und über den südwestlichen Theil Arabiens*. Reprint of the 1st edition Hildesheim: Olms Verlag, 2004.

Malcolm X. 2001 [1965]. *The Autobiography of Malcolm X*. London: Penguin.

Manāʿ, ʿAbdullāh. 2008. *Baʿḍu al-ayām baʿḍu al-layālī: aṭrāf min qiṣṣat ḥayātī*. Jeddah: Dār al-Mursī.

____. 2011. *Tārīkh mā lam yuʾarrakh. Jiddah: al-insān wa-l-makān*. Jeddah: Dār al-Mursī.

Mandeli, K. N. 2008. 'The Realities of Integrating Physical Planning and Local Management into Urban Development: A Case Study of Jeddah, Saudi Arabia.' *Habitat International* 32 (4): 512–33.

Maneval, Stefan. 2010. 'Die liberale Reformbewegung in Saudi-Arabien: Analyse und Übersetzung der Reformpetition vom 2. Februar 2007.' In *Saudi-Arabien: Ein Königreich im Wandel*, edited by Ulrike Freitag, 61–87. Paderborn: Schöningh.

____. 2012a. 'Die Einstürzenden Altbauten. Ein Bericht über den Verfall der Altstadt von Dschidda.' *Zenith: Zeitschrift für den Orient*, March/April: 70–4.

____. 2012b. 'Abdullah, wir müssen reden.' *Zenith: Zeitschrift für den Orient*, December/January: 82–91.
____. 2014. 'Niemand hat die Absicht, einen Aufsatz zu zensieren.' *Forum Kritische Archäologie* 3: 1–10.
____. 2019. 'Counterpublics in Saudi Shopping Centres, Beach Resorts, and Gated Communities.' *Middle East: Topics & Arguments* 12: 76–86.
Marçais, William. 1928. 'L'Islamisme et la vie urbaine.' *Comptes rendus des séances de l'Académie des Inscriptions et Belles-Lettres* 72 (1): 86–100.
Marcus, Abraham. 1986. 'Privacy in Eighteenth-Century Aleppo: The Limits of Cultural Ideals.' *International Journal of Middle East Studies* 18 (2): 165–83.
Mashāṭ, Fāṭima Aḥmad. 1998/9 [1419 AH]. 'Qaṣr Khuzām.' In *al-Malik ʿAbd al-ʿAzīz fī Jiddah*, edited by Hānim Ḥāmid Yārkandi, 73–82. Jeddah: al-Riʾāsa al-ʿāmma li-taʿlīm al-banāt.
Massey, Doreen. 2005. *For Space*. London: Sage.
Matthiesen, Toby. 2009. '*Diwaniyyas*, Intellectual Salons, and the Limits of Civil Society.' In *The Kingdom of Saudi Arabia, 1979–2009: Evolution of a Pivotal State*. Viewpoints, Middle East Institute, Washington, DC, 13–15.
____. 2012. 'Saudi Arabia: The Middle East's Most Under-reported Conflict.' *Guardian*. 23 January. www.theguardian.com/commentisfree/2012/jan/23/saudi-arabia-shia-protesters (accessed 23 April 2015).
McKernan, Bethan. 2018. 'Mohammed bin Salman: Saudi Arabia's Great Young Reformer May Struggle to Control the Forces He Has Unleashed.' *Independent*. 7 February. https://www.independent.co.uk/news/world/middle-east/saudi-arabia-mohammed-bin-salman-crown-prince-social-reforms-women-yemen-conservatism-a8199431.html (accessed 28 March 2019).
Meijer, Roel. 2010. 'Reform in Saudi Arabia: The Gender-Segregation Debate.' *Middle East Policy* 17 (4): 80–100.
Meijer, Roel, and Joas Wagemakers. 2013. 'The Struggle for Citizenship of the Shiites of Saudi Arabia.' In *The Dynamics of Sunni-Shia Relationships*, edited by Brigitte Maréchal. 117–38. London: Hurst.
Menoret, Pascal. 2014. *Joyriding in Riyadh: Oil, Urbanism, and Road Revolt*. New York: Cambridge University Press.
Meuser, Michael. 2005. 'Frauenkörper – Männerkörper: Somatische Kulturen der Geschlechterdifferenz.' In *Soziologie des Körpers*, edited by Markus Schroer, 272–94. Frankfurt am Main: Suhrkamp.
Meuser, Michael and Rüdiger Lautmann. 1997. '"Menschen und Frauen": Die Geschlechtslosigkeit des Mannes in der Moderne.' In *Sie und Er: Frauenmacht und Männerherrschaft im Kulturvergleich*, edited by Gisela Völger, vol. 2, 253–8. Cologne: Rautenstrauch-Joest-Museum.
Miran, Jonathan. 2009. *Red Sea Citizens: Cosmopolitan Society and Cultural Change in Massawa*. Bloomington/Indianapolis, IN: Indiana University Press.
Morphy, Howard. 2009. 'Art as a Mode of Action: Some Problems with Gell's Art and Agency.' *Journal of Material Culture* 14 (1): 5–27.
Mortada, Hisham. 1992. 'Islamic Principles and the Modern Housing of Jeddah.' Ph.D. diss., University of Edinburgh.
____. 2003. *Traditional Islamic Principles of Built Environment*. London/New York: RoutledgeCurzon.
al-Mutawea, Fahad Mohammed. 1987. 'The Housing of the Academic Staff of King Abdulaziz University, Jeddah, Saudi Arabia.' Ph.D. diss., University of Newcastle upon Tyne.
al-Nafea', Nada A. 2005. 'Home Environment in Transition: Women and House Design in the City of Riyadh, Saudi Arabia.' Ph.D. diss., London South Bank University.
National Oceanic and Atmospheric Administration. 'Jeddah.' ftp://ftp.atdd.noaa.gov/pub/GCOS/WMO-Normals/RA-II/SD/41024.TXT (accessed 16 June 2015).
Neglia, Giulia Annalinda. 2008. 'Some Historiographical Notes on the Islamic City with Particular Reference to the Visual Representation of the Built City.' In *The City in the Islamic World*, edited by Salma K. Jayyusi, Renata Holod, Attilio Petruccioli and André Raymond, 3–46. Leiden: Brill.
Nelson, Cynthia. 1974. 'Public and Private Politics: Women in the Middle Eastern World.' *American Ethnologist* 1 (3): 551–63.
Nissen, Sylke. 2008. 'Urban Transformation from Public and Private Space to Spaces of Hybrid Character.' *Czech Sociological Review/Sociologický časopis* 6: 1129–49.

Ochsenwald, William. 1981. 'Saudi Arabia and the Islamic Revival.' *International Journal of Middle East Studies* 13 (3): 271–86.
____. 1984. *Religion, Society and the State in Arabia: The Hijaz under Ottoman Control, 1840–1908*. Columbus, OH: Ohio State University Press.
Okruhlik, Gwenn. 2002. 'Networks of Dissent: Islamism and Reform in Saudi Arabia.' *Current History* 101 (651): 22–8.
Panofsky, Erwin. 1957. *Gothic Architecture and Scholasticism*. New York: Meridian.
Park, Robert E. 1915. 'The City: Suggestions for the Investigation of Human Behavior in the City Environment.' *American Journal of Sociology* 20 (5): 577–612.
Park, Robert E., Ernest W. Burgess and Roderick D. McKenzie. 1967 [1925]. *The City*. Chicago: University of Chicago Press.
Pesce, Angelo. 1976. *Jiddah: Portrait of an Arabian City*. N.p.: Falcon Press.
Peteet, Julie. 1986. 'Women and the Palestinian Movement: No Going Back?' *Middle East Report* 138: 20–24, 44.
Pétriat, Philippe. 2016. *Le négoce des lieux saints: Négociants hadramis de Djedda, 1850–1950*. Paris: Publications de la Sorbonne.
Prokop, Michaela. 2003. 'Saudi Arabia: The Politics of Education.' *International Affairs* 79 (1): 77–89.
____. 2005. 'The War of Ideas: Education in Saudi Arabia.' In *Saudi Arabia in the Balance*, edited by Paul Aarts and Gerd Nonneman, 57–81. London: Hurst.
Qian, Junxi. 2014. 'Public Space in Non-Western Contexts: Practices of Publicness and the Socio-spatial Entanglement.' *Geography Compass* 8 (11): 834–47.
al-Rasheed, Madawi. 1996. 'God, the King and the Nation: Political Rhetoric in Saudi Arabia in the 1990s.' *Middle East Journal* 50 (3): 359–71.
____. 1998. 'The Shi'a of Saudi Arabia: A Minority in Search of Cultural Authenticity.' *British Journal of Middle Eastern Studies* 25 (1): 121–38.
____. 2002. *A History of Saudi Arabia*. New York: Cambridge University Press.
____. 2004. 'The Capture of Riyadh Revisited: Shaping Historical Imagination in Saudi Arabia.' In *Counter-narratives: History, Contemporary Society, and Politics in Saudi Arabia and Yemen*, edited by Madawi al-Rasheed and Robert Vitalis, 183–200. New York: Palgrave Macmillan.
____. 2012. 'No Saudi Spring: Anatomy of a Failed Revolution.' *Boston Review*. 1 March. www.bostonreview.net/madawi-al-rasheed-arab-spring-saudi-arabia (accessed 23 April 2015).
____. 2013. *A Most Masculine State: Gender, Politics and Religion in Saudi Arabia*. Cambridge: Cambridge University Press.
____. 2015. 'Caught between Religion and State: Women in Saudi Arabia.' In *Saudi Arabia in Transition*, edited by Bernard Haykel, Thomas Hegghammer and Stéphane Lacroix, 292–313. New York: Cambridge University Press.
Rathjens, Carl, and Hermann von Wissmann. 1947. 'Landschaftskundliche Beobachtungen im südlichen Hedjaz.' *Erdkunde: Archiv für wissenschaftliche Geographie* 1: 61–89, 200–5.
Raymond, André. 2008. 'The Spatial Organisation of the City.' In *The City in the Islamic World*, edited by Salma K. Jayyusi, Renata Holod, Attilio Petruccioli and André Raymond, 47–70. Leiden: Brill.
Ross, Andrew. 1999. *The Celebration Chronicles: Life, Liberty and the Pursuit of Property Value in Disney's New Town*. New York: Ballantine.
Ryan, Mary P. 1992. 'Gender and Public Access: Women's Politics in Nineteenth-Century America.' In *Habermas and the Public Sphere*, edited by Craig Calhoun, 259–88. Cambridge, MA/London: MIT Press.
Ṣabbān, Suḥayl. n.d. *Jiddah fī wathā'iq al-arshīf al-'uthmānī*. Jeddah: Markaz Mawsū'a Jiddah.
Salvatore, Armando. 2007. *The Public Sphere: Liberal Modernity, Catholicism, Islam*. New York: Palgrave.
Salvatore, Armando, and Dale Eickelman, eds. 2004. *Public Islam and the Common Good*. Leiden: Brill.
Sanger, Richard H. 1954. *The Arabian Peninsula*. Ithaca, NY: Cornell University Press.
Sauvaget, Jean. 1934. 'Esquisses d'une histoire de la ville de Damas.' *Revue des Etudes Islamiques* 8: 421–80.
____. 1941. *Alep: Essai sur le développement d'une grande ville syrienne, des origines au milieu du XIXe siècle*. Paris: P. Geuthner.
Savignac, Raphaël. 1917. 'Carnet de guerre de 1914–1918.' Unpublished manuscript, transcribed by Jean-Michel de Tarragon, École biblique et archéologique française de Jérusalem.

Scharoun, Lisa. 2012. *America at the Mall: The Cultural Role of a Retail Utopia*. Jefferson, NC: McFarland.

Schmid, Larissa. 2010. 'Symbolische Geschlechterpolitik in Saudi-Arabien.' In *Saudi-Arabien: Ein Königreich im Wandel*, edited by Ulrike Freitag, 89–105. Paderborn: Schöningh.

Schroer, Markus. 2009. 'Materielle Formen des Sozialen: Die "Architektur der Gesellschaft" aus Sicht der sozialen Morphologie.' In *Die Architektur der Gesellschaft: Theorien für die Architektursoziologie*, edited by Joachim Fischer and Heike Delitz, 19–48. Bielefeld: transcript.

Scott, James C. 1985. *Weapons of the Weak: Everyday Forms of Peasant Resistance*. New Haven, CT: Yale University Press.

____. 1998. *Seeing Like a State: How Certain Schemes to Improve the Human Condition Have Failed*. New Haven, CT/London: Yale University Press.

Sedgwick, Mark. 1997. 'Saudi Sufis: Compromise in the Hijaz, 1925–40.' *Die Welt des Islams* 37 (3): 349–68.

Sennett, Richard. 1994. *Flesh and Stone: The Body and the City in Western Civilization*. New York: W.W. Norton.

al-Shahrani, Mohammad Ali. 1992. 'An Inquiry into Leisure and Recreation Patterns and their Relationship to Open Space and Landscape Design: The Case of Jeddah, Saudi Arabia.' Ph.D. diss., University of Edinburgh.

Siddiqui, Aisha M., and Hayat Z. Kamfar. 2007. 'Prevalence of Vitamin D Deficiency Rickets in Adolescent School Girls in Western Region, Saudi Arabia.' *Saudi Medical Journal* 28 (3): 441–7.

Sijeeni, Tariq. 1995. 'Contemporary Arabian City: Muslim *Ummah* in Sociocultural and Urban Design Context.' Ph.D. diss., University of Michigan.

Silvey, Rachel. 2004. 'Transnational Domestication: State Power and Indonesian Migrant Women in Saudi Arabia.' *Political Geography* 23 (3): 245–64.

____. 2006. 'Consuming the Transnational Family: Indonesian Migrant Domestic Workers to Saudi Arabia.' *Global Networks* 6 (1): 23–40.

al-Simari, Fahd A. 2011. 'The Birth of the Kingdom of Saudi Arabia.' In *Roads of Arabia: The Archaeological Treasures of Saudi Arabia*, edited by Ute Franke and Joachim Gierlichs, 282–7. Tübingen: Wasmuth Verlag.

Sorkin, Michael. 1992. *Variations on a Theme Park: The New American City and the End of Public Space*. New York: Noonday Press.

Stapleton, Stephen, and Edward Booth-Clibborn, eds. 2012. *Edge of Arabia: Contemporary Art form Saudi Arabia*. London: Booth-Clibborn Editions.

Steinberg, Guido. 2002. *Religion und Staat in Saudi-Arabien: Eine Sozialgeschichte der wahhabitischen Gelehrten 1912–1953*. Würzburg: Ergon.

Stern, S.M. 1970. 'The Constitution of the Islamic City.' In *The Islamic City*, edited by Albert H. Hourani and S.M. Stern, 25–50. Oxford: Bruno Cassirer.

Stolleis, Friederike. 2004. *Öffentliches Leben in privaten Räumen: Muslimische Frauen in Damaskus*. Würzburg: Ergon.

Talen, Emily. 2005. *New Urbanism and American Planning: The Conflict of Cultures*. New York/London: Routledge.

Tamisier, Maurice. 1840. *Voyage en Arabie*, vol. 1: *Séjour dans le Hedjaz*. Paris: Louis Desessart.

Ṭarābulsī, Muḥammad Yūsuf Muḥammad. 2008. *Jiddah: ḥikāyat madīna*. Jeddah: al-Madīna al-Munawwira li-l-ṭibāʿa wa-l-nashr.

Teitelbaum, Joshua. 2000. *Holier Than Thou: Saudi Arabia's Islamic Opposition*. Washington, DC: Washington Institute for Near East Policy.

Telmesani, Abdullah, Fuad Sarouji and Adnan Adas. 2009. *Old Jeddah: A Traditional Arab Muslim City in Saudi Arabia*. Jeddah: self-published.

Thābit, Nādiyya ʿUmar. 1998/9 [1419 AH]. 'Al-malik ʿAbd al-ʿAzīz fī dhākirat ahālī Jiddah.' In *al-Malik ʿAbd al-ʿAzīz fī Jiddah*, edited by Hānim Ḥāmid Yārkandī. 83–100. Jeddah: al-Riʾāsa al-ʿāmma li-taʿlīm al-banāt.

Thompson, Mark C. 2014. *Saudi Arabia and the Path to Political Change: National Dialogue and Civil Society*. London: I.B. Tauris.

Toledano, Ehud R. 1982. *The Ottoman Slave Trade and Its Suppression: 1840–1890*. Princeton: Princeton University Press.

____. 1998. *Slavery and Abolition in the Ottoman Middle East*. Seattle, WA: University of Washington Press.

____. 2007. *As If Silent and Absent: Bonds of Enslavement in the Islamic Middle East*. New Haven, CT: Yale University Press.

Tuncalp, Secil, and Abdullah al-Ibrahim. 1990. 'Housing Finance in Saudi Arabia.' *Habitat International* 14 (1): 111–21.

al-Turkī, Thurayā, and Abū Bakr Bāqādir. 2006. *Jiddah, umm al-rakhā wa-l-shidda: taḥawwulāt al-ḥayāt al-usriyya bayna fatratayn*. Cairo: Dār al-Shurūq.

Um, Nancy. 2009. *The Merchant Houses of Mocha: Trade and Architecture in an Indian Ocean Port*. Seattle, WA: University of Washington Press.

Vassiliev, Alexei. 2000. *The History of Saudi Arabia*. London: Saqi.

Vitalis, Robert. 2007. *America's Kingdom: Mythmaking on the Saudi Oil Frontier*. Stanford, CA: Stanford University Press.

Warner, Michael. 2002. *Publics and Counterpublics*. New York: Zone.

Weber, Max. 1958 [1921]. *The City*. Translated and edited by Don Martindale and Gertrud Neuwirth. Glencoe: Free Press.

Weber, Stefan. 2009. *Damascus: Ottoman Modernity and Urban Transformation (1808–1918)*. Aarhus: Aarhus University Press.

Welt, Die. 2001. 'Jeder darf bauen, was er will.' 13 June. www.welt.de/print-welt/article456612/jeder-darf-bauen-was-er-will.html (accessed 13 April 2015).

Whitworth, Damian. 2012. 'Flowering in the Sand.' *The Times*. 24 January.

Wilson, Elizabeth. 1992. *The Sphinx in the City: Urban Life, the Control of Disorder, and Women*. Berkeley, CA: University of California Press.

Wirth, Eugen. 2000. *Die orientalische Stadt im islamischen Vorderasien und Nordafrika*. Mainz: Philipp von Zabern.

Yamani, Mai. 1996. 'Some Observations on Women in Saudi Arabia.' In *Feminism and Islam: Legal and Literary Perspectives*, edited by Mai Yamani, 263–81. New York: New York University Press.

____. 2000. *Changed Identities: The Challenge of the New Generation in Saudi Arabia*. London: Royal Institute of International Affairs.

____. 2004. *Cradle of Islam: The Hijaz and the Quest for an Arabian Identity*. London: I.B. Tauris.

Zacharia, Janine. 2011. 'Signs of Dissent Becoming More Visible among Saudi Arabian Youths.' *Washington Post*. 11 March. www.washingtonpost.com/wp-dyn/content/article/2011/03/10/AR2011031006107.html (accessed 5 August 2015).

Za'zū', Laylā bint Ṣāliḥ Muḥammad. 2004. *Riḥlat al-mar'a al-yaumiyya li-l-'amal fī Jiddah. Dirāsa taṭbīqiyya fī al-jughrāfiyyā al-ijtimā'iyya*. Beirut: al-Dār al-'arabiyya li-l-'ulūm/Arab Scientific Publishers.

Index

abāya 155, 162, 187, 209–11, 218
ʿAbd al-ʿAzīz bin Saʿūd, King 26, 35, 45, 127
ʿAbd al-ʿAzīz bin Bāz, *see* Ibn Bāz
ʿAbdullāh, King 185–7, 189, 201, 223–4
activists xiv, 201–3, 216 n. 25, 226; Islamic 122; women's rights 6, 128; *see also* Islamic Revival; protests
affect 17–18, 20, 21 n. 8, 139–40
air conditioning 145, 173, 174
Alireza, Marianne 27, 73–4, 80, 100–3
Āl Saʿūd 123–5, 127, 175, 202, 205, 215 n. 13; *see also* family, royal family
Altorki, Soraya 4–5, 70, 103–5, 190–1
Ammann, Ludwig 8, 66–7, 69, 85 n. 21, 132
apartments: social life in 139, 147, 157, 163, 182, 184; within old buildings 56, 58, 77, 82; *see also* architecture of apartment buildings
ARAMCO 111–12, 151
architectural criticism 93, 109–11, 114–16, 119–21, 130, 134–5, 136 n. 3, 222
architecture: of apartment buildings 33, 92–3, 97–9, 118–20, 136 n. 4, n. 6, 142–7, 173; and Islam 64, 71, 109, 113, 115, 119–22, 130, 134–5, 137 n. 12, 158, 222; private space and 2–3, 11, 13–17, 41, 54, 63–4, 71–4, 76, 81–2, 98–9, 106–7, 117–22, 133, 135, 137 n. 10, 139, 141–2, 147, 153, 158–9, 163, 166–8, 211, 213–14, 220–3; of public space 2–3, 10, 13–17, 41, 54, 63–4, 72, 81–2, 98–9, 106–7, 133, 141–2, 167, 171, 200, 205, 211, 213–14, 220–1, 223; residential 16, 20, 54, 81–2, 88, 91–3, 95–8, 106–8, 110–11, 113–15, 119, 121, 133, 139–42, 162–3, 166, 221–2; of single-family houses 92, 94, 98–9, 103, 108, 115, 119, 141–2, *144*, 147, 153, 164, 174, 183 (*see also* villas); and social control 56, 72, 77, 82, 104–5, 117, 120, 133, 163–4, 167, 168 n. 3, 221–2; sociology of 3, 14–20, 21 n. 6, n. 9, 163; studies on 4, 8, 18–20, 21 n. 7, 100, 109, 113–16, 119, 121, 133; and style 32, 109, 111, 113, 121, 141–2, 151, 166
art 129, 137 n. 21, 160–1, 199–200, 217, 226
assemblage 10, 12, 17–20, 71–2, 223
automotive city 33, 173, 179, 213
al-ʿAwda, Salmān 123–4, 126

Baghdādiyya 87, 107 n. 2, 145
al-Balad, *see* Jeddah, al-Balad
Basic Law of Governance 127
bazaar, *see sūq*
beach 152, 174, 187, 192, 205–7, 213, 224–5
Bokhari, Abdulla 19, 32, 93, 108–9, 111, 120–2, 135
Burckhardt, Johann Ludwig 23, 26, 28

cafes: and gender segregation xii–xiii, 187–9, 193–4, 215 n. 10, 220, 223–4; and leisure 160, 193, 196, 205; as men's meeting places 47–8, 82, 96–7, 107, 117; and public expression 198–200, 216 n. 23
cars: and contact between men and women 181–2, 194–5; and privacy 180–2, 212–13, 224–5; and public space 107, 173–4, 180–2, 202–4, 212; and safety 153–4; and urban development 31, 33, 90, 94, 96, 99, 101, 107, 117, 136 n. 2, 173–5; and women's mobility 101–2, 107, 126, 160, 189; *see also* drifting, driving
caravans 23, 25
city gates 23, 39 n. 8, 40, 42, 45
climate 35, 131, 162, 180
Committee for the Promotion of Virtue and Prevention of Vice, *see* religious police
concrete: as building material 28, 31, 73, 91–2, 97, 120, 140; factory 87, 91; road blocks 160–1
counterpublics xv, 9–10, 165, 168, 207–8, 211–14, 219–20, 224–6; Islamic 79, 85 n. 25, 138 n. 22, 214

Delitz, Heike 17–18
Deleuze, Gilles 17–18, 71
demonstrations 124–5, 128, 176, 198, 216 n. 25; *see also* protests
Doumato, Eleanor 5, 126, 159
drifting 10, 173, 202, 204–5, 226
driving 6, 117, 153, 180, 202; women's ban on xiii, 124–6, 128, 160, 189

Edge of Arabia 129, 137 n. 21, 160–1, 188, 199–200
Effat University 1–4, 21, 160, 165, 195–7, 205
entrances: of public buildings and spaces 1, 173, 188, 191; of shops and shopping centres 40, 194; of residential houses 55–8, 60, 72, 74–5, 81–2, 103–4, 119, 136 n. 6, 142, 148, 153; to gated communities and resorts 152–3, 206–7, 225
Eve's Tomb *24*, 84 n. 9

expatriates: architecture constructed by 93; lifestyle of 151–4, 160, 162, 166, 195–7; networks of 166, 202; Western expatriates 102, 111, 151–4, 162, 177; *see also* migrant workers
Eyuce, Ahmet 19, 119, 121, 131, 147

Facebook 12, 201
Fadan, Yousef 110–13, 115–16, 119, 131, 135, 145
Fahd, King 124–5, 127
al-Faqīh, Sa'd 124
family: extended family 5, 58–9, 73–4, 76, 82, 93–4, 100, 102–5, 107, 114–17, 136 n. 2, 142, 157, 167, 221–2; families-only spaces xv, 21, 187–92, 194; and gender segregation 2, 53–7, 59, 61, 71–3, 80–1, 97–8, 102, 119–20, 132, 142, 147–8, 157–8, 188–9, 191; and income 52–3, 76, 82, 84 n. 12, 96, 155–6, 169 n. 5, 221; and Islam 64, 71, 116, 122, 137 n. 10, 159; nuclear family 5, 103–7, 115–17, 121, 167, 221–2; and patriarchy 55, 78, 216 n. 16; reputation 69, 76, 82, 154, 221; royal family 5, 35, 123–4, 128, 151, 175, 205, 214, 215 n. 13; and women's roles 51–3, 75–8, 80–1, 155–7, 160, 185, 187, 196
fatwas 125–7, 137 n. 18, 156–7, 189
Fayṣal, King 27, 32, 35, 90
feminism 7–9, 11, 40, 70, 79
Foucault, Michel 14, 18, 128
Fraser, Nancy 8, 78, 79

gated communities: and counterpublics 205, 211, 213–14, 224–5; and mixing of men and women 207–9, 211, 213–14; and public space 206–7, 211, 224; gated family compounds: history of 151, 168 n. 2; and lifestyle 151–3, 162, 166; and safety 18, 151–4, 160–1
gender: gendered publics 63, 78, 82–3, 220, 223; inequality 6, 185, 190–1, 217, 219; and research data and methods 4, 9, 11, 13, 69–70, 100; and slaves 75; and the state xv, 5, 126, 185–9, 223
gender segregation: abolition of xii–xiii, xv, 216 n. 20; implications for men 188, 191–4, 214; and Islamic Revival 126, 154–6, 186, 222; and public activities of women 5, 54, 80–3, 100, 190–1, 197–8, 214, 224; in residential houses 57–61, 72, 75, 98, 100, 119, 147, 162; Saudi debate on, *see ikhtilāṭ*; Western discourse on 6–7, 40–1, 191, 217–19
Gilsenan, Michael 52
Gulf War 123–4, 126–7, 137 n. 13, 151

Habermas, Jürgen 7–10, 69, 207, 218
ḥajj (pilgrimage): and economy 22–3, 25, 43; and migration 25–6; as a pillar of Islam 112; and residential architecture 43, 47, 56; and urban space 23, 45, 54, 86–91; *see also* pilgrims

ḥāra (neighbourhood) 27, 45; al-Baḥr 27, 45, 48, 53; al-Maẓlūm 27, 45; al-Shām 27, *29*, *30*, 31, 45, *46*, 57; al-Yaman 27, 45–6; *shaykh al-ḥāra*, *see* 'umda
harbour 22–3, *25*, 31–2, 35, 39–42, *51*, 53, 79, 83 n. 1, 87, 175, 188
al-Ḥawālī, Safar 123–4, 126
hay'a, *see* religious police
hegemonic masculinity 9, 70
al-Ḥijāz: architecture and urban space in 60, 71–2, 113, 121, 222; gender relations in 51–2, 78, 101–2; history of 23, 26; social hierarchies in 79; Sufism in 45–6, 105, 165
Hindāwiyya 31, *92*, 96, 147–9, 174, 177, 210
Hirschkind, Charles 79, 129
Hurgronje, Christiaan Snouck 19, 48–50
huts 28, *30*, 31, 74, 113, 163

Ibn 'Abd al-Wahhāb, Muḥammad 127
Ibn Bāz, Shaykh 'Abd al-'Azīz 125–6, 156
Ibn Sa'ūd, *see* 'Abd al-'Azīz bin Sa'ūd, King
Ibn 'Uthaymīn, Shaykh Abū 'Abdullāh 12
ikhtilāṭ (mixing of men and women): attitudes to 182, 197–9, 205, 212–14, 223–4; practices of xv–xvi, 187–9, 209, 211–12, 215 n. 10, 224; public debate on 127, 137 n. 18, n. 19, 185–9, 215 nn. 8–9, 223
Indian Ocean 23
internet: and architectural sociology 17; and communication between men and women 162, 195–6, 198; and criticism 186, 201, 204, 226; and counterpublics 9, 211–12, 216 n. 29
Islamic Awakening, *see* Islamic Revival
Islamic City 7, 61, 130, 132–3
Islamic Revival 122–4, 126, 128–30, 134–6, 137 n. 16, 138 n. 22, 141, 146, 155, 158–9, 163, 187, 213, 222

Jeddah: al-Balad (the old town) 38, 115–16, 148, 170, 174, 176, 196, 210; Jeddah Strategic Plan 179; Municipality of 145, 173, 175, 179, 201, 222
Jomah, Hisham 19, 51–2, 71–3, 85 n. 22, 98, 115, 119–20, 122, 131, 135, 137 n. 12, 167

Kandara 31, 94–6, 139, 145, *146*, 174, 177, 203, 210
khalwa (intimacy) 182, 184–5, 197–98, 213, 223
King Abdulaziz University (KAU) 21, 60, 100, 109, 147, 151, 170, 187, 189
King Abdullah University of Science and Technology (KAUST) 185, 187

Le Renard, Amélie 5, 10, 154, 187, 190–1
limestone 16, *24*, 27–8, 92
Löw, Martina 3, 7, 63
Low, Setha 18, 161

Mahmood, Saba 21 n. 5, 159
maḥram (close kin) 58, 60, 62, 72–3, 76, 81–2, 98

majlis (living room) 57–9, 61, 72–3, 75, 77, 79–81, 98, *150*
majlis (social gathering) 165–6, 169 n. 9, 200
majlis al-shūrā (consultative council) 124, 127
Makhlūf, ʿAbd al-Raḥmān 32
Malcolm X 86, 88–91
Maltzan, Heinrich von 28, 74
Manāʿ, ʿAbdullāh 22, 48, 52–3, 57, 59–60, 76, 90–1
marriage 27, 59, 75, 80–1, 154, 190
Massey, Doreen 7, 63, 78
Mecca 22–6, 32, 54, 71, 86, 88–91, 113, 123, 126
Medina 22–3, 25–6, 32, 91, 123
Menoret, Pascal 5, 10, 175, 202
merchants 22–3, 28, 40, 42, 45, 57, 77
migrant workers: economic development and 31–3; and housing 38, 91, 93, 96, 103, 111, 147–8, 151, 153, 175, 225; and protest 202–4, 226; from rural parts of Saudi Arabia 175, 214 n. 3, 215 n. 15; social/legal status of 9, 111, 190, 202–4, 206, 216 n. 17–19, 225; and social life and practices 96, 99, 162, 174, 179
mirkāz (men's gathering place) 46, 56–7, 61, 65, 72, 77–9, 81, 94–8, 105, 133, 148, *149*, 177, 207
Mortada, Hisham 116–17, 119–20, 122, 133–5
mosques: and gender segregation 97, 187; as meeting places 45–6, 82, 95, 97; al-Miʿmār Mosque *44*; occupation of the Grand Mosque in Mecca 123, 126; at the pilgrims' city at the airport 88–9; al-Shāfiʿī Mosque *37*, 45; and the state 105, 126; Sulṭān Ḥasan Mosque/Pasha Mosque 45, *46*, 83 n. 7; al-ʿUkāsh Mosque 42, *44*; and urban planning 64, 109, 131
mudun al-ḥujjāj, *see* pilgrims, mass accommodation for
Muḥammad bin ʿAbd al-Wahhāb, *see* Ibn ʿAbd al-Wahhāb
Muḥammad bin Salmān xii–xv
Municipality, *see* Jeddah, Municipality of
al-Mutawea, Fahad Mohammed 64, 72, 118–20, 122, 133, 135
muṭawwif (pilgrimage guide) 25, 43, 49, 89–91

New Islamic Urbanism: discourse of 134–5, 141–2, 155, 168, 215 n. 6, 220, 222; in practice 139, 141–5, 166–7, 182, 220, 222–3
New Urbanism 130–2, 134
Niebuhr, Carsten 23, *24*
al-Nuzla al-Yamāniyya 31, 35, 53, 96, 99, 147

Ottoman Empire 22, 25–7, 29, 75

patriarchy 6, 13, 78, 190, 216 n. 16, 217
petitions 124–5, 127–8, 201
photographs 9, 19, 28, 40, 48–50, *208*, 209–11, 222
piety 126, 129, 136, 156–7, 166, 181, 214
pilgrimage, see *hajj*
pilgrimage guides, *see muṭawwif*
pilgrims 22–3, 25–6, 40, 42–3, 45, 56, 77, 86–91, 112, 203; mass accommodation for 42, 87–91, 106, *183*; *see also hajj*
pious forefathers 122–23, 130, 135, 137 n. 17, 222
port, *see* harbour
privacy: and family 73–4, 76, 82, 104–5, 107, 118–19, 132, 142, 148, 181, 221–2; and gender 63, 69, 72, 74, 76–7, 81–2, 107, 180, 184, 193, 197, 213, 218, 220–1, 223–4; of the individual 73–4, 81, 117, 120, 163, 181, 212, 224; and Islam 3, 7, 11–14, 64–8, 84 n. 20, 85 n. 21, 118–20, 122, 135, 158, 222; local conceptions of 11–12, 61, 64–5, 71–4, 76–7, 81–2, 119–20, 136 n. 7, 137 n. 10, 139, 141–2, 158–9, 167–8, 181–2, 197, 205, 213, 220, 223; and protection against intrusion 67–8, 75–7, 81, 119, 153, 171; and social status 63, 74–7, 82, 220–1; and the state 105, 165, 220, 223, 225; theory and methods 2, 10–15, 61–3, 66–9, 85 nn. 21–2, 219; visual 72, 74–5, 77, 82, 105, 118–19, 136 n. 4, n. 6, 142, 148, 153, 158, 162–3, 166–8, 180, 213, 221–3, 225; *see also* architecture, private space and
privatisation 207, 216 n. 28, 224
prostitution 27, 74–8, 82, 113, 163, 181, 221, 225
protest 111, 176, 201, 204–5, 214, 216 n. 25
public sphere 2, 6–13, 40, 54, 63, 66, 69–70, 78, 80, 83, 85 n. 21, 168, 198, 202, 211–13, 217–18, 220, 225–6
public space, *see* architecture, of public space

al-Rasheed, Madawi 5, 127, 157, 190
Real Estate Development Fund (REDF) 33, 108, 176
Red Sea 23, 26, 39 n. 1
reform: liberal reformers 124–5, 128, 186; Islamic, *see* Islamic Revival; state responses to calls for 124–8, 201; Tanzimat 29
religious police 125–6, 154, 156, 159, 186, 195, 199, 206, 208, 216 n. 29
resistance, *see* protests
resorts 152, 157, 174, 187, 205–8, 213, 224–5
restaurants 3, 10, 89, 96, 117, 151–2, 173–4, 177, 179, 187–90, 196, 205
Riyadh 5, 10, 13, 31, 111, 124, 126, 142, 154, 165, 168, 175–6, 187, 196, 204
Robert Matthew, Johnson-Marshall & Partners (RMJMP) 32–3, 35–6, 38
rūshān (bay window) 28, 58–61, 92, 95, 97, 99, 148, 151
Ruways 31, 92, 100, 102–3

al-Sabīl 31, 94, 147, 174, 177
Salafism 126, 134, 137 n. 17, 153, 222
al-salaf al-ṣāliḥ, *see* pious forefathers
Salmān, King 194, 215 n. 10, 224
salons 57, 63
Salvatore, Armando 8, 69
ṣaḥwa islāmiyya, *see* Islamic Revival

shuyūḫ al-ṣaḥwa 123, 125, 186
Savignac, Raphaël 19, 49–50, 52, 84 n. 9
securitisation 207, 216 n. 29, 224
segregation, *see* gender segregation
shūrā Council, *see majlis al-shūrā*
slaves 9, 27, 49, 51, 53, 75–9, 82–3, 113, 204, 221, 225
social media 5, 12, 162, 195, 197
social status 8–9, 52, 62–3, 75–6, 81–3, 94, 207, 216 n.19, 220–1, 225
stairs 58, 60, 72–4, 77, 104, 119, 163, 182, 184, 221
students 1–2, 151, 189; and activism 198, 202; of architecture and urban planning 109, 135, 222; and gender relations 1, 4, 188, 195–7; and mobility 160, 196–7
Suez Canal 23
Sufism 45–6, 69, 78, 105, 165, 200
sūq (market) 23, 40–2, 56, 64, 155, 174, 177, 207, 220
Sūq al-ʿAlawī 23, 40, 42, 45, 83 n. 3, n. 6

Taif 23, 32, 102
Tihama 23, 167
travelogues 19, 26, 28, 39 n. 6, 45, 74, 88

ʿulamāʾ (religious scholars) 8, 45, 122–7, 137 n. 16, 159, 184–6
ʿumda (neighbourhood representative) 27, 57, 78
al-ʿUtaibī, Juhaimān 123
ʿUthmān, caliph 22

veiling (of women) 2, 49, 52, 54, 66–7, 73, 76, 101, 224; and the Islamic Revival 155–7, 159; and Western discourse 6–7, 218–19
villas 31, 92–3, 100, 103, 111–12, 136 n. 2, n. 4, n. 6, 141–5; *see also* architecture, of single-family houses

Wahhabism: disaccordance with 162, 165, 168, 181, 222–3; and the Islamic Revival 126, 155–6; and moral standards 162, 164, 181; and religious diversity 45; and politics of gender 5, 155–6, 217
waqf 37, 69, 126
Warner, Michael 9–10, 12, 79, 138 n. 22, 208, 211–13, 225
water sellers 25, 49–50
water supply 26, 36, 39 n. 4, 87, 91, 111
Westernisation 114, 121–4, 130, 222
Winckelsen, Charles 19, 50, 52, 84 n.10
Wissmann, Hermann von 45, 83 n. 6
women: and driving 101–2, 125–6, 128, 154, 180–4, 189; and sexual harassment 75, 154, 156, 204, 214; visibility of 6, 41, 49–52, 75–6, 82, 99, 126, 130, 154–5, 218, 220–1, 223; and work 5, 51–3, 70, 75–6, 78, 84, 101, 124–6, 147, 155–7, 159–60, 168 n. 4, 185, 187, 189

Yamani, Mai 4–5, 142, 155–7, 190–1

zāwiya 45, 105